FEMINIST MORALITY

WOMEN IN CULTURE AND SOCIETY
A Series Edited by Catharine R. Stimpson

FEMINIST MORALITY
Transforming Culture, Society, and Politics

Virginia Held

THE UNIVERSITY OF CHICAGO PRESS
Chicago and London

Virginia Held is professor of philosophy at the City
University of New York, Hunter College and Graduate School. Her previous books include *Women's Realities, Women's Choices* (coauthor), and *Rights and
Goods: Justifying Social Action.*

THE UNIVERSITY OF CHICAGO PRESS, CHICAGO 60637
THE UNIVERSITY OF CHICAGO PRESS, LTD., LONDON
© 1993 by The University of Chicago
All rights reserved. Published 1993
Printed in the United States of America
02 01 00 99 98 97 96 95 94 93   1 2 3 4 5

ISBN 0-226-32591-1 *(cloth)*
0-226-32593-8 *(paper)*

Library of Congress Cataloging-in-Publiction Data

Held, Virginia.
    Feminist morality : transforming culture, society,
and politics / Virginia Held.
        p.   cm.—(Women in culture and society)
    Includes bibliographical references and index.
    1. Feminist theory—Moral and ethical as-
pects.   2. Feminism—Moral and ethical aspects.
I. Title.   II. Series.
HQ1190.H44   1993
305.42—dc20   93-16954
                                             CIP

Contents

Contents

Series Editor's Foreword

Oh, what a lovely book this is. Virginia Held is the author of two earlier, much-respected books of moral theory. She has now written a beautifully lucid and comprehensive account about the meaning of feminism for anyone, philosopher or not, who asks, "How can I be good in my life? How can I do well?" Sane and radical, visionary and reasonable, exploratory and judicious, *Feminist Morality: Transforming Culture, Society, and Politics* also proves the stupidity of the canard that feminist philosophy is junk and bunk.

Held builds on, synthesizes, and adds to the work of other feminist thinkers. With habitual clarity and scope, she takes on three related tasks. The first is to remind us persuasively, without snide rancor, of the inadequacies of traditional Western moral and political thought, especially in its treatment of women. There have been startling errors of commission and omission. Think, for example, of the pernicious equation of the female with the irrational, crude contemporary variants of which are "bimbo" and "airhead." Think, to take another example, of the historic evasion of the pervasiveness and power of sex/gender systems. Think, to take still another example, of the belief in freedom. Held realizes that freedom is the treasured soul of liberal political theory, but she also realizes how much blood has been spent in order to extend freedom to women of all races and men of despised races. Moreover, my right to liberty is empty if I lack the material ability to exercise it. My freedom is then just another word for nothing left to lose.

Held's second task is to amplify our analysis of culture by viewing such major institutions as the media *and* such major philosophical and political questions as the nature of democracy through the lens of feminism. Her feminist lens does more than catch the lives of women and the structure of sex/gender systems, important though this is. A feminist gaze re-sees and re-figures everything. Finally, and most constructively, Held sets out a table of the elements of a feminist moral theory. Because of her pragmatic commitment to the interplay of thought and action, she imagines the culture and society that we might have if we were to act on her ideas.

Central to Held's ethics is her belief that women, although they vary widely among themselves, have a commonality. Most of them are able to give birth. No man can. This is the significant difference between women and men. In the past, sexual difference has led to male domination and female subordination, but Held, like such other feminist philosophers as Sara Ruddick, believes that women's difference has generated redeeming values as well.

Crucially, both women and men can be feminists. To act as a feminist is also to redress the balance between the claims of the individual and of the community, to reground and rebuild social relations. To do so, Held argues, we must limit the use of our model of the human as rational, economic man, deliberately entering into contracts with others. We can find a supplementary model—in women's lives, more specifically in the relationships between mothers and children. If we accept this model, a moral agent, female or male, will be a "mothering person." A mothering person respects an ethics of care as well as the right to liberty and equality. If mothering is central to morality, our picture of the good society will be that of the "postpatriarchal family." Equitable, peaceable, such a family will be neither a tool of the state nor a respite from its rigors, but its teacher.

Logically, to act as a feminist also means the rejection of domination and violence as an instrument of domination. Held's ethics extend the practice of integrating feminism with the movement for nonviolence. A commitment to nonviolence, she remarks rather tartly, is the sign not of the weak but of the courageous. In summary, she writes, "Instead of a society determined by violent conflict modified by the authority and restraints of law and preoccupied with economic gain, we might have a society which saw as its *most* important task the flourishing of children and the creation of human relationships worthy of the aspirations of the children who will become women as well as men" (p. 214).

In the last decade of the twentieth century it has become fashionable, as well as profitable, to talk about the decline of American and Western civilization. Held refuses to join the chorus of mopes and jeremiads. What the chorus ignores, she suggests, are the profound, invaluable changes in our thinking about gender and in our sex/gender systems. So far, these changes have been largely in the domain of culture, but culture has tremendous power. The existence of *Feminist Morality*, which could not have been written and published thirty years ago, is one sign of change. Held declares, "To replace the order of male domination with gender equality would be even more fundamental than replacing the order of feudalism with democratic institutions. There can be little doubt that movement towards [democratic institutions] has had profound effects on a society's place in the world; movement towards [gender equality] is no doubt doing so now" (p. 216). To the feminist, these developments are largely for the good. With *Feminist Morality*, Held becomes the author/creator of a significant feminist ethic to guide and undergird change. As she urges us to connect feminist moral principles with daily life, she welcomes us to the historic party of hope for us paltry, striving, human beings.

Catharine R. Stimpson
Rutgers University

Acknowledgments

The development of feminist thought has been so shared an endeavor that it is often hard to remember, to name, to single out, those who have contributed to one's own expression of it. All the same I wish to thank in particular Sara Ruddick, who has read the whole manuscript at various stages and been very generous and helpful with her comments, Alison Jaggar and Catharine Stimpson for their valuable thoughts and suggestions, and the anonymous readers for the University of Chicago Press for their extensive and helpful recommendations. Others to whom I am especially grateful for comments on earlier versions or on papers which have become chapters of this book or for relevant conversations include Annette Baier, Seyla Benhabib, Karin Ben-Zvi, Larry Blum, Patricia Hill Collins, Nancy Fraser, Marilyn Friedman, Celeste Friend, Carol Gould, Marsha Hanen, Nancy Hartsock, Julia Held, Eva Kittay, Patricia Mann, Diana Meyers, Kathryn Pauly Morgan, Kai Nielsen, Lucius Outlaw, Carole Pateman, Amélie Rorty, Sibyl Schwarzenbach, Joan Tronto, and Margaret Urban Walker. I am grateful to the Center for Advanced Studies in the Behavioral Sciences at Stanford for a fellowship during which I began to work on some of the issues explored in this book, to Hamilton College for a visiting appointment with unusually light teaching obligations, and to Hunter College and the Graduate School of the City University of New York for a sabbatical leave enabling me to complete the book. Finally, I thank Wilma Ebbitt, Beth Goldstein, and Karen Wilson for admirable editorial and research assistance.

ONE

The Feminist Transformation of Consciousness and Culture

Feminism is transforming the ways in which we think and live and express ourselves. I focus in this book on how feminism is transforming our understanding of morality and its implications, as we grope in the present currents of change for patches of solid ground on which to steady ourselves. I explore how feminism is changing our views of almost everything about which we make moral choices: how to care about and care for others and ourselves, in what ways to maintain and in what ways to change our relationships, what goals to strive for and how to go about shaping our cultural and social and political arrangements.

To upset the gender hierarchy that permeates society is surely revolutionary. Male dominance has not been overcome, but the revolution to free humanity from it is proceeding. In this book I indicate how, more than any comparable social transformation, the feminist revolution is cultural. In changing culture we are changing society. The ways in which we see the world and think and feel about ourselves in it, and thus the ways we and others act, are undergoing upheavals, reversals, and, especially, gradual and cumulative and profound transformation.

When the author of a book on the women's movement in the United States since 1960 was asked, in 1992, "What impact did the women's movement have on your life?" she answered, "It was like a total shift in perspective. I joined a consciousness-raising group in late '70 or '71. We had a list of issues, and we would sit around one night a week and just explore them. I began to see the whole world differently and myself differently . . . I had really felt that what a woman should be was unselfish, unaggressive, unambitious, nurturant, the whole female stereotype. I bought it a hundred percent. I had always thought of myself as a follower rather than a leader, and I just began to see all kinds of potential in myself and potential for women. It was always there, but I never saw it. It was like having your eyeballs peeled. Nothing ever looked quite the same again."[1]

1

Culture and Liberation

For many feminists, the transformation of almost everything brought about by women's movements is most apparent, most important, and most promising in the domain of culture.[2] When we begin to think along these lines, instead of sharing the concentration of the liberal tradition on legal remedies and political power, instead of sharing the concentration of the Marxist tradition on economic power, and even instead of sharing the concentration on causal explanation of any kind, some of us may pay special attention to the moral and social and cultural forms in which we experience our lives being led and changed and to the ways we may express this change. For some feminists, our intent may be directed especially toward shaping the forms and aspects of culture and its expression. If one can change the interpretations given to, the values placed on, and especially the intended uses of configurations of power, one can change society. If one can change people's aspirations for the kinds of lives to be led and change the way persons experience a sense of self and of a life as satisfactory, one can change the ways political and economic and other forms of power are used to pursue the goals of persons and groups.

The feminist revolution, thus, may have somewhat less to do with changing forms of government or economic systems than other revolutions, and somewhat more to do with transforming the culture and thereby the society. We often address questions of how we ought to think and feel as well as act. We often argue that the feminist voice should be adequately heard in the production and replication and transformation of symbolic reality, from the household to the media to the classroom, as well as in the more traditionally recognized locations of power. We often think that feminist values should permeate the culture, whose values should then permeate economic and political and personal life. How can this happen? And will it?

Feminists are, of course, not a unified group. We all belong to other groups, such as those that make our racial or class or ethnic backgrounds, and thus our experiences, very different. None of us can claim to present "the feminist view," but we can try to articulate aspects of it. It seems to me that we are trying to construct the kinds of feminist cultural reality which encourage human connection yet discourage domination and that we seek these changes both in the family and among friends and gradually in the community, the society, and the world.

To note the extent to which we look to culture for the changes sought is not to downgrade the vital importance of organization and political action. It is not to revert to Enlightenment deceptions, which suppose that changed ideas can produce changed societies while ignoring material realities. A feminist view of culture includes, though it may not be limited to, an understanding of the material forms of the production and development of culture, and of the material lives of those who make culture and are shaped by it. A feminist view of culture recognizes the expensiveness of the equipment and the vastness of the economic resources needed to exert influence through the media in contemporary society. It includes recognition of the embodied reality of human life, as women strive to assure the security of our persons and as mothers struggle to earn enough to feed and safeguard the fragile bodies of children. But it includes, as well, awareness of the everyday symbolism of such nonhierarchical activities as women together doing what needs to be done in caring cooperatively for children or publishing a newsletter. And it understands the cultural change involved in women and men working together as genuine equals in jobs of equal standing—and feeling comfortable doing so.

A feminist view of the importance of culture assuredly knows that there will have to be transformations of the material realities of women's and men's lives to achieve liberation. Women's capacities to resist oppression in the political system, in the economy, and in the family will have to be greatly strengthened. There will have to be changes in the institutions of the corporation and the workplace, of government at all levels, and in the university and the media. There will have to be changes in how labor is divided in the household and how sexuality is experienced.

Nevertheless, through their imagination and expression women can to some degree escape existing material bounds. They should escape not into utopian or romantic fantasies that serve to uphold existing structures but into the feminist culture that can be nurtured by and for women and feminist men. Without such a culture, change in the material realities may be subverted into superficial improvements that belie the goal of liberation, if such improvements are possible at all.[3] For decades after women had gained the right to vote, their votes merely mirrored the votes of men, until a feminist consciousness began to produce a gender gap in voting patterns and, following that, demands that serious attention be paid to women's issues.[4] And the very high degree of participation of women in the labor force in the former Soviet Union and in Eastern Europe, unaccompanied as it was by feminist critiques of male domination, did not go far to reduce the subordination of women; the burdens of housework and child care remained unshared, and the shapings of sexuality and personality continued to uphold male dominance.[5]

Although a feminist culture brought about by the imagination and expression of feminist women and men will by itself be wholly inadequate to overcome the oppression of women and of many men, it is a sufficiently important component of what feminists must work for to merit much focused attention in our inquiry and activity.

The transformations explored in this book are largely philosophical ones and thus largely cultural. The focus is on concerned moral inquiry, on understanding from a feminist point of view, on making recommendations, on imagining more suitable social arrangements than those now in place. In a sense, all philosophical analysis and recommendation is cultural: philosophers do not have political or economic power at their disposal. But as feminists transform what we seek to achieve, how we interpret our experiences, and how we express ourselves, we contribute to transforming our lives and the lives of others.

I am dealing in this book with what Arthur Danto calls, after Hegel, "the realm of spirit," which Danto enumerates as "the area of politics, law, morality, religion, art, culture, and philosophy itself." Philosophy, he says, has largely left this territory unexplored. Although in his view, "it is in the realm of spirit that we exist as human beings," this realm, he holds, is "dark and difficult *terra incognita* so far as philosophical understanding is concerned."[6] Not all of philosophy has been as powerless to offer understanding of this territory as has the philosophy his book describes, but when we approach these regions from the perspective of feminism, we must admit that we venture into this dark and difficult terrain with little guidance and few maps from those often thought to be the leading lights of contemporary philosophy. And to so venture we must discount misleading advice from nearly every tradition. But we are, thankfully, accompanied in our search by many sisterly explorers with abundant curiosity and insight.

Patriarchy and Its Causes

The term 'patriarchy' (meaning literally "rule by the fathers") has been used in various ways, and feminists have debated its utility. Traditional political thought has claimed that the patriarchy defended by theorists such as Robert Filmer has been replaced by the democracy advocated by Locke, Jefferson, and others. Feminists, however, have shown that the social contract theory that based political rule on a hypothetical contract among equals instead of on inherited rule by a paternal monarch still maintained the rule of men over women. Many feminists have come to think of patriarchy as a view about male domination in all or most spheres of life and society, not a theory focusing only on political authority. They see domination by men as built into the basic structure of all societies and as something that must be overcome.

To many feminists, the term 'patriarchy' conveys well the pervasiveness and structural nature of the dominance of men over women. Others think the term obscures the domination resulting from class and race as well as gender hierarchy, and still others find it too vague or ahistorical to be helpful. Sheila Rowbotham, for instance, thinks that patriarchy "implies a universal and ahistorical form of oppression which returns us to biology." But Carole Pateman argues that if the concept of patriarchy is abandoned because of its problems, "feminist political theory would then be without the only concept that refers specifically to the subjection of women, that singles out the form of political right that all men exercise by virtue of being men. If the problem has no name, patriarchy can all too easily slide back into obscurity."[7]

Throughout this book I use the term 'male dominance' to indicate the gender hierarchy that pervades and structures society. Why it should not be thought of as biologically determined I discuss at various points. I also speak frequently of 'patriarchal' attitudes or arrangements, seeing no need to avoid a term I find descriptively useful, especially in contexts influenced, as most are, by the view of man as head of his family or household.

Much important feminist theory tries to understand the causes of women's subordination on the grounds that before we can understand how to achieve the liberation of women, we need to understand what causes the oppression of women and how these causes operate. Alison Jaggar's influential and impressive book, *Feminist Politics and Human Nature,* is organized around these questions, showing how feminists are united in the goal of ending the oppression of women, though divided in our views of what causes this oppression.[8] Ann Ferguson, in *Blood at the Root,* considers a variety of causal questions: (1) the causes of the origins of male dominance; (2) the causes of its persistence, once it is established; and (3) the causes of its "reproduction" in society after society and over time.[9]

Ferguson's own causal explanation of male dominance in North American capitalist society is formulated in terms of the organization of "sex/affective production." Her thesis concerns the ways in which women are dominated through the use and control of our energy—energy directed toward sexuality, the provision of affection, and the satisfaction of human needs for care. She shows how this has taken different forms in different historical periods: father patriarchy in feudal Europe and colonial North America, husband patriarchy in nineteenth-century capitalist society, and now public patriarchy.

Ferguson follows Carol Brown in calling the contemporary form of male dominance in advanced capitalist societies "public patriarchy."[10] Men still have much control over women in family situations, but the primary social mechanisms of control, these feminists believe, lie in state regulations and media influences. I would not describe the contemporary form of the subordination of women in the United States as public patriarchy, partly because of the difficulties in designating as "public" what capitalist culture calls "private enterprise," and the fact that the media are overwhelmingly in this domain. But I share Ferguson's view of the influence the media exert in sustaining the dominance of men.

Though many examinations of the causes of women's oppression offer new and interesting theses, they often employ a rather traditional model of causal explanation, a model based on an assumption that there are always scientific laws or law-like generalizations in accordance with which certain kinds of causes determine certain kinds of effects. Such explanations may include the irrational causes recognized by Freudian theory along with the economic causes recognized by Marxist theory, both revised with an awareness provided by feminists of causes omitted by both previous theories. But the conception of causality itself in human life is close to the scientific one.

Although I think the causes of the oppression of women are multiple, I do not focus in this book on questions of causality. One reason is that I am skeptical of the model of causality on which such questions rest. It seems to me doubtful that any of the familiar models of causal explanation can adequately deal with women's experience (or men's). This becomes most apparent when we listen with a feminist receptivity to women's efforts to express the choices we make and how we make them. The human experiences of agency and change are not the same as an observer's supposition that one event causes another. Instead of focusing on what we can see within the framework of observation, I will be chiefly concerned with what we do when we change our lives and create new lives.

Even if the kinds of explanation considered in causal accounts were adequate to indicate how male domination came about and how it replicates itself, it does not follow that these explanations can yield an understanding of how feminist liberation is to occur. In dealing with this question, we are likely to pay far more attention than causal explanations can to the moral and political recommendations we devise and act on, to how we respond to or resist social influences, and especially to the cultural images and ideas we create.

When the social sciences import into the study of human beings the causal models familiar from the physical sciences, their results are often unimpressive. Concepts of causality developed in Marxist and psychoanalytic theories may be an improvement, but not by much. As historical events unfold, they can frequently be better understood through the alternative contexts of the recommendations of morality and political and social theory, the insights of literature, and the images of cultures and countercultures. Recent transformations in the lives of women can often illustrate the way we, as human beings, change our interpretations of existing realities, give ourselves reasons to act differently than in the past, and think and feel and live differently than before. We can often understand how clumsily accounts of these changes fit into any familiar framework of causal explanation.

The history of Western philosophy and science is a history of picturing the world, including the human beings in it. But this concentration on "seeing," on depicting, may itself by a biased way of living in a world we also need to understand in ways that picturing overlooks. We do not merely observe strangers, we live with other human beings whom we listen to and hear, whom we touch and feel as well as look at. Many feminists note that the metaphors of voice—of listening, hearing, and speaking—are central to women's efforts to discuss our intellectual development, in contrast with the metaphors of sight so central to traditional, male conceptions of knowledge.[11] And whole categories of empathetic understanding, of sensitivity to others' feelings, may be missing from the enterprise of observation, as generations of poets have tried to remind us.

Our language for dealing philosophically with experience other than "seeing," whether that seeing is with our eyes or our minds, is underdeveloped so far, and it needs to be cultivated. Although I speak often in this book of the feminist "point of view," of the feminist "perspective," or the feminist "outlook," employing metaphors from vision, I use this language because it is hard to find terms to convey these concerns in an alternative framework.[12] My use reflects not an acceptance of the overemphasis on "seeing" but an indication of the paucity of alternative metaphors and concepts.

7

Most feminists recognize the way human relationships are central to and color human experience. Repeatedly, feminist approaches indicate to us that we ought to pay far more attention than most inquiry does to relationships among people, relationships that we cannot see but can experience nevertheless. I will often focus on such relationships. They can be felt and understood but, as experienced, are not reducible to the properties of individual entities that can be observed by an outsider and mapped into a causal scientific framework.

To understand experience, we need to attend to cultural interpretations and recommendations, to the realms of expression and imagination, far more than have the social sciences, and, given their assumptions drawn from the natural sciences, more than they are at present equipped to do. Culture shapes social reality. But to deal adequately with how a cultural image or idea or norm leads us to act or to change the way we think and feel and act, we need to think in ways that are different from those of the causal explanations developed out of scientific worldviews.

Let's consider an example that is by now banal. An image of a glamorous woman draped over an automobile in an advertisement can lead a given woman who views it to spend more time worrying about her appearance than she otherwise would. But the image doesn't cause her to do so in a way the model of causal explanation can well handle. Further, if the same woman discusses with other women how those who pay for the advertisements of a commercial culture use the images of women for their own gain and in the process damage the aspirations of girls and women, this woman can come to be less influenced by the advertising that surrounds her. Again, this change in her consciousness and activity cannot well be dealt with in the causal explanations developed for the sciences.

Or consider the potential of televised reports to elicit moral approval and disapproval. Few images elicit more shared condemnation than that of a large adult brutally beating a small child. Although the disapproval will not be nearly as unanimous, images of armed men brutally beating peaceful demonstrators will also elicit widespread disapproval and can become one of the most effective forces leading to the development of greater freedom of expression. While governments can attempt to keep cameras away from demonstrations, their efforts to suppress the news are often unsuccessful. And where pictures cannot be taken or recordings made, stories can still be told. And the stories, added to other stories, can lead to further expression and action in ways that the social sciences may be inherently unsuited to understand. Subjectivity must be taken seriously in human experience.

Catharine MacKinnon gives an illuminating description of the feminist method of consciousness-raising, and how it contrasts with the epistemology of the natural and social sciences. Feminist consciousness-raising, she writes, is "the collective critical reconstruction of the meaning of women's social experience, as women live through it." It is, in MacKinnon's view, the key to the development of feminist theory; it is not confined to what goes on in consciousness-raising groups. Scientific method, including social scientific method, tries to overcome the limitations of the knower by positing a mind that gets outside its particular, situated circumstances, as, for instance, of being a nineteenth-century Englishman. Feminist method, in contrast, MacKinnon writes, is such that women are presumed able to understand society and its structure "because they live in it and have been formed by it, not in spite of those facts. Women can know society because consciousness is part of it, not because of any capacity to stand outside it or oneself." Through consciousness-raising, MacKinnon continues, "women grasp the collective reality of women's condition from within the perspective of that experience, not from outside it."[13]

Feminist consciousness-raising, which has been a central part of the cultural change that has propelled the women's movements of recent decades, now often occurs in the classroom, in conversation at the workplace, and in the letters columns of newspapers, and it often includes men, in contrast with the "consciousness-raising sessions" of the 1970s. But it continues apace.

I am not, then, trying to deal directly with the causes of the oppression of women, though some assumptions have to be made and some assertions ventured about, for instance, the relative importance of culture for social change. I am chiefly trying to address questions about what we, as feminists, ought to do and to believe. At one level, the answer is obvious: we ought to end the subordination of women. But when we pull apart the strands of that subordination, looking at their ideological, cultural, economic, political, psychological, and other components, we need detailed guidance, and we need to assemble arguments for our various recommendations.

Whatever one holds concerning the need to understand the causes of the oppression of women, it seems to me important, in any case, to welcome a division of feminist labor in which some persons focus on such causal questions as I neglect, and others, making certain plausible assumptions, focus on the conceptual questions that arise as feminists strive to overcome the subordination of women. My efforts belong to the latter category. I hope to show that certain traditional conceptions and normative recommendations rest on dubious images and metaphors, and that they lead to patterns of thinking and acting which need to be changed. I avoid claiming that such thinking or such change in thinking causes women and men to act in certain ways, because the process may be more like one story leading to another than one event causing another. As we change our stories we can change our lives, at least to some extent. In place of explanations or causes, then, I offer recommendations—my own and others'—for change. They will be recommendations for further transforming how we think about morality and culture and society and how we should try to live our lives.

What Is Culture?

To decide what we wish to mean by the term 'culture' is among the most difficult of questions.[14] Let me begin with an offered characterization. For the cultural anthropologist Clifford Geertz, 'culture' denotes "an historically transmitted pattern of meanings embodied in symbols; a system of inherited conceptions expressed in symbolic forms by means of which [human beings] communicate, perpetuate, and develop their knowledge about and attitudes toward life."[15]

The area of inquiry known as cultural studies can best be described as a loose network or intellectual movement influential in such established fields as English, sociology, history, communications, and linguistics. Some of those working in this area argue persuasively that at this stage 'culture' should not be precisely defined. One writer who expresses this view says: "It is a rationalist illusion to think we can say, 'henceforth this term will mean . . .' and expect a whole history of connotations (not to say a whole future) to fall smartly in line."[16]

There are good reasons to keep the term open for the time being. Yet we can clarify some alternatives about which more needs to be said. Within the area of cultural studies, there are some who argue, more nearly in accord with anthropological approaches, that a culture must be studied as a whole way of life in particular historical circumstances; culture thus includes the characteristic ways in which people live, produce, consume, settle disputes, govern themselves, as well as the ways they worship or tell stories or fashion artifacts or interpret the meanings of what they say and do. Others engaged in cultural studies argue for a more limited focus on a relatively independent domain of meaning—consciousness, subjectivity, signification, symbols, art, entertainment; these are thought of as distinct from the social structure of society, with its economic and political and other configurations of power.

To some extent the distinctions break down, wherever one focuses. For some persons to have economic power, they and others must accept whole sets of meanings about property, ownership, money, contract, and so forth. For those in government to have power, others must believe that governmental decisions must or ought to be obeyed; that is, the meanings attached to the governmental positions in question confer authority or legitimacy. Even such means of exercising power as firing guns and killing opponents constitute power only if those who have guns know how to use them and accept certain beliefs concerning the permissibility of using force. So meanings and subjective understandings and interpretations of symbols are almost never absent in human affairs, even in those circumstances most determined by physical forces. When we focus on gender, we can see vividly how unclear the distinction is. Gender is, of course, part of the basic social structure of society, though this has only recently been acknowledged.[17] We now recognize that societies structure themselves along lines of gender, allocating power, privilege, and appropriate roles for women and men, in accordance with their conceptions of and attitudes about gender. At the same time, since gender orders virtually all human life, both public and private, both symbolic and material, and since it colors virtually all human thought and imagination, it should not be associated with social structure *rather than* with culture as if the two could be separated. It permeates culture as well. We now recognize, too, the many ways in which knowledge is power or in which the ability to gain and keep an audience is a form of power, and we certainly understand the ways that words, the most symbolic and the least material of realities, have force. So no lines between the symbolic and the material in human affairs are likely to be firm or precise or lasting.

Still, a book is not a rifle, a rock concert is not a police force, and entertainment does not provide the caloric intakes needed to sustain life. We may want to distinguish more explicitly the domain of symbolic, meaning-laden human expression from what is more clearly dependent on material resources, such as economic power or political force or military strength. We may find it useful to limit the concept of culture so that it is not coextensive with everything that happens in human society. I find the distinction between culture and social structure sufficiently helpful to lean more in the direction of accepting it than rejecting it altogether.

When I speak of the transformations discussed in this book as primarily cultural, that is because they are transformations in how we think about and evaluate various domains of society, and this thinking and evaluating belong to the realm of culture. But when we describe society itself, it seems to me helpful to distinguish economic and political structures in which power is exercised from the cultural phenomena that express and create meanings in symbolic forms. The term 'culture' can then designate somewhat more narrowly the production and reception of images and narratives and information, the development and imparting of what is considered art or knowledge, and the expressive and evaluative practices of, say, singing or applauding or reading.

Among those engaged in cultural studies, some have paid attention especially to the making of cultural products, largely in England and in the United States—who produces them, who finances and gains from the enterprise, and how the culture industry is organized. Others have paid attention especially to the "texts" of the culture, the products themselves. They have explored the formal aspects of texts, their genres, their messages (often masked), their dramatic or ideological meanings, and how the meanings for creators and recipients may differ. A feminist sensibility encourages a much more perceptive understanding of the meanings of such cultural products. And it often opens up new understandings of the place of culture in society. We can see how culture upholds what may be the deepest and most pervasive aspect of social structure, the structure of gender. We can see how culture affects other uses of power based on gender. And we can, most interestingly, gain a glimpse of how cultural changes can change the gender structure and thereby, perhaps, many other areas of domination and many other structures of oppression.

The Challenge of Postmodernism

Postmodern critiques of universal claims, of totalizing theory, of impartial truth, of the Cartesian "I" have become ubiquitous in contemporary cultural life and have influenced many feminists.

Postmodernist culture has been given diverse characterizations. To Frederic Jameson's influential list of terms by which it can be described—pastiche, collage, and schizophrenia—Dana Polan adds *incoherence,* in the sense of "the inability or unwillingness of culture to cohere, to follow an evident logic."[18] Patricia Mellencamp thinks that television can serve as a "theoretical object for modeling postmodernism . . . Epitomizing every blemish or glow, television is the quintessential embodiment (or emblem of decline) of postmodernism's central traits."[19]

Some theorists have offered enlightening parallels between postmodern and feminist criticisms of Enlightenment certainties.[20] The modern concept, from Descartes on, of the rational, knowing finder of truth has been subjected to poststructuralist and postmodernist attacks that have shown it to be one historically constructed point of view among others, rather than the bedrock or privileged point of view from which to find universal knowledge.[21] Such critiques have illuminated feminist analyses of philosophical positions shown to reflect a male and Western perspective rather than a universal one, and have been followed by postmodern rejections of any totalizing claims about women or about what women essentially are. Catharine Stimpson concludes her book *Where the Meanings Are* by accepting postmodern fragmentation and by suggesting that we should not even try to achieve unified views. "The question," she writes, "is not how to paste and staple a consensus together again but rather how to live culturally and politically with fragmentation."[22]

At the same time, a growing number of feminists are developing resistance to what is seen as postmodern excess; these feminists are wary of how postmodern theoretical positions may undermine feminist projects. Indeed, Linda Alcoff fears that the nominalism of poststructuralist critiques of subjectivity "threatens to wipe out feminism itself."[23] Perhaps at first instinctively, and then reflectively, many feminists resist the dangerous relativism and particularism into which postmodern analyses often seem to lead.

Postmodernism's challenge to an earlier version of feminism that made claims about Woman as such, or about All Women, needs to be taken seriously and addressed, but not given the last word. Though arguments in behalf of recognizing differences among women are often valid, they can be made independently of postmodern attacks. The postmodern suggestions that there is no category "woman" and that *no* general claims about women are justifiable may go so far as to render women unable to demand an end to our subordination and even in no position to construct our own theories.[24] As Alison Jaggar insists, a feminist commitment is "incompatible with any form of moral relativism that condones the subordination of women or the devaluation of their moral experience."[25]

Lynda Lange makes the useful point that many feminists have had to argue for "the legitimacy of *any* woman's perspective of any kind in theory building." Rather than seeing feminist claims as a totalizing forcing of all women into a single, essentialized category, when one looks historically at the emergence of the current wave of the women's movement, Lange says, one sees how it has made its case by "pointing to the minimizing, and even outright rejection of the concerns of women, by otherwise democratic movements . . . The problem has been that when women's concerns are 'one strand among others,' they have always tended to be subordinated to those other concerns."[26]

Susan Bordo notes that in postmodern writing, "metaphors of dance and movement have replaced the ontologically fixing stare of the motionless spectator." But, she argues, the fantasy of transcendence "has not yet been abandoned. The historical specifics of the modernist, Cartesian version have simply been replaced with a new postmodern configuration of detachment, a new imagination of disembodiment: a dream of being *everywhere*." And, she asks, "What sort of body is it that is free to change its shape and location at will, that can become anyone and travel everywhere?" In short, the postmodern body, like the Cartesian I, is "no body at all."[27] Along with many feminists, I share her view that the thinking of women must never become unmoored from the embodied reality of women and men.

Postmodern critiques, in Bordo's view, have been applied selectively, targeting gender more than race or class. But postmodern arguments can undercut a commitment to change along various lines. Mary Hawkesworth fears that "should postmodernism's seductive text gain ascendancy, it will not be an accident that power remains in the hands of the white males who currently possess it. In a world of radical inequality, relativist resignation reinforces the status quo."[28] And if we recognize the need for critiques of the status quo in terms of the inequalities of class and race, then surely, Lynda Lange argues, "for liberatory purposes we need the category 'women' in at least as basic a way as we need categories such as class, race, or ethnicity." Without such categories of feminist analysis as sexuality, reproduction, or child care, "and some notion of women as a category of the oppressed, women stand to continue to be more silenced than men within the class, culture, race, or nation, where they find themselves," as they always have been.[29]

Susan Hekman defends the postmodern rejection of the Cartesian "constituting" subject against arguments that this critique robs women of our subjectivity and agency just as we are beginning to find our voices and to act decisively to free ourselves from our subordination.[30] Feminist

14

thought is committed to keeping experience in mind, and feminist experience must include personal test cases of a self, a female subject, taking responsibility for resisting the language and thought and practices that confront us and maintain our subordination. Female experience must include some generalizations as we share our stories.

Hekman, following Julia Kristeva, argues that "part of learning a language is learning to be creative within these constraints," and though "subjects are constituted by multiple and sometimes contradictory discourses," we can "resist, mutate, and revise these discourses from within them."[31] But many feminists, skeptical of postmodernism's implications, deem it necessary to focus also on the female self or subject who learns the language and provides resistance to dominant discourses and materially embodied oppression. Although the relational female self or subject or person of these feminists does not resemble the female-transcending and body-denying Cartesian self, as will be seen in later chapters, it does not resemble the fractured postmodern self either. Among the many notions which feminists are trying to reconceptualize into some adequate form is that of the embodied, related persons we experience ourselves to be. At least some of the time we are sufficiently integrated to strive to end the oppression of women, and we can build on that experience.

To Nancy Hartsock the theories of postmodernism "present less an alternative to the overconfident theories of the Enlightenment than a parasitic continuation of its preoccupations." In her view, "the situated knowledges of the oppressed make no claim to the disembodied universality of reason."[32] However, because of their "embodied, social, and collective nature, they can also avoid the opposite problem of a descent into a particularistic relativism." What she sees as the postmodern abandonment of theory and of the goal of a just society is "a dangerous approach for any marginalized group to adopt."[33] Though many postmodernist feminists deny that they reject theory and forsake the pursuit of justice, the questions concern the implications of various assumptions.

In a clever and amusing discussion of how postmodernism is contributing to a loss of political activism among those engaged in women's studies, Ailbhe Smyth of University College, Dublin, writes that postmodernism "is an increasingly sophisticated, articulate, and prevalent strand which threatens to occupy (if it's not already there) and dominate hardwon space for women's thought and knowledge, paralysing action. The world is not, after all, reducible to a text, is not a matter of rhetoric . . . The dismantling of the notion of identity . . . the privileging of the concept of fragmentation as process are extraordinarily unhelpful in enabling women—or other groups—to develop collective practices."[34] Such qualms seem likely to have an increasing influence.

Normative Validity

Certainly the term 'postmodernism' means many things to many persons. If one accepts Andreas Huyssen's identification of it with the breakdown of a sharp distinction between high art and mass culture and with a vindication of interest in mass culture and the ethical and political questions it raises, many of the critics of postmodernism cited might identify themselves with it, as might I. But many critics focus rather, as do I, on the theoretical stance postmodernists have often adopted toward normative judgment, a stance which risks exactly the "mindless pluralism of anything goes" that Huyssen claims he will avoid. Critics of postmodernism can as easily claim to be committed to meaningful normative judgment while avoiding the "sterile modernist dogma" that insists on a "necessary separation of high art from mass culture, politics, and the everyday" and that dismisses popular culture as trash, a notion which Huyssen appealingly rejects.[35]

Postmodern approaches may be especially attractive to those whose primary interest or background is literary. To my mind, the distinction between philosophy and literature is important and should be maintained. Philosophy seeks a general understanding of reality, knowledge, methods of inquiry, and morality. Literature calls our attention to particular lives, loves, despairs, persistences. Though the interpretations of literary criticism may see the general in the particular, the aim of illuminating an instance prevails. For philosophy, while no instance should be thought irrelevant, the aim of progressing toward unifying the disparate, of approaching wider truth or more inclusive validity, remains salient.

I think we need a sustained feminist *and* philosophical focus on culture, including popular culture, but this focus should resist the pull toward a literary postmodern fragmentation that may dissipate the concentrated effort needed to strive for liberation. Many of the feminists who devote their attention to culture embrace postmodernism. I try, in contrast, to focus on culture while diverging from a postmodernist skepticism so deep as to disperse attention centered on gender. Gender seems to me at the heart of culture and at the center of what will be needed to transform culture and change society. As I intend to demonstrate, the alternative to a philosophy which has become a handmaiden of the sciences should not be a philosophy which becomes a handmaiden to literature.

Normative philosophy and moral recommendations are not merely the expressions of subjective, personal perspectives and preferences. They can progress toward what may resemble objective validity, as subjective understanding is shared and confirmed in the experience of others.[36]

We need philosophically defended methods of inquiry to make such progress possible. I will argue for a method of feminist moral inquiry and delineate some recommendations it might yield for social arrangements. Such a method does not surrender subjective understanding to the purportedly wholly objective points of view of scientific observers or of universal rational theories. But neither does it surrender to the limiting subjective points of view of many creators of art and literature or of postmodern relativism.

Speaking for Each Other

There has been much valid criticism that assertions by feminists are often based on excessively simplified generalizations.[37] Such criticisms may seem to resemble postmodern attacks, but they can be fundamentally different in calling for more satisfactory general claims rather than for an end to a search for unified views.[38] Persuasive arguments have been offered that we need to recognize more than we have the differences among women, differences especially of race and class, of historical context and sexual orientation. As these critics point out, what has been claimed about the experience of women has often been based on the views of white, relatively privileged, heterosexual Western women, and as such may overlook or misrepresent the experience of women of color in given historical circumstances, of working-class women with quite different life patterns, of women with different sexual attachments, of non-Western women in all their variety.[39]

What we think of as Woman is a social construction, not an essential reality. I agree that we should be wary of tendencies toward essentialism based on an inadequate understanding of the experiences of different women. At the same time I believe we should hesitate to deny ourselves the language and concepts with which to speak of certain experiences that are common to many or most women. Emily Martin provides her list of such experiences:

> Women in our society . . . do share some experiences: all are defined
> as 'women,' one of two usually permanent gender categories to

17

which everyone in our society must be assigned; all (some more than others, some more aware than others) occupy subordinate positions to men, if not in their jobs, then in their families, and if not in their families, then in general cultural imagery and language; all have female bodies and experience common bodily processes such as menstruation and childbirth (however various the meanings such diverse groups as black Americans or Jewish Americans can give these processes); all are affected in one way or another by medical and scientific views of female bodily processes.[40]

Though some of these statements could be qualified, many apply usefully well beyond "our society."

There are oppressions women share, and there are incapacities that men share. That no men give birth, for instance, and that the capacity to give birth belongs only to women is an important aspect of experience. Although the meanings attached to birth differ in different cultures and historical periods, there may well be a significance to the commonalities with respect to giving life. I do not suggest at all that women are only or "essentially" or "primarily" givers of life, or that the capacity to give life should in any way determine women's occupations, but rather that we should raise various questions about that reality of human life: that every person is born of a woman. We need to understand whatever resentment exists about such dependency on women and whatever envy of female creativity.[41] And we need to explore the promise suggested for the transformation of the human world as women begin to see that world from *our* point of view.

We should be aware of the enormous differences among women. No woman should presume to speak for those whose experiences and aspirations may be very different. The ways we understand the world and the recommendations we make may not be especially similar. On the other hand, we should all be encouraged to imagine alternatives to the oppressions of contemporary society, to express our thoughts and evaluations concerning the problems we face and how to deal with them.[42] Those who share our views and those who do not may be glad to have heard them. It is in this spirit and in line with a practice fairly common in feminist writing that I use the pronoun "we" to refer to women in this book. It is not that we suppose any one of us can speak for all but that since almost no women have spoken for any women for so long, we welcome the many voices which are progressing, much of the time, toward harmony.

In this book I examine feminist transformations occurring in morality and moral theory, in cultural images and institutions, and in social and political thought. I propose new ways of thinking and feeling about the personal and social worlds we inhabit and some new ways of imagining and expressing our hopes for change.

In chapters 2, 3, and 4, I suggest what I believe our methods of inquiry into moral questions ought to be, I consider some central moral concepts that are being transformed in the process of developing what can be viewed as feminist ethics, and I explore what feminist moral theory might be like. In chapter 5, I consider changes needed in our view of culture, in how culture shapes society, and in the way culture is produced. In the next two chapters, I look at how dominant images of birth and life and death are distorted along lines of gender and suggest how they might be reimagined; I consider what links may exist between gender and violence and how the links between violence and social organization might be changed. In chapters 8 and 9, I inquire into the ways feminism may change our thinking about and our striving for freedom, equality, democracy, and personal development. In chapter 10, I suggest that society may look very different from a feminist point of view from the way it has traditionally been presented. Finally, in a brief epilogue, I trace some imagined outlines of a possible feminist future.

Speaking for Myself

The philosophical tradition that has purported to present the view of the essentially and universally human has, masked by this claim, presented instead a view that is masculine, white, and Western. Doubting that anyone can truly reflect the essentially and universally human, and suspicious of those who presume to do so, feminists often ask that speakers openly acknowledge the backgrounds from which they speak so that their hearers can better understand the contexts of their experiences. Annette Baier, for instance, suggests that in deciding how much we ought to trust a moral theorist, we need to know something of that theorist's life and experience.[43]

By psychological inclination, I am not given to discussing my background and personal life, but I recognize that here there are good reasons to do so. Accordingly I provide this brief account. I am a white woman born the day after the Great Crash of 1929, the third of four children of parents of modest economic privilege, whose ancestors had been in this country for many generations, in New York State and Rhode Island. Early in life I acquired a strong affinity for solitude, as I spent much time in the woods surrounding the house in which I grew up. In adolescence, I largely abandoned the Protestant doctrines I had been offered. By the age of fifteen I plunged into the challenges of social life and, by sixteen, the excitements of urban stress.

I finished college shortly after my twentieth birthday and married later that year, thinking, unbelievably, that it was time to settle down after what had been, for those times, an adventurous youth. My husband, having been pressed into the German army when virtually a child, was intimately acquainted with a vast range of experience of which I was ignorant: violence, horror, terror, guilt. For many years we experienced economic hardship together, in Europe and then in the United States, where I began what might have been a career as a reporter and writer while he pursued graduate studies in political science. When I was twenty-seven, we had a daughter and, five years later, a son. My development as an independent yet deeply connected person proceeded. At thirty-two, I returned to philosophy, which had been my first strong intellectual attachment. My years away from it had led me to believe that philosophy was not the mere intellectual luxury I had earlier come to fear it was, but profoundly influential in society.

I am old enough to have lived through, before they even had these names, pervasive patriarchal attitudes and assumptions shared by almost everyone I knew, blatant sex discrimination in employment, and damaging instances of sexual harassment. My relationships with men, both occupational and personal, were often fraught with conflict, until the changes brought about by the recent phase of the women's movement made greater mutuality more likely. By the time I was forty-two, my marriage had ended, and I was now responsible, even more than before, for two children as well as for myself. My children are still close to the core of my being; my grandchildren provide additional joy. A respectful love has brought pleasure to the most recent decade of my life.

Deep personal and professional associations with persons of other cultures, races, and outlooks have, I believe, enriched my philosophical understanding, as did my early years as a journalist. My years as a graduate student in philosophy were nightmare years, with part-time studying and mothering, part-time working and teaching, and almost no time sleeping. But good fortune did allow me to progress in the profession. As a philosopher, I have focused especially on social and political philosophy, on ethics, and in recent years on feminist philosophy.

I have a longer background acquaintance with Anglo-American analytic philosophy than with continental philosophy, and almost no familiarity with non-Western thinking. The issues with which I have been concerned have led me to take a much broader view of philosophy than that preferred by the tradition in which my "training" occurred. Still, this book is written from an admittedly white and largely North American point of view. When I speak of women or mothering or contractual society or the media, I am reflecting an experience of them limited to what is often called a Eurocentric perspective. Rather than trying to give a superficial account of a much wider range of feminist views, I express those that have developed out of my philosophical background and experience.

Feminism is overturning so much of established theory and uncovering so many biases in what has been taken to be knowledge that those of us involved in feminist inquiry have ventured far beyond anything for which our backgrounds could have well prepared us. We gain strength and insights and orientation from each other. This book reflects a gradual bringing together of my thoughts about feminism, about ethics, about social and political philosophy, and about the cultures in which we fashion our lives.

TWO

Feminist Moral Inquiry:
Method and Prospects

Among the most central inquiries we engage in are those of morality: What ought we to do as we lead our lives, care for our families, choose our occupations, frame our goals, and pursue those goals for ourselves, our communities, our globe? In this chapter I suggest a methodology for the development of feminist moral understanding.

A focus on methodology is appropriate. In historical terms, feminist inquiry is in its infancy. Of course we have not yet adequately worked out feminist moral theories with which to live our lives. And of course we are still groping for adequately developed views of the deep and fundamental ways in which culture and the organization of society and the pursuit of scientific knowledge will all have to be changed to be compatible with feminist morality. Feminist moral inquiry is an ongoing process that will need to continue far into the future. To get our methodological bearings in this process is a good first step.

We might think of this topic as feminist moral epistemology, but the term 'epistemology' may be too closely tied to scientific inquiry to serve my purposes. To speak of moral epistemology may suggest that morality is primarily a matter of knowledge, as science is usually thought to be. In contrast, most feminists see morality as a matter of practice and art as well as of knowledge. Practice is involved both in understanding what we ought to do and in carrying out the norms of morality. I share this view, and I take moral inquiry to involve activity and feeling as well as thought and observation. Moral inquiry involves living our lives and actively shaping our relationships with others rather than accurately registering and theorizing about the impressions made upon us by what some take to be an external world. To engage in the development of feminist morality is to seek to improve practices in which knowledge is only one component, though an important one. It is to cultivate the art of living a life as admirable for women as for men.

Inquiry and Experience

When, some years ago, I developed my views on how moral inquiry should be conducted, I did not think of my positions on the questions involved as specifically feminist.[1] Only in retrospect can I see how well the insights offered by feminists concerning the development of moral theory and concerning moral theory itself can be meshed with the views I was developing concerning the conduct of moral inquiry. At the time, the locus of my interest in moral inquiry tended to. be in politics, law, and economic activity. Having written on issues in these areas, I tried to spell out explicitly the methodology by which I thought we should conduct moral inquiry and develop moral theories suitable for human experience.

The method I argued for relied on actual rather than hypothetical experience. Moral theories, I thought and still think, should give us guidance in confronting the problems of actual life in the highly imperfect societies in which we live. We need moral theories about what to do and what to accept here and now. Ideal theories of perfect justice or purely rational theories for ideal societies leave the problems of what to do here and now unsolved, even unaddressed. They usually provide no way to connect moral theory with our actual experience, except through suggestions that once we have a clear view of our goals, we can take up, separately, questions about how to reach them. The moral theory seldom goes on to tell us how such means to our goals should be evaluated in *moral* terms, rather than merely in the instrumental terms of efficiency—which questions, it is said, belong more to the social scientists than to moral philosophers.

In my view, not only must moral theories be applicable to actual problems, they must in some way be "tested" in actual experience. They must be made to confront lived reality; they must be found satisfactory in the actual situations people find themselves in. Otherwise they are intellectual exercises that may be intriguing and impressively coherent, but they are not adequate as *moral theories*.

The method of moral inquiry for which I argued some time ago made room for what I call "moral experience." This is quite different from the "experience" of most philosophical writing, in ethics as well as in epistemology, where the term refers to empirical experience. Empirical observation is of course part of experience, but so is choosing what to do, so is the experience of feeling either disapproval or empathy, and so is the awareness that we share social relationships with other persons. In my view, moral theories need to be found to withstand the trials of actual moral experience, which is not at all the same as to advocate naturalistic moral theories that can meet the tests of empirical experience. To the extent that moral theories include judgments about empirical matters, such as that the consequences of x will be y and y is morally bad, the empirical component should of course be empirically accurate. But moral theories are not empirical theories; they address themselves to questions about what we *ought* to do, and they judge outcomes and feelings in distinctively *moral* terms.

Moral experience is the experience of consciously choosing to act, or to refrain from acting, on grounds by which we are trying conscientiously to be guided. *Moral* experience is the experience of accepting or rejecting moral positions for what we take to be good moral reasons or well-founded moral intuitions or on the basis of what we take to be justifiable moral feelings. *Moral* experience is the experience of approving or disapproving of actions or states of affairs of which we are aware and of evaluating the feelings we have and the relationships we are in.

When I first started using the term 'moral experience' in talks I gave in the 1970s and in papers published soon after, I encountered incredulity: What can you mean by moral experience? To most philosophers, "experience" meant empirical observation. By now the term seems to present fewer problems; a president of the Midwestern Division of the American Philosophical Association used it throughout his address to the annual meeting of that group in 1990, without expressing any need to explain it.[2] I count that as progress.

The view I developed of moral experience and its relation to moral theory seems to me entirely compatible with and strengthened by a feminist view of experience. The central category of feminist thought, at least in its contemporary phase, is experience. It is not the constricted experience of mere empirical observation. It is the lived experience of feeling as well as thought, of acting as well as receiving impressions, and of connectedness to other persons as well as to self. Time and time again, feminist inquiry begins here and returns to the experience of women so inadequately reflected in the thought that has been taken as standard, which we can now so often recognize as constructed from points of view privileged in terms of gender as well as of race, class, and culture. When women test male constructs against our own experience, we often experience conflict. Because of male domination, we may have attributed the clash to what we imagined to be our limited capacities, in comparison to men, to think or to act. But in times of flourishing feminist expression, the theories men have constructed are often undermined by our lived experience.

Few feminists identify ourselves specifically as pragmatists, but perhaps most of us could offer more support for pragmatism at its best than most pragmatists realize. We would, however, have to transform pragmatism as so far developed for it to be compatible with feminism. Since experience, as feminists understand it, is not limited to the perceptual experience on which Charles Pierce had theory rely, nor to experience as the predictor of future experience, as with William James, nor to the empirical, problem-solving experience invoked by John Dewey, feminists may never be in large numbers feminist pragmatists the way many are socialist feminists. But it is experience all the same to which we constantly return, at least in the United States. As Catharine Stimpson observes, "The trust in women's experience in North American feminist writing has been as common and as pervasive as city noise."[3] And Catharine MacKinnon writes of feminism that "its project is to uncover and claim as valid the experience of women."[4]

It is from experience that we adopt our critical stance toward what has been claimed as "knowledge" in male-dominated society. It is experience with which we confront and protest existing institutions and distributions of power. It is experience on which we trace suggested patterns for the future. And, I believe, it is moral experience to which we are now subjecting traditional moral theories and our own proposals for how we ought to live.

Experience and Belief

A large question in ethics is whether or not our experience of moral approval or disapproval is always a function of our beliefs, whatever they are. To use an example made familiar by Gilbert Harman, if we already *believe* that setting fire to a cat is wrong, then when we see some children pouring gasoline on a cat and lighting it, we will disapprove. But the disapproval, according to this view, is never independent of the belief. My view, in contrast, is that the moral experience of disapproval or approval *may* sometimes be independent of our beliefs, including our moral beliefs, at any given time, and that, indeed, we ought to decide what moral theories to *believe* in conjunction with the *independent* moral experience to which such theories should be subjected.

Let's consider another example relating to animals. A person may grow up believing that eating meat is beneficial to one's health and pleasing to the taste, that a diet rich in meat is appropriate to the kind of life one wishes to live, and that eating meat is morally permissible in an unproblematic way. But after learning about "factory farming" and about the painful and degrading conditions in which animals are raised and slaughtered, this person may decide that one ought not to eat animals raised under these conditions if doing so contributes to the perpetuation or increase of this kind of farming. We can grant that one's beliefs about the costs and benefits to health of eating meat may be revised on purely empirical grounds. An awareness of how much a wealthy society's high meat consumption contributes to inequities in world distribution of available food may also affect one's judgment about whether to eat meat. And knowledge of various aspects of meat production may gradually affect the enjoyment gained from its taste. But here I am concerned with moral experience *other than* empirical experience.

Let's concentrate on the single issue of factory farming. If one already believes that to cause unnecessary pain to animals is wrong and then judges that a method of raising calves causes them severe and quite unnecessary pain, then a judgment of disapproval of that farming method follows. But one might well have been previously undisturbed by knowledge of the pain inflicted on animals raised for meat. Then, let us suppose, on a visit to a factory farm one sees at firsthand how small the space is that the animal is confined in and how the animal struggles to escape confinement. One may still doubt whether the animal is aware of its situation in a way that would make it "conscious" of its dissatisfaction. But if one comes to a judgment that, other things being equal, the animal should not be kept in such conditions, this judgment may be arrived at independently of any general beliefs about how animals ought to be treated and how the profits of farming and the satisfaction of consumers ought to be weighed against the distress of animals.

The particular judgment disapproving the treatment of the animal can, in my view, be based on what persons feel, on what positions they choose to take in the particular context in question, rather than on the basis of beliefs they already have. It can be a judgment independent of previous moral beliefs. This does not mean that such a judgment is irrevocable or "foundational"—it may well be revised in the light of all the other judgments and principles by which a person decides to be guided. But it means that it is one of the judgments between which coherence should be sought. And that the judgment is based on feelings or is a choice colored by emotion does not, in my view, invalidate it, as many moral theories suppose. On the contrary, such particular judgments are often justifiably based on feelings.

Once one has arrived at a particular judgment, one needs to bring it into coherence with other related judgments. In doing so, one may decide that in some cases the needs of people for food outweigh some levels of distress to animals. But a previous web of judgments that did not include them may be replaced by a web that includes the general judgments that the pain caused by humans to animals should be decreased, and that various methods of factory farming cause so much pain as to be morally unacceptable.

Moral experience, as I understand it, includes the sort of judgment we arrive at independently of moral theory. It includes the sort of choices we make about how to act, arrived at independently of general moral judgments to which we think we are committed. Sometimes we already have moral theories or general judgments recommending how we ought to act, and we act in accordance with them and judge that we acted rightly. Or, if we fail to act in accordance with them, we judge that we acted wrongly, out of weakness of will perhaps, but we maintain our belief in the theory or judgment. At other times, we choose to act because that particular act seems right to us regardless of any moral theory or abstract generality. And sometimes we continue to suppose that the particular act was morally justified. This may then require us to revise our moral beliefs because the act we judge right conflicts with what a theory we previously thought satisfactory would recommend. But rather than suppose that the act was wrong because the theory said so, we might *justifiably* retain the judgment arrived at in the moral experience of acting, and we might reject the theory. And if this is part of a sincerely pursued process of trying to develop a coherent network of moral beliefs by which to be guided, it need not be thought of as rationalization, but rather as part of an appropriate internal dialogue aiming to continually improve one's moral understanding.

Certainly not all our experience can serve as the kind of "test" of theory I am discussing. And the experience that can so serve need not be actively sought; sometimes we stumble upon an experience that clashes with our previous moral beliefs.[5] What is needed is that the moral inquirer interpret the experience, either before, during, or after its occurrence, as such a test, and interpret the perspective in question, whichever it is, as the most valid.

For instance, suppose that a woman has grown up believing that a fetus's right to life makes abortion wrong in all cases except when failure to abort violates the mother's right to life. And then suppose that the woman is already a single parent, working to support her child, and that she finds herself pregnant as a result of rape. She realizes that if she remains pregnant and gives birth, it will be possible to place the infant for adoption, but she decides, instead, to have an abortion. Afterwards she continues to feel that she did the right thing. The judgment, in actual circumstances, that her abortion was justified requires her to revise her view on the nearly absolute right of the fetus. Reasons such as how the fetus was brought into being and the effects of the pregnancy on her and her child are now seen as relevant, in a way they were not before, to decisions about the morality of abortion.

This method resembles to some extent that of John Rawls's "reflective equilibrium" with a very significant difference.[6] The judgments between which equilibrium is to be sought will in my view deliberately include rather than deliberately exclude particular judgments based on feelings and arrived at in actual circumstances in which we are not necessarily impartial. This is a difference that also distinguishes the method I advocate from the "wide reflective equilibrium" frequently discussed among philosophers interested in moral theory.

"Reflective equilibrium" requires that coherence be sought between our particular judgments (about justice, for instance) and our general normative principles (of justice, for instance). "Wide reflective equilibrium" requires that these be coherent as well with our background philosophical ways of thinking—with contractualism, say, for those who find it persuasive—and with our reasons for subscribing to them.[7]

Rawls counsels us to seek equilibrium between our particular "considered" judgments and our general principles, such as our principles of justice and equality. He offers his principles of justice as a means for us to do so. But he counsels us to admit into our pool of "considered judgments" only those which have been laundered of their entanglements with self-interested or other emotional colorings. Rawls thinks we should discount any judgments we make "when we are upset or frightened, or when we stand to gain one way or the other."[8] I argue, in contrast, that judgments based on feelings can and should be included among those between which we seek coherence.

The Process of Inquiry

Moral inquiry is an ongoing process. To see it as rational reflection providing theory, followed by the straightforward application of that theory to particular cases, is, in my view, unsatisfactory. Rather, it should be seen as a process of continual adjustment of theory in the light of moral experience, as well as of particular judgments and actions in the light of theory.

I worked out these views chiefly in connection with examples of political decisions taken on moral grounds, such as whether to engage in civil disobedience to protest the war in Vietnam or whether government has an obligation to provide basic necessities for the poor and unemployed. When I did so, I was not consciously approaching the issues from a feminist perspective, although, as a feminist, I was concerned about the way those views, if implemented, would affect women. But I had not yet explicitly thought about feminist moral theory and whether it would be different from any other moral theory I could find adequate.

My first explorations into feminist moral theory were approached as if this were a new topic, and I remained unclear for some time about how to mesh moral theory developed from a feminist point of view with what I took to be moral theory as such, from any point of view. But gradually I came to recognize that what could be thought of as the methodology implicit in feminist moral theory coincided closely with what I had come to believe should be the method of moral inquiry appropriate from any point of view.

For instance, one of the claims made by many feminist moral theorists is that room must be made for what some call the moral emotions. The rationalism of many traditional moral theories, both the pure rationalism of Kantian ethics and the calculating rationalism of utilitarian approaches, is suspect in its denigration of emotion, in its advocacy of morality as involving a suppression of the emotions or a distancing of the self from feelings that may cloud what a rational man would hold or what an ideal observer would judge.

Feminists often insist on the importance of the emotions in moral understanding.[9] We value emotion not only in the way traditional moral theories do—as feelings to be cultivated to help us carry out the dictates of reason or as preferences setting goals toward which utilitarian calculations will recommend rational means. Although such theorists as Mill and Rawls applaud the cultivation of certain appropriate feelings, they value these feelings for their assistance in carrying out the requirements of morality, not in helping us to understand what these requirements are. And although utilitarianism and rational choice theory recognize the emotions as giving us the desires whose satisfaction we should seek to maximize, emotions are to be discounted in calculating how we morally ought to act so as to maximize the satisfaction of these desires among all those affected.

Many feminists argue, in contrast, that the emotions have an important function in developing moral understanding itself, in helping us decide what the recommendations of morality themselves ought to be. Feelings, they say, should be respected by morality rather than dismissed as lacking impartiality. Yes, there are morally harmful emotions, such as prejudice, hatred, desire for revenge, blind egotism, and so forth. But to rid moral theory of harmful emotions by banishing all emotion is misguided. Such emotions as empathy, concern for others, hopefulness, and indignation in the face of cruelty—all these may be crucial in developing appropriate moral positions. An adequate moral theory should be built on appropriate feelings as well as on appropriate reasoning. And that such a view requires us to suppose we already understand what feelings are appropriate is no more insurmountable an obstacle than that other views require us to suppose we already understand what train of reasoning is appropriate for morality. *Some* circularity may be inescapable on any plausible view of inquiry.

The emphasis of many feminists working in ethics and in moral development is on the concerns and implications of *caring:* caring for children, caring for the ill or infirm, caring about the feelings of others, and understanding how to care for human beings, including ourselves, enmeshed as we are in human relationships, and finally, also, caring about the globe. The caring so central here is partly emotional. It involves feelings and requires high degrees of empathy to enable us to discern what morality recommends in our caring activities.

Many philosophers emphasize the way reason and emotion are interconnected, pointing out that reasoning characteristically has an affective component and that our emotions characteristically have a cognitive content.[10] I am inclined to keep the concepts distinct for the sake of descriptive clarity but to acknowledge that the human moral experience against which we should test our moral theories characteristically involves both feeling and thought experienced together.

The practice of mothering brings out the way reason and emotion are entwined in the task of what Sara Ruddick names "preservative love":

> Rather than separating reason from feeling, mothering makes reflective feeling one of the most difficult attainments of reason. In protective work, feeling, thinking, and action are conceptually linked; feelings demand reflection, which is in turn tested by the

feelings it provokes. Thoughtful feeling, passionate thought, and protective acts together test, even as they reveal, the effectiveness of preservative love.[11]

Returning to the method of moral inquiry sketched before, one can see how well it incorporates the feminist concern for emotion along with reason and the feminist appreciation of appropriate feelings. This method holds that when particular judgments are arrived at independently of moral theory, they may justifiably include judgments based on the feelings of care and concern that we experience. Instead of dismissing judgments based on such feelings as incompatible with the demands of impartial reason, the method of moral inquiry I advocate should develop theories that are capable of being as compatible with these particular judgments as with abstract principles divorced from emotional experience.

Experience and Impartiality

Let's consider the concern a parent may feel for her child. Plato, in *The Republic,* is perhaps the best known of those for whom parental feelings are seen as a threat to the moral well-being of the whole society, at which well-being the members of the society ought to aim. Hegel, appreciating women's devotion to our families but finding it threatening to the state, writes that the state "creates for itself in what it suppresses and what it depends upon an internal enemy—womankind in general."[12]

Many other moral theorists suggest that such feelings as parental concern are at best irrelevant to morality. They are simply part of the empirical given within which morality makes its recommendations. A Kantian approach will, for instance, from the perspective of pure reason, indicate what obligations to respect other persons any one person owes any other. Special feelings of affection between a parent and child are among the emotional attitudes to be discounted as a parent reasons about what the Categorical Imperative requires. *It* may require that all parents provide their children, to the best of their ability, with such necessities as food and shelter. But then the moral course of action would be to do so out of respect for the moral law, not because of parental feelings of affection. A utilitarian theory may also calculate that for parents to provide for their children will be conducive to maximizing the happiness of all, counting each person's happiness as of equal worth. But again, the judgment of what a parent ought to do will be based on the principle of utility, rationally applied, not on parental feelings except to the extent that the satisfaction of them enters into the calculation.

But consider now a situation in which schoolchildren riding a bus are endangered. The parent of one child is present; those of the other children are not. The parent is in no way responsible for the other children being on the bus (as she would be if this were an outing in which she had invited them to participate). She has no role obligation to all the children equally as has the bus driver. Can this parent justifiably act to protect her child before acting to protect the other children? Does morality require her to treat every child impartially, including her own child as just one among all? Or may she act on her feelings of concern for her child, and must any adequate moral theory *allow* for such special feelings?

A legitimate question to ask would be whether the parent enjoys some special privilege that permits her to accompany her child on bus rides, while the parents of other children enjoy no comparable advantage, and whether that privilege is unfair. But let us assume that this is not the case. The parent's action, once the parent is on the bus, still raises moral issues concerning further fairness, and the impartiality that may or may not be required by morality.

This example resembles one discussed by Charles Fried and Bernard Williams. Fried had suggested that a man able to save one of two persons in equal peril could of course choose the one who was his wife, rather than treating both equally and making a random choice of whom to save.[13] Williams suggests that a man searching for some higher-order thought, such as one a rule-utilitarian might give—that each should look out for his own, a rule that would justify his choosing to save his wife rather than a stranger from drowning—has "one thought too many." He concludes that somewhere "one reaches the necessity that such things as deep attachments to other persons will express themselves in the world in ways that cannot at the same time embody the impartial view."[14] Williams sees these attachments as what gives a man's life enough "substance or conviction" for him to go on living.

Feminist moral theorists might share the views of Fried and Williams that the requirements of moral impartiality should not always be dominant and that one may give special consideration to one's spouse or child, but the feminist interpretation is apt to be different from that of nonfeminists. Instead of an individual man and his projects or attachments as the contrasting model opposing the dominance of impartiality, feminists tend to focus on relationships that contrast with impersonal impartiality and that are at least partially constitutive of the individuals in them.[15]

Feminist moral theories tend to acknowledge as central, rather than overlook or even condemn, relationships between actual persons. Hegel recognized relationships between parents and children and found the guarding of them appropriate for women, but he feared them as subversive of morality for male citizens, whose primary loyalty should be to the universal rationality realizable, in his view, only at the level of the state.[16] Other moral theories see family relationships as the natural bonds from which a rational individual will seek to free himself insofar as he is deciding what morality requires and is acting morally; the ideal of autonomy makes suspect relationships that are permanent and not chosen. Still other moral theories overlook family relationships altogether, employing such individualistic categories that relationships between persons become all but invisible.

In contrast, feminist moral theories almost never lose sight of such bonds as those of friendship and those that link parents and children. And in the situation under consideration, a feminist perspective would almost surely suggest that a parent who did not act to protect her own child might damage her relationship with that child in morally unacceptable ways. If we employ the method of moral inquiry recommended above, no moral theory would be acceptable that required a parent to disregard the relationship between her and her child or to fail to consider the health of that *relationship*, based as it needs to be on trust and concern. Moral theories would have to be tested for acceptability in the light of just those particular judgments of actual experience that might be based on a strong sense of the value of relationships between parents and children and on feelings about the importance of a child's trust.

Older children, or spouses, may come to value a parent's or a spouse's commitment to a moral principle requiring impartial treatment of all, even one's own child or spouse. A relationship of respect can be based on understanding such commitments. But then the issue might change. In the case I am considering, the issue is this: If trust *were* to be eroded by such treatment, would the commitment to principle still have priority for the morally conscientious person, regardless of the damage to the relationship between parent and child, or between spouses? On some traditional theories there could be principles yielding obligations to maintain the expectations of special relationships such as these. But if we take these obligations as questionable, we can consider the case I am suggesting, where the conflict is between actual relationship and abstract principle. A feminist approach to morality might give a felt relationship of trust priority over principle and seek a morality compatible with this priority.

Actual versus Hypothetical Experience

Another way in which a feminist approach to moral inquiry seems to coincide with the approach I earlier advocated is in its greater reliance on actual rather than on hypothetical experience. Traditional moral theory is frequently built on what a person might be thought to hold from the point of view of a hypothetical ideal observer, or a hypothetical purely rational being. Morality is to reflect what Thomas Nagel calls "the view from nowhere."[17] A hypothetical moral being is thought able to distance himself from the particular selfish interests and distorting passions of actual, embodied human beings, located in particular social and historical contexts. Feminists have often been critical of these attempts to ignore the reality of embodiment. We have seen how Susan Bordo puts it: the view from nowhere embodies the ideal of being everywhere, and the individual who is everywhere is necessarily disembodied. And as Alison Jaggar argues, "We must never forget that consent given hypothetically is never the moral equivalent of actual consent. Constructions of hypothetical consent have no independent moral force, any more than hypothetical experiments have independent evidential force."[18]

The method of moral inquiry I earlier developed relies on actual rather than hypothetical moral experience. It is suspicious of the inapplicability or remoteness of the theory developed from a hypothetical point of view, and it is critical of the inability of such theory to address actual moral problems as they arise for embodied, feeling human beings in specific historical and social contexts. In its development of relevant theory through a process of revising general principles in the light of particular judgments, it values the particular judgments arrived at in actual experience over those imagined to be acceptable in hypothetical circumstances.

Feminist moral inquiry, in like manner, often relies on actual, lived, moral experience. It pays attention to the neglected experience of women and to such a woefully neglected though enormous area of human moral experience as that of mothering. It attends to the actual experience of suffering domestic violence, of being conceptualized in terms of one's sexual availability or capacity to please men, of being exploited in the provision of care and affection. It suggests that moral theory will be adequate only if it can address moral problems in this kind of actual experience as well as in the actual experience for which traditional moral theories have claimed, though have often failed, to have relevance. And feminist moral inquiry suggests that women must be listened to as we express our actual experience and our efforts to act morally and to arrive at morally sound judgments in our actual, not hypothetical, lives.

Most feminist moral theory rejects a pure reliance on particular judgments. General principles are recognized as necessary.[19] For instance, principles demanding equal respect for women and an end to gender oppression are basic to almost all feminist theory. Feminist moral theory is thus seldom a kind of situation ethic; it does not embrace a pure case-by-case approach.[20] Neither is it characteristically relativistic.[21] But it does suggest that the principles that might be found adequate by feminist moral inquiry will have to be compatible with particular judgments based, often enough, on feelings of empathy and on caring concern rather than on rational calculation or abstract reasoning. And it does suggest that these judgments should be arrived at in actual rather than hypothetical experience, in the kind of experience which acknowledges the embodied and relational reality of human beings in actual historical contexts.

The Abstract Rational Agent

An example of a contemporary moral theorist who relies on abstract reason as the foundation of morality is Stephen Darwall. Because his views are characteristic of a highly influential contemporary approach to moral inquiry, I shall discuss them in some detail.

Darwall suggests that what we seek in our ethical inquiries are *unqualified* reasons to act, not just reasons to do something if it accords with our interests or with the ends we happen to have. With this I and many feminists would agree. But he goes on to locate the source of such justifying reasons in "what we would will for all from the perspective of an autonomous agent as such."[22] He thus relies, for devising answers to our questions about what we ought to do, on our conception of a purely rational, abstract individual and on what such an individual, from such an impartial position, would recommend.

Many feminists doubt that in trying to figure out what morality requires of us, we should adopt the point of view of the impartial, abstract "agent as such." Why not instead, we ask, approach the questions of morality from the points of view of embodied, related, actual persons? And many of us conclude that moral inquiry can more fruitfully be conducted from the points of view of actual persons in actual relationships than from the point of view of an abstract individual agent.

The persons from whose points of view I would hope for improvement in the development of morality would try to progress toward coherence between their particular moral judgments and their general principles. But the particular moral judgments between which they should seek coherence would not be the judgments of an abstract rational individual from whose perspective all particular emotions and interests had been washed out. They would be the particular judgments of embodied persons, persons with feelings for others and for themselves, with interests shared and unshared with others, and with ties to others that help make them the persons they are. Darwall's agent as such would have none of these feelings, interests, or ties. He would reason for hypothetical agents in hypothetical actions. Can this be persuasive as a basis for a morality that addresses the moral concerns we have in our actual lives?

One way moral theory based on impartial rationality has managed to overlook its unsuitability for much human moral experience has been through supposing that emotional ties and interactions between family members are not matters of *moral* import because they belong to the realm of "nature" rather than to the realm of "morality." A mother caring for a child, for instance, has been supposed to be acting on natural sentiment rather than moral principle. Behavior thus "governed" by natural impulses and not subject to moral deliberation is then treated as "outside morality." But how can the care of children possibly be imagined to lie outside morality? A parent trying to decide when to punish and when to forgive, or how to divide her attention between several children, or what ideals to hold up to her child, is of course engaged in acting morally. Certainly she is involved in moral deliberation. That this whole vast region of human experience can have been dismissed as "natural" and thus as irrelevant to morality is extraordinary. It may be outside moralities built entirely on abstract rationality, modeled as these are on an abstraction of the supposed "public" realm. But that only shows how deficient these moralities are for the full range of human moral experience.

Can the kind of pure rationality Darwall espouses yield the kinds of improvements in moral understanding we all should seek? I doubt it. This is not to say that rationality should be abandoned; it is to say that rationality must be tried out in and revised in the light of moral experience and must be supplemented by the moral understanding that can only be cultivated by embodied, empathetic actual persons.

Let's take a familiar illustration of the issues. Religious and practical instructions throughout the world at most times in history have included the directive addressed to wives: Obey your husbands. But do wives then really have reasons to obey our husbands? Many of us would say no. Even if some wives have promised to obey, that would at most be a prima facie reason that usually would be outweighed by other reasons. And even if we were to have reason to fear retaliation if we did not obey, that would at most recommend outward conformance together with inner resistance. But could such conclusions be drawn from the point of view of the abstract, autonomous individual upon whose rational judgments Darwall and many others would have moral justification rest?

One familiar argument is that such a point of view would indeed yield principles of equality for husbands and wives and that prescriptions that wives ought to obey our husbands would be incompatible with such principles. But we know that principles of equality must recognize some differences as relevant in deciding how equal treatment for equals is to yield plausible results rather than results which require the sick and the well to be treated so equally that both receive the same medication. Throughout most of the history of principles of equality, gender has been supposed to be a relevant difference permitting different treatment, and directives to wives to obey our husbands have thus not been recognized as in conflict with the point of view of the autonomous rational moral legislator. Neither Rousseau nor Kant saw any conflict. And if we add the formulation of the veil of ignorance, and ask, not knowing if one will be husband or wife, whether one could accept the principle that wives ought to obey husbands, it is unclear how an agent as such would reason. Reasoning alone might *not* preclude the conclusion: *If* I turn out to be a wife I should obey my husband. Only lived experience enables us to assert with conviction that gender is *not* a relevant difference on which to make exceptions to rational principles requiring equal treatment with respect to rights to vote or to occupational opportunities or to relations between husbands and wives.

To arrive at a convincing rejection of the directive that wives ought to obey our husbands requires, in addition to reasoning, the experience that families in which husbands and wives make decisions by consensus, and neither obeys the other, are not only empirically "workable," contrary to what Rousseau thought, but that they are built on a relation between husbands and wives that is morally better than the relation of obedience. Though such a judgment may begin in rational reflection, it should not end there. And to justify such a judgment morally we need not only to apprehend the rational validity of a principle of equality and to derive from it a judgment in a particular case, but to experience a relationship of equality and of respect and especially, perhaps, of trust.

Annette Baier thinks that trust is *the* fundamental concept of morality.[23]

If we only go so far as to think with her that trust is *a* central concept of morality, consider how it is overlooked by the reasoning of the autonomous agent as such. Trust is a relationship *between* actual persons; one agent reasoning about what he would will for all does not connect with it. Would he will that all be trusting? But sometimes trust is misplaced, and one ought *not* to trust another; to do so only increases the likelihood that some others will take advantage of one, as empirical studies of prisoner's dilemma situations have shown, for those whose own experience has not so instructed them. What should be sought by a morality recognizing the importance of trust would have to deal with real and felt relationships between actual persons. But an abstract, autonomous agent as such cannot be in such real and felt relationships. So a morality of autonomous agents as such may be ill suited to be a morality for actual human families and communities.

The moral experience in which the principles of morality should be tried out, and revised in the light of, must include not only those regions traditionally thought of as providing arenas for moral choice and application—the regions of law and state and public policy—but also such neglected regions as those of friendship and of the family, of bringing up children and caring for the vulnerable. Then, it seems, to decide *what* morality counsels will require a much richer experience than that available to the abstract agent of so much traditional moral theory. We do not play with our children out of respect for the moral law. Though the moral law may provide moral minimums beneath which we should not sink, flourishing childhoods and joyful friendships rest on a wide range of moral considerations beyond what the moral law requires.

The experience needed for morality is the experience of persons who are at least partly constituted by relations with other persons, not autonomous individual agents as such. What we may look to morality to provide is guidance as we navigate within our actual, embodied, historically located relationships. The morality that will then give us unqualified reasons to act, when it can give us reasons at all, will be quite different from what would be prescribed for innumerable autonomous but essentially abstract and timeless and nonexistent individuals.

A Morality of Contexts

The moral theory that would result from reliance on a feminist method of moral inquiry would be highly unlikely to proclaim any single, simple principle such as the Categorical Imperative or the Principle of Utility as applicable to all moral problems. Much more likely would be a pluralistic ethics, containing some principles at an intermediate level of generality, relevant to given domains, and many particular judgments sensitively arrived at in these various domains. For instance, principles about how conflict ought to be settled nonviolently could be offered for small numbers of persons: children in a household, adolescents in school, rivals for a lover's affection. Different contexts might have different procedures. Principles advocating nonviolence would also be offered for conflicts among large numbers of persons, such as ethnic groups, and for methods of achieving social change. The principle would be more sound if approached from the points of view of those experienced with the former, rather than solely from the point of view of purely rational, nonexistent beings. As Sara Ruddick has shown in *Maternal Thinking*, the context of mothering can be a fruitful source of insight concerning how peace should be sought in other domains. And moral principles need to be appropriate for given domains, not so remote and abstract as to lose sight of the differences between different contexts and between the persons and groups in them.

Even principles that are only at an intermediate level of generality may be of no more than tentative use in interpreting actual complex moral problems. Sensitivity to a wide range of moral considerations may often be more important than rigid adherence to principle. While the dangers of arbitrary ad hoc decisions are real, so are the dangers of distorting actual situations in order to fit them into the abstract legalistic categories of general principles. Persons cannot increase the trust between them by misinterpreting each others' problems and pains.

To whom does a principle apply? What does the principle provide? Although these are different questions, we cannot decide on the validity of a principle independently of the question of its applicability. If we hold that each living creature has a right not to be killed, does that mean we cannot swat a mosquito or that we must protect rabbits from foxes? When we reject these edicts, we must reject the principle, unless we qualify its applicability. On the other hand, principles providing that human beings ought to be treated with equal respect have not been applied across gender and racial lines. When they are so applied, we may continue to support the principle, while widening its applicability, although recognizing that equal respect cannot imply the same treatment of children and comatose human beings as it does of competent adults.

It is quite true that subordinate groups have often used an abstract, clear principle of equality to argue against their subordination. They have not taken issue with the principle of equality but have argued that a widely accepted principle should apply to a previously excluded group—that their members are also entitled to the equality that has been denied 'them. In such cases, a call by the dominant group to recognize the complexity of particular situations is often used to distract the aggrieved and to excuse the exclusion, and should be rejected. In such cases, clear principles can be of the utmost importance. But as soon as we try to interpret what equality may require in given contexts, we must move beyond the abstract principle to a consideration of particular factors.[24] And we see that such principles can give us, at most, a view of certain moral minimums which have a high priority but which hardly constitute an adequate morality.

By now, many moral theorists have gone on to suggest, in behalf of previously subordinated groups, that there is more to an adequate morality than can be seen from the point of view of the autonomous individual agent as such, the rational man of liberal theory. What more is needed is not merely an optional extra which liberal theory can permit those so inclined to pursue. As Annette Baier explains, "The liberal morality, if unsupplemented, may *unfit* people to be anything other than what its justifying theories suppose them to be, ones who have no interest in each others' interests."[25] And such people will be unfit to care for and bring up with appropriate affection and concern the next generation in a suitably cared-for environment.

Feminist morality will develop its principles with awareness of the differences between the contexts for which such principles are deemed suitable and with attention to the moral experience of those actually in such contexts. It will be more open than theories which rely on a single, simple, universal moral principle that can be invoked for every moral problem.

Achieving Consensus

Traditional approaches to moral theory often suggest that where individuals and groups have conflicting views on what ought to be done and how people ought to act, what they may be able to agree on are abstract principles, especially procedural ones, arrived at from the point of view of the abstract, rational individual. Thus John Rawls writes that "while men may put forth excessive demands on one another, they nevertheless acknowledge a common point of view from which their claims may be adjudicated."[26] From that point of view he offers his principles of justice as what would be agreed to. And Alan Gewirth, seeking even more clearly a moral rather than a merely political consensus, observes that "widely

different ideals and conceptions of well-being and benefit have been upheld as morally relevant, right, or good by different persons or groups."[27]
He argues that a supreme moral principle based entirely on the reasoning
available to the rational individual is the only satisfactory solution to such
conflict, and he offers his version of such a principle.

Many feminists, in contrast, suggest that agreement is much more
likely, and much more likely to be satisfactory, if it rests on actual dialogue between actual persons. Iris Young defends a "dialogic conception
of normative reason":

> Precisely because there is no impartial point of view in which a sub-
> ject stands detached and dispassionate to assess all perspectives, to
> arrive at an objective and complete understanding of an issue or ex-
> perience, all perspectives and participants must contribute to its dis-
> cussion. Thus dialogic reason ought to imply reasons as contextual-
> ized, where answers are the outcome of a plurality of perspectives
> that cannot be reduced to unity. In discussion speakers need not
> abandon their particular perspective nor bracket their motives and
> feelings. As long as the dialogue allows all perspectives to speak
> freely, and be heard and taken into account, the expression of need,
> motive and feelings will not have merely private significance, and
> will not bias or distort the conclusions because they will interact
> with other needs, motives and feelings.[28]

And in an influential article on how to develop feminist theory that
avoids cultural imperialism on the part of white Anglo women, Maria
Lugones and Elizabeth Spelman present the voice of a woman of color:

> If white/Anglo women are to understand our voices, they must un-
> derstand our communities and us in them . . . From within friend-
> ship you may be moved by friendship to undergo the very difficult
> task of understanding the text of our cultures by understanding our
> lives in our communities . . . [This learning] does not consist in a
> passive immersion in our cultures, but in a striving to understand
> what it is that our voices are saying. Only then can we engage in a
> mutual dialogue that does not reduce each one of us to instances of
> the abstraction called "woman."[29]

These calls do not ask that we all agree to take the point of view of the
abstract rational man, or woman, but that we listen to each other in actual
conversations in actual communities.

Many women of color have felt that in the women's movement in the
United States, relatively privileged white women were presuming to
speak for all women and that the claims made were often distorted ver-

sions of the experience of various minorities. The book entitled *All the Women Are White, All the Blacks Are Men, But Some of Us Are Brave: Black Women's Studies* is an example of black women expressing this resentment and seeking to give voice to actual experience.[30] By now many of us have learned to listen to each other across the divisions of race and class and ethnicity. The understanding we seek may be much more likely to arise out of actual conversation (some of it on paper) than out of a search for abstract principles to be chosen from the point of view of what some of us might think of as "woman as such."

Darwall claims that "the very search for unqualified justification is an exercise in autonomy."[31] But why? We might think instead that it should be an exercise in dialogue, in which embodied persons listen to other embodied persons, and try to adjust not only their own particular embodied and felt judgments to their own principles, but their own sense of what a reasonable morality demands to the comparable sense of others. This is a different process from that of reasoning to what we would will for all from the standpoint of the impartial, autonomous agent as such, and many feminists find nothing in nonfeminist moral theory to refute the claim that it might be a better process.

The morality such a dialogue might produce would be a morality suitable for existing rather than merely hypothetical agents. To the extent that this morality will give us reasons to act, along with its judgments of moral worth and its cultivations of moral emotions, these reasons will be unqualified in Darwall's sense. But they will never be unqualified in the sense of absolute or certain. And they will not be reasons that rest on reasoning alone.

It may well be that for *some* types of moral problems, the point of view of the autonomous agent as such *is* morally appropriate. But to make such a judgment we need a fuller and richer and more nuanced view of morality within which to decide that we have unqualified reasons to treat some but *not* all moral problems in that way. And the search for *that* morality and *its* justification must continue. A feminist approach offers prospects for coming closer to achieving such a morality.

Is there anything really new about feminist moral inquiry, and will the theory that results be different from nonfeminist moral theory? In the next two chapters, I will look further at feminist moral concepts and theory in an attempt to answer these questions.

THREE

Transformations of
Moral Concepts

If we turn to the history of philosophy, including the history of ethics, we can see that it has been constructed from male points of view and has been built on assumptions and concepts that are by no means gender-neutral.[1] Lorraine Code points out the significance of the way feminists characteristically begin with different concerns and give different emphases to the issues we consider: "Starting points and focal points shape the impact of theoretical discussion."[2] Far from merely providing additional insights that can be incorporated into traditional theory, feminist explorations often require radical transformations of existing fields of inquiry and theory.[3] From a feminist point of view, moral theory, along with almost all theory, will have to be transformed to take adequate account of the experience of women.

Bias in the History of Ethics

Consider the ideals embodied in the phrase "the man of reason." As Genevieve Lloyd has told the story, what has been taken to characterize the man of reason may have changed from historical period to historical period, but in each, the character ideal of the man of reason has been constructed in conjunction with a rejection of whatever has been taken to be characteristic of the feminine. "Rationality," Lloyd writes, "has been conceived as transcendence of the 'feminine,' and the 'feminine' itself has been partly constituted by its occurrence within this structure."[4]

This has, of course, fundamentally affected the history of philosophy and of ethics. The split between reason and emotion is one of the most familiar of philosophical conceptions. The advocacy of reason "controlling" unruly emotion, of rationality guiding responsible human action against the blindness of passion, has a long and highly influential history, almost as familiar to nonphilosophers as to philosophers. Lloyd sums it up:

> From the beginnings of philosophical thought, femaleness was symbolically associated with what Reason supposedly left behind—the

43

dark powers of the earth goddesses, immersion in unknown forces associated with mysterious female powers. The early Greeks saw women's capacity to conceive as connecting them with the fertility of Nature. As Plato later expressed the thought, women "imitate the earth."[5]

In asserting its claims and winning its status in human history, Reason was thought to have to conquer the female forces of Unreason. Reason and clarity of thought were early associated with maleness, and as Lloyd says, "What had to be shed in developing culturally prized rationality was, from the start, symbolically associated with femaleness." In later Greek philosophical thought, the form/matter distinction was articulated, with a similar hierarchical and gendered association. Maleness was aligned with active, determinate, and defining form; femaleness with mere passive, indeterminate, and inferior matter. Plato, in the *Timaeus*, compared the defining aspect of form with the father, and indefinite matter with the mother; Aristotle also compared the form/matter distinction with the male/female distinction. To quote Lloyd again, "This comparison . . . meant that the very nature of knowledge was implicitly associated with the extrusion of what was symbolically associated with the feminine."[6]

The associations among Reason, form, knowledge, and maleness have persisted in various guises and have permeated what has been thought to be moral knowledge as well as what has been thought to be scientific knowledge and what has been thought to be the practice of morality. The associations between the philosophical concepts and gender cannot be merely dropped and the concepts retained regardless of gender, because gender has been built into them in such a way that without it, they will have to be different concepts. As feminists repeatedly show, if the concept of "human" were built on what we think about "woman" rather than what we think about "man," it would be a very different concept. Ethics, thus, has not been a search for universal, or truly human guidance, but a gender-biased enterprise.

Other distinctions and associations have supplemented and reinforced the identification of reason with maleness, and of the irrational with the female; on this and other grounds "man" has been associated with the human, "woman" with the natural. Prominent among distinctions reinforcing the latter view has been that between the public and the private. Again, these provide as familiar and entrenched a framework as do reason and emotion, and they have been as influential for nonphilosophers as for philosophers. It has been supposed that in the public realm man transcends his animal nature and creates human history. As citizen, he creates government and law; as warrior, he protects society by his willingness to risk death; and as artist or philosopher, he overcomes his human mortality. Here, in the public realm, morality should guide human decisions. In the household, in contrast, it has been supposed that women merely "reproduce" life as natural, biological matter. Within the household, the "natural" needs of man for food and shelter are served, and new instances of the biological creature that man is are brought into being. But what is distinctively human and what transcends any given level of development to create human progress have been thought to occur elsewhere.

This contrast was made explicit in Aristotle's conceptions of polis and household; it has continued to affect the basic assumptions of a remarkably broad swath of thought ever since. In ancient Athens, women were confined to the household; the public sphere was literally a male domain. The associations of the public, historically male sphere with the distinctively human, and of the household, historically a female sphere, with the merely natural and repetitious, have persisted, even though women have been permitted to venture into public space. These associations have deeply affected moral theory, which has often supposed the transcendent, public domain to be relevant to the foundations of morality in ways that the natural behavior of women in the household could not be.

To take some representative examples, David Heyd, in his discussion of supererogation, dismisses a mother's sacrifice for her child as an example of the supererogatory because it belongs, in his view, to "the sphere of natural relationships and instinctive feelings (which lie outside morality)."[7] J. O. Urmson had earlier taken a similar position, saying, "Let us be clear that we are not now considering cases of natural affection, such as the sacrifice made by a mother for her child; such cases may be said with some justice *not to fall under the concept of morality*" (emphasis added).[8] And in his article "Distrusting Economics," Alan Ryan argues persuasively about the questionableness of economics and other branches of the social sciences built on the assumption that human beings are rational, self-interested calculators. He discusses various examples of behavior, such as that of men in wartime, which is not self-interested and which shows the assumption to be false; but nowhere in the article is there any mention of the activity of mothering, which would seem to be a fertile locus for doubts about the usual picture of rational man.[9] Although Ryan does not provide the kind of explicit reason offered by Heyd and Urmson for omitting mothering from consideration as relevant to his discussion, it is difficult to understand the omission without a comparable assumption being implicit here, as it so often is elsewhere. Without feminist insistence on the relevance for morality of the experience in mothering, this context is largely ignored by moral theorists. And yet from a gender-neutral point of view, how can this vast and fundamental domain of human experience possibly be imagined to lie "outside morality"?

The result of the distinction between public and private, as usually formulated, has been to privilege the points of view of men in the public domains of state and law, and later in the marketplace, and to discount the experience of women. Mothering has been conceptualized as a primarily biological activity, even when performed by human beings, and virtually no moral theory in the history of ethics has taken mothering, as experienced by women, seriously as a source of moral insight, until feminists in recent years began to.[10] Women have been seen as emotional rather than rational beings, and thus incapable of full moral personhood. Women's behavior has been interpreted as either "natural" and driven by instinct, and thus as irrelevant to morality and to the construction of moral principles, or it has been interpreted, at best, as in need of instruction and supervision by males better able to know what morality requires and better able to live up to its demands.

The Hobbesian conception of reason is very different from the Platonic or Aristotelian conceptions before it and from the conceptions of Rousseau or Kant or Hegel later; all have in common the habit of ignoring and disparaging the experience and reality of women. Consider Hobbes's account of man in the state of nature contracting with other men to establish society. These men hypothetically come into existence fully formed and independent of one another, and decide either to enter civil society or stay outside of it. As Christine Di Stefano writes, "What we find in Hobbes's account is a vital concern with the survival of a gendered subject conceived in modern masculine terms . . . In the state of nature, Hobbes's masculine egoism carries the day . . . the specifically gendered dimension of this egoism is underscored by a radical atomism erected on the denial of maternity."[11]

In *The Citizen,* where Hobbes gave his first systematic exposition of the state of nature, he asks us to "consider men as if but even now sprung out of the earth, and suddenly, like mushrooms, come to full maturity, without all kind of engagement with each other."[12] Di Stefano points out that it is an incredible feature of Hobbes's state of nature that the men in it "are not born of, much less nurtured by, women, or anyone else" and that to abstract from the complex web of human reality an abstract man for rational perusal, Hobbes has "expunged human reproduction and early nurturance from his account of basic human nature and primordial human relations. Such a descriptive strategy ensures that Hobbes can present a thoroughly atomistic subject."[13]

From the point of view of women's experience, such a subject or self is unbelievable and misleading, even as a theoretical construct. The man-made political Leviathan Hobbes erects on these foundations "is effectively composed," Di Stefano writes, "of a body politic of social orphans who have socially acculturated themselves." Hence, Hobbesian man "bears the tell-tale signs of a modern masculinity in extremis: identity through opposition, denial of reciprocity, repudiation of the (m)other in oneself and in relation to oneself."[14]

Rousseau and Kant and Hegel paid homage respectively to the emotional power, the aesthetic sensibility, and the familial concerns of women. But since in their views morality must be based on rational principle and since women were incapable of full rationality, or a degree or kind of rationality comparable to that of men, women were deemed to be inherently wanting in morality. For Rousseau, women must be trained from childhood to submit to the will of men lest their sexual power lead both men and women to disaster. For Kant, women were thought incapable of achieving full moral personhood, and women lose all charm if they try to behave like men by engaging in rational pursuits. For Hegel, women's moral concern for our families could be admirable in its proper place, but it is a threat to the more universal aims to which men, as members of the state, should aspire.[15]

These images of the feminine as what must be overcome if knowledge and morality are to be achieved, of female experience as naturally irrelevant to morality, and of women as inherently deficient moral creatures are all built into the history of ethics. Examining these images, feminists find that they are not the incidental or merely idiosyncratic suppositions of a few philosophers whose views on many topics depart far from the ordinary anyway; they are the nearly uniform reflection in philosophical and ethical theory of patriarchal attitudes pervasive throughout human history. Or they are exaggerations of ordinary male experience, which exaggerations then reinforce rather than temper other conceptions and institutions reflective of male domination. At any rate, they distort the actual experience of many men as well as women. Annette Baier has speculated why it is that moral philosophy has so seriously overlooked the trust among human beings that in her view is an utterly central aspect of moral life. "The great moral theorists in our tradition," she says, "not only are all men, they are mostly men who had minimal adult dealings with (and so were then minimally influenced by) women." For the most part they were "clerics, misogynists, and puritan bachelors," and thus it is not surprising that they focus their philosophical attention "so single-mindedly on cool, distanced relations between more or less free and equal adult strangers."[16]

As feminists, we deplore the male domination that so much of philosophy and moral theory reflect. But we recognize that the problem requires more than changing patriarchal attitudes, for moral theory as so far developed is incapable of correcting itself without almost total transformation. It cannot simply absorb the gender that has been "left behind," even if both genders want it to. To continue to build morality on rational principles opposed to the emotions and to include women among the rational will leave no one to reflect the promptings of the heart, which promptings can be moral rather than merely instinctive. To simply bring women into the public and male domain of the polis will leave no one to speak for the household. Its values have been hitherto unrecognized, but they are often moral values. Or to continue to seek contractual restraints on the pursuits of self-interest by atomistic individuals and to have women join men in devotion to these pursuits will leave no one involved in the nurturance of children and cultivation of social relations, which nurturance and cultivation can be of the greatest moral import.

There are very good reasons for women not to want simply to be accorded entry as equals into the enterprise of morality as so far developed. In a recent survey of types of feminist moral theory, Kathryn Morgan laments that "many women who engage in philosophical reflection are acutely aware of the masculine nature of the profession and tradition, and feel their own moral concerns as women silenced or trivialized in virtually all the official settings that define the practice."[17] Clearly women should not agree, as the price of admission to the masculine realm of traditional morality, to abandon our own moral concerns as women.

And so we are trying to shape new moral theory. Understandably, we are not yet ready to offer fully developed feminist moral theories. But we can suggest some directions our project is taking. As Morgan points out, there is not likely to be a "star" feminist moral theorist on the order of a Rawls or a Nozick:

> There will be no individual singled out for two reasons. One reason is that vital moral and theoretical conversations are taking place on a large dialectical scale as the feminist community struggles to develop a feminist ethic. The second reason is that this community of

feminist theoreticians is calling into question the very model of the individualized autonomous self presupposed by a star-centered male-dominated tradition . . . We experience it as a common labour, a common task.[18]

Promising dialogues are proceeding on feminist approaches to moral theory. As Alison Jaggar makes clear in her useful overview, there is no unitary view of ethics that can be identified as "feminist ethics." Feminist approaches to ethics share a commitment to "rethinking ethics with a view to correcting whatever forms of male bias it may contain." While those who develop these approaches are "united by a shared project, they diverge widely in their view as to how this project is to be accomplished."[19]

Not all feminists, by any means, agree that there are distinctive feminist virtues or values. Some are especially skeptical of the attempt to give positive value to such traditional "feminine virtues" as a willingness to nurture, or an affinity with caring, or reluctance to seek independence. They see this approach as playing into the hands of those who would confine women to traditional roles.[20] Other feminists are skeptical of all claims about women as such, emphasizing that women are divided by class and race and sexual orientation in ways that make any conclusions drawn from "women's experience" dubious.[21]

Still, it is possible, I think, to discern some focal points in current feminist attempts to transform ethics into an acceptable theoretical and practical activity. In the glimpse I have presented of bias in the history of ethics, I focused on what, from a feminist point of view, are three of its most questionable aspects: the split between reason and emotion and the devaluation of emotion; the public/private distinction and the relegation of the private to the natural; and the concept of the self as constructed from a male point of view. In the remainder of this chapter, I will examine further how some feminists are exploring these topics. We are showing that previous treatment of them has been distorted, and we are trying to reenvision the realities and recommendations with which these aspects of moral theorizing should deal.

Reason and Emotion

In the area of moral theory in the modern era, the priority accorded to reason has taken two major forms. On the one hand has been the Kantian, or Kantian-inspired, search for very general, abstract, deontological, universal moral principles by which rational beings should be guided. Kant's Categorical Imperative is a prime example. It suggests that all moral problems can be handled by applying an impartial, pure, rational principle to particular cases. It requires that we try to see what the general features of the problem before us are and that we apply to the problem an abstract principle or rules derivable from it. This procedure, it is said, should be adequate for all moral decisions. We should thus be able to act as reason recommends, and resist yielding to emotional inclinations and desires in conflict with our rational wills.

On the other hand, the priority accorded to reason in the modern era has taken a Utilitarian form. The Utilitarian approach, reflected in rational choice theory, recognizes that persons have desires and interests, and suggests rules of rational choice for maximizing the satisfaction of these desires and interests. While some philosophers in the tradition espouse egoism, especially of an intelligent and long-term kind, many do not. They begin, however, with assumptions that what is morally relevant are the gains and losses of utility to theoretically isolable individuals and that morality should aim to maximize the satisfaction of individuals. Rational calculation about such an outcome will, in this view, provide moral recommendations to guide all our choices. Like the Kantian approach, the Utilitarian approach relies on abstract general principles or rules to be applied to particular cases. And it holds that although emotion is, in fact, the source of our desires for certain objectives, the task of morality should be to instruct us on how to pursue those objectives most rationally. Emotional attitudes toward moral issues themselves interfere with rationality and should be disregarded.

Although the conceptions of what the judgments of morality should be based on and how reason should guide moral decision are different in Kantian and Utilitarian approaches, they share a reliance on a highly abstract, universal principle as the appropriate source of moral guidance, and they share the view that moral problems are to be solved by the application of such an abstract principle to particular cases. Both admire the rules of reason to be appealed to in moral contexts, and both denigrate emotional responses to moral issues.

Many feminist philosophers have questioned whether the reliance on abstract rules, rather than the adoption of more context-respectful approaches, can possibly be adequate for dealing with moral problems, especially as women experience them. Though Kantians may hold that complex rules can be elaborated for specific contexts, there is nevertheless an assumption in this approach that the more abstract the reasoning applied to a moral problem, the more satisfactory. And Utilitarians suppose that one highly abstract principle, the Principle of Utility, can be applied to every moral problem no matter what the context.

A genuinely universal or gender-neutral moral theory would be one that would take account of the experience and concerns of women as fully as it would take account of the experience and concerns of men. When we focus on women's experience of moral problems, however, we find that they are especially concerned with actual relationships between embodied persons and with what these relationships seem to require. Women are often inclined to attend to rather than to dismiss the particularities of the context in which a moral problem arises. And we often pay attention to feelings of empathy and caring to help us decide what to do rather than relying as fully as possible on abstract rules of reason.

Margaret Walker, for instance, contrasts feminist moral "understanding" with traditional moral "knowledge." She sees the components of the former as involving "attention, contextual and narrative appreciation, and communication in the event of moral deliberation." This alternative moral epistemology holds that "the adequacy of moral understanding decreases as its form approaches generality through abstraction."[22]

The work of psychologists such as Carol Gilligan has led to a clarification of what may be thought of as tendencies among women to approach moral issues differently from men. Rather than seeking solutions to moral problems by applying abstract rules of justice to particular cases, many of the women studied by Gilligan were concerned with preserving actual human relationships and with expressing care for those for whom they felt responsible. Their moral reasoning was typically more embedded in a context of particular others than was the reasoning of a comparable group of men.[23] One should not equate tendencies women in fact display with feminist views, since the former may well be the result of the sexist, oppressive conditions in which women's lives have been lived. But many feminists see our own consciously considered experience as lending confirmation to such psychological studies.

Feminist philosophers are in the process of reevaluating the place of emotion in morality in at least two respects. First, many think morality requires the development of the moral emotions, in contrast to moral theories emphasizing the primacy of reason. As Annette Baier observes, the rationalism typical of traditional moral theory will be challenged when we pay attention to the role of parent:

> It might be important for father figures to have rational control over their violent urges to beat to death the children whose screams en-

rage them, but more than control of such nasty passions seems needed in the mother or primary parent, or parent-substitute, by most psychological theories. They need to love their children, not just to control their irritation.[24]

So the emphasis in traditional theories on rational control over the emotions, rather than on cultivating desirable forms of emotion, is challenged by feminist approaches to ethics.

Second, emotion will be respected rather than dismissed by many feminist moral philosophers in the process of gaining moral understanding. The experience and practice out of which we can expect to develop feminist moral theory will include embodied feeling as well as thought. In an overview of a vast amount of writing, Kathryn Morgan states that "feminist theorists begin ethical theorizing with embodied, gendered subjects who have particular histories, particular communities, particular allegiances, and particular visions of human flourishing. The starting point involves valorizing what has frequently been most mistrusted and despised in the western philosophical tradition."[25] Foremost among the elements being reevaluated are women's emotions. The "care" of the alternative feminist approach to morality appreciates rather than rejects emotion, and such caring relationships cannot be understood in terms of abstract rules or moral reasoning. And the "weighing" so often needed between the conflicting claims of some relationships and others cannot be settled by deduction or rational calculation. A feminist ethic will not just acknowledge emotion, as do Utilitarians, as giving us the objectives toward which moral rationality can direct us; it will embrace emotion as providing at least a partial basis for morality itself and certainly for moral understanding.

Trust is essential for at least some segments of morality.[26] Achieving and maintaining trusting, caring relationships is quite different from acting in accord with rational principles or satisfying the individual desires of either self or other. Caring, empathy, feeling for others, being sensitive to each other's feelings—all may be better guides to what morality requires in actual contexts than may abstract rules of reason or rational calculation.

The fear that a feminist ethic will be a relativistic "situation ethic" is misplaced. Some feelings can be as widely shared as are rational beliefs, and feminists do not see their views as reducible to "just another attitude." In her discussion of the differences between feminist medical ethics and nonfeminist medical ethics, Susan Sherwin shows why feminists reject the mere case-by-case approach that prevails in nonfeminist medical ethics. This approach also rejects the excessive reliance on abstract rules characteristic of standard ethics, and in this way resembles feminist ethics. But the very focus on cases in isolation rules out attending to general features in the institutions and practices of medicine that, among other faults, systematically contribute to the oppression of women.[27] The difference of approach can be seen in the treatment of issues in the new reproductive technologies that may further decrease the control of women over reproduction.

This difference is not one of substance alone; Sherwin shows its implications for method as well. With respect to reproductive technologies one can see clearly the deficiencies of the case-by-case approach: what needs to be considered is not only choice as seen in the purely individualistic terms of this approach, but control at a more general level and how such control affects the structure of gender in society. Thus, a feminist perspective does not always counsel attention to specific case versus appeal to general considerations, as some sort of methodological rule. But the general considerations are often not the purely abstract ones of traditional and standard moral theory; they are the general features and judgments to be made about cases in actual (which means, so far, male-dominated) societies. A feminist evaluation of a moral problem should never omit the political elements involved; and it is likely to recognize that political issues cannot be dealt with adequately in purely abstract terms any more than can moral issues.

The liberal tradition in social and moral philosophy argues that in a pluralistic society and even more clearly in a pluralistic world, we cannot agree on our visions of the good life, on what is the best kind of life for human beings, but we can hope to agree on the minimal conditions for justice, for coexistence within a framework allowing us to pursue our visions of the good life.[28] Many feminists contend that the commitment to justice needed for agreement *in actual conditions* on even minimal requirements of justice is as likely to demand relational feelings as a rational recognition of abstract principles. Human beings can and do care—and are capable of caring far more than most do at present—about the suffering of children quite distant from them, about the prospects for future generations, and about the well-being of the globe. The mutually disinterested rational individualists of the liberal tradition would seem unlikely to care enough to take the actions needed to achieve moral decency at a global level, or environmental sanity for decades hence, since they seem unable to represent caring relationships within the family and among friends. Annette Baier puts it thus:

A moral theory, it can plausibly be claimed, cannot regard concern for new and future persons as an optional charity left for those with a taste for it. If the morality the theory endorses is to sustain itself, it must provide for its own continuers, not just take out a loan on a carefully encouraged maternal instinct or on the enthusiasm of a self-selected group of environmentalists, who make it their business or hobby to be concerned with what we are doing to mother earth.[29]

The possibilities as well as the problems (and we are well aware of some of them) in a feminist reenvisioning of emotion and reason need to be further developed, but we can already see that the views of nonfeminist moral theory are unsatisfactory.

The Public and the Private

A second questionable aspect of the history of ethics is its conception of the distinction between the public and the private. As with the split between reason and emotion, feminists are showing how gender bias has distorted previous conceptions of these spheres, and we are trying to offer more appropriate understandings of "private" morality and "public" life.

Feminists reject the implication that what occurs in the household occurs as if on an island beyond politics. In fact, the personal is highly affected by the political power beyond, from legislation about abortion to the greater earning power of men, to the interconnected division of labor by gender both within and beyond the household, to the lack of adequate social protection for women against domestic violence.[30] Of course we recognize that the family is not identical with the state, and we still need concepts for thinking about the private and the personal, the public and the political; but we do know they will have to be very different from the traditional concepts.

Feminists have also criticized deeper assumptions about what is distinctively human and what is "natural" in the public and private aspects of human life, and what is meant by "natural" in connection with women.[31] Consider the associations that have traditionally been built up: the public realm is seen as the distinctively human realm in which man transcends his animal nature, while the private realm of the household is seen as the natural region in which women merely reproduce the species. These associations are extraordinarily pervasive in standard concepts and theories, in art and thought and cultural ideals, and especially in politics. So entrenched is this way of thinking that it was reflected even in Simone de Beauvoir's pathbreaking feminist text, *The Second Sex*, published in

1949.[32] Here, as elsewhere, feminists have had to transcend our own early searches for our own perspectives.

Dominant patterns of thought have seen women as primarily mothers, and mothering as the performance of a primarily biological function. Then it has been supposed that while engaging in political life is a specifically human activity, women are engaged in an activity which is not specifically human. Women accordingly have been thought to be closer to nature than men, to be enmeshed in a biological function involving processes more like those in which other animals are involved than like the rational discussion of the citizen in the polis, or the glorious battles of noble soldiers, or the trading and rational contracting of "economic man."[33] The total or relative exclusion of women from the domain of public life has thus been seen as either fitting or inevitable.

The view that women are more determined by biology than are men is still extraordinarily prevalent. From a feminist perspective it is highly questionable. Human mothering is a far different activity from the mothering engaged in by other animals, as different as the work and speech of men is from what might be thought of as the "work" and "speech" of other animals. Of course all human beings are animal as well as human. But to whatever extent it is appropriate to recognize a difference between "man" and other animals, so is it appropriate to recognize a comparable difference between "woman" and other animals, and between the activities—including mothering—engaged in by women and the behavior of other animals.

Human mothering shapes language and culture, it forms human social personhood, it develops morality. Animal behavior can be highly complex, but it does not have built into it any of the consciously chosen aims of morality. In creating human social persons, human mothering is different in kind from merely propagating a species. And human mothering can be fully as creative an activity as those activities traditionally thought of as distinctively human, because to create *new* persons and new types of *persons* can surely be as creative as to make new objects, products, or institutions. *Human* mothering is no more "natural" or "primarily biological" than is any human activity.

Consider nursing an infant, often thought of as the epitome of a biological process with which mothering is associated and women are identified. There is no more reason to think of human nursing as simply biological than it is to think this way of, say, a businessman's lunch. Eating is a biological process, but what and how and with whom we eat are thoroughly cultural. Whether and how long and with whom a woman nurses an infant are also human, cultural matters. If men transcend the natural by conquering new territory and trading with their neighbors and making deals over lunch to do so, women can transcend the natural by choosing not to nurse their children when they could, or choosing to nurse them when their culture tells them not to, or singing songs to their infants as they nurse, or nursing in restaurants to overcome the prejudices against doing so, or thinking human thoughts as they nurse, and so forth. Human culture surrounds and characterizes the activity of nursing as it does the activities of eating or governing or writing or thinking.

We are continually being presented with images of the humanly new and creative as occurring in the public realm of the polis or in the realms of marketplace or of art and science outside the household. The very term 'reproduction' suggests mere repetition, the bringing into existence of repeated instances of the same human animal. But human reproduction is not repetition. This is not to suggest that bringing up children in the interstices of patriarchal families, in society structured by institutions supporting male dominance, can achieve the potential of transformation latent in the activity of human mothering. But the activity of creating new social persons and new kinds of persons is potentially the most transformative human activity of all. And it suggests that morality should concern itself first of all with this activity, with what its norms and practices ought to be, and with how the institutions and arrangements throughout society and the world ought to be structured to facilitate the right kinds of development of the best kinds of new persons. The flourishing of children ought to be at the very center of moral and social and political and economic and legal thought, rather than, as at present, at the periphery, if attended to at all.

Revised conceptions of public and private have significant implications for our conceptions of human beings and relationships between them. Some feminists suggest that instead of interpreting human relationships on the model of the impersonal "public" sphere, as standard political and moral theory has so often done, we might consider interpreting them on the model of the "private," or of what these relationships could be imagined to be like in postpatriarchal society. The traditional approach is illustrated by those who generalize, to regions of human life other than the economic, assumptions about "economic man" in contractual relations with other men. It sees such impersonal, contractual relations as paradigmatic, even, on some views, for moral theory. Many feminists, in contrast, consider the realm of what has been misconstrued as the "private" as offering guidance to what human beings and their relationships should be like in regions beyond those of family and friendship as well as in more intimate contexts. Sara Ruddick looks at the implications of the practice of mothering for the conduct of peace politics. Marilyn Friedman and Lorraine Code consider friendship, especially as women understand it, as a possible model for human relationships.[34] Others see society as noncontractual rather than as contractual.

Clearly, a reconceptualization is needed of the ways in which every human life is entwined with both personal and social components. Feminist theorists are rethinking and reorganizing the private and the public, the personal and the political, and thus morality.

The Concept of Self

Let me turn now to the third aspect of the history of ethics which I discussed and which feminists are reenvisioning: the concept of self. A major emphasis in a feminist approach to morality is the recognition that more attention must be paid to the domain between the self as ego, as self-interested individual, and the universal, everyone, others in general. Traditionally, ethics has dealt with these poles of individual self and universal all. Often it has called for impartiality against the partiality of the egoistic self; sometimes it has defended egoism against claims for a universal perspective. But most standard moral theory has hardly noticed as morally significant the intermediate realm of family relations and relations of friendship, of group ties and neighborhood concerns, especially from the point of view of women.

When it has noticed this intermediate realm it has often seen its attachments as threatening to the aspirations of the man of reason or as subversive of "true" morality. In seeing the problems of ethics as problems of reconciling the interests of the self with what would be right or best for "everyone," standard ethics has neglected the moral aspects of the concern and sympathy that people actually feel for particular others, and what moral experience in this intermediate realm suggests for an adequate morality.

The region of "particular others" is a distinct domain, where what can be seen to be artificial and problematic are the very egoistic "self" and the universal "all others" of standard moral theory. In the domain of particular others, the self is already constituted to an important degree by relations with others, and these relations may be much more salient and significant than the interests of any individual self in isolation.[35] The "others" in the picture, however, are not the "all others," or "everyone," of traditional moral theory; they are not what a universal point of view or a view from nowhere could provide.[36] They are, characteristically, actual flesh-and-blood other human beings for whom we have actual feelings and with whom we have real ties.

From the point of view of much feminist theory, the individualistic assumptions of liberal theory and of most standard moral theory are suspect.[37] Even if we were freed from the debilitating aspects of dominating male power to "be ourselves" and to pursue our own interests, we would, as persons, still have ties to other persons, and we would at least in part be constituted by such ties. Such ties would be part of what we inherently are. We are, for instance, the daughter or son of given parents or the mother or father of given children, and we carry with us at least some ties to the racial or ethnic or national group within which we developed into the persons we are.

If we look at the realities of the relation between mothering person (who can be female or male) and child, we can see that what we value in the relation cannot be broken down into individual gains and losses for the individual members in the relation. Nor can it be understood in universalistic terms. Self-development apart from the relation may be much less important than the satisfactory development of the relation. What matters may often be the health and growth and development of the relation-and-its-members in ways that cannot be understood in the individualistic terms of standard moral theories designed to maximize the satisfaction of self-interest. Neither can the universalistic terms of moral theories grounded in what would be right for "all rational beings" or "everyone" handle what has moral value in the relation between mothering person and child.

Feminism is, of course, not the only locus of criticism of the individualistic and abstractly universalistic features of liberalism and of standard moral theory. Marxists and communitarians also see the self as constituted by its social relations. But in their usual form Marxist and communitarian criticisms pay no more attention than liberalism and standard moral theory to the experience of women, to the context of mothering, or to friendship as women experience it.[38] Some nonfeminist criticisms, such as offered by Bernard Williams, of the impartiality required by standard moral theory, stress how a person's identity may be formed by personal projects in ways that do not satisfy universal norms yet ought to be admired. Such views still interpret morality from the point of view of an individual and his project, not a social relationship such as that between mothering person and child. And nonfeminist criticisms in terms of traditional communities and their moral practices, as seen for instance in the work of Stuart Hampshire and Alasdair MacIntyre, often take traditional gender roles as given or else provide no basis for a radical critique of them.[39] There is no substitute, then, for feminist exploration of the area between ego and universal, as women experience this area, or for the development of a refocused concept of relational self that could be acceptable from a feminist point of view.

Relationships can be evaluated as trusting or mistrustful, mutually considerate or selfish, harmonious or stressful, and so forth. Where trust and consideration are appropriate, which is not always, we can find ways to foster them. But to understand and evaluate relationships and to encourage them to be what they can be at their best require us to look at relationships between actual persons and to see what both standard moral theories and their nonfeminist critics often miss. To be adequate, moral theories must pay attention to the neglected realm of particular others in the actual relationships and actual contexts of women's experience. In doing so, problems of individual self-interest versus universal rules may recede to a region more like background, out-of-focus insolubility, or relative unimportance. The salient problems may then be seen to be how we ought best to guide or to maintain or to reshape the relationships, both close and more distant, that we have, or might have, with actual other human beings. Particular others can be actual children in need in distant continents or the anticipated children of generations not yet even close to being born. But they are not "all rational beings" or "the greatest number," and the self that is in relationships with particular others and is shaped to a significant degree by such relations is not a self whose ego must be pitted against abstract, universal claims.

The concept of a relational self is evolving within feminist thought. Among the interesting inquiries it is leading to is the work being done at the Stone Center at Wellesley College.[40] Psychologists there have posited a self-in-relation theory and are conducting empirical inquiries to try to establish how the female self develops. In working with a theory that a female relational self develops through a mutually empathetic mother-daughter bond, they have been influenced by Jean Baker Miller's reevaluation of women's psychological qualities as strengths rather than weaknesses. In 1976, Miller identified women's "great desire for affiliation" as one such strength. Nancy Chodorow's *Reproduction of Mothering*, published in 1978, has also had a significant influence on the work done at the Stone Center, as it has on much feminist inquiry.[41] Chodorow argued that a female sense of self is reproduced by a structure of parenting in which mothers are the primary caretakers and that sons and daughters develop differently in relation to a parent of the same sex, or a parent of different sex, as primary caretaker. Daughters come to define themselves as connected to or in relation with others. Sons, in contrast, come to define themselves as separate from or less connected with others. An implication often drawn from Chodorow's work is that parenting should be shared equally by fathers and mothers so that children of either sex can develop with caretakers of both same and different sex.

In 1982, Carol Gilligan offered her view of the "different voice" with which girls and women express their understanding of moral problems.[42] Like Miller and Chodorow, Gilligan valued tendencies found especially in women to affiliate with others and to interpret their moral responsibilities in terms of their relationships with others. In all, to value autonomy and individual independence over care and concern for relationships was seen as an expression of male bias. Psychologists at the Stone Center have tried to elaborate on and to study a feminist conception of the relational self. In a series of working papers, researchers and clinicians have explored the implications of the conception of the relational self for various issues in women's psychology (for example, power, anger, work inhibitions, violence, eating patterns) and for therapy.

The self as conceptualized in these studies is seen as having both a need for recognition and a need to understand the other, and these needs are seen as compatible. They are created in the context of mother-child interaction and are satisfied in a mutually empathetic relationship. This does not require a loss of self, but a relationship of mutuality in which self and other both express an understanding of each other's subjectivity. Both give and take in a way that not only contributes to the satisfaction of their needs as individuals but also affirms the "larger relational unit" they compose.[43] Maintaining this larger relational unit then becomes a goal, and maturity is seen not in terms of individual autonomy but in terms of competence in creating and sustaining relations of empathy and mutual intersubjectivity.

The Stone Center psychologists contend that the goal of mutuality is rarely achieved in adult male-female relationships because of the traditional gender system, which leads men to seek autonomy and power over others and to undervalue the caring and relational connectedness that is expected of women. Women rarely receive the nurturing and empathetic support they provide. Accordingly, these psychologists look to the interaction that occurs in mother-daughter relationships as the best source of insight into the promotion of the healthy relational self. This research provides an example of exploration into a refocused, feminist conception of the self and into empirical questions about its development.

In a quite different field, that of legal theory, a refocused concept of self is leading to reexamination of such concepts as property and autonomy and the role these have played in political theory and in constitutional law. For instance, the legal theorist Jennifer Nedelsky questions the imagery that is dominant in constitutional law and in our conceptions of property: the imagery of a bounded self, a self contained within boundaries and having rights to property inside a wall—rights to exclude others and to exclude government. The boundary metaphor, she argues, obscures and distorts our thinking about human relationships and what is valuable in them: "The boundedness of selves may seem to be a self-evident truth, but I think it is a wrong-headed and destructive way of conceiving of the human creatures law and government are created for." In the domain of the self's relation to the state, the central problem, she argues, is not "maintaining a sphere into which the state cannot penetrate, but fostering autonomy when people are already within the sphere of state control or responsibility." What we can from a feminist perspective think of as the male "separative self" seems on an endless quest for security behind such walls of protection as those of property. Property focuses the quest for security "in ways that are paradigmatic of the efforts of separative selves to protect themselves through boundaries."[44] But surely property is a social construction, not a thing; it requires the involvement of the state to define what it is and to defend it. Only constructive relationships can provide what we seek to assure through the concept of property.

In a discussion of autonomy, Nedelsky recognizes that of course feminists are centrally concerned with the freedom and autonomy to live our own lives. But, she argues, to express these concerns we need a language that will also reflect "the equally important feminist precept that any good theorizing will start with people in their social contexts. And the notion of social context must take seriously its constitutive quality; social context cannot simply mean that individuals will, of course, encounter one another." The problem, then, is how to combine the claim that social relations are a large part of what we are with the value of self-determination. Liberalism has been the source of our language of freedom and self-determination, but it lacks the ability to express comprehension of "the reality we know: the centrality of relationships in constituting the self."[45]

In developing a new conception of autonomy that avoids positing self-sufficient and thus highly artificial individuals, Nedelsky points out, first, that "the capacity to find one's own law can develop only in the context of relations with others (both intimate and more broadly social) that nurture this capacity," and, second, that "the 'content' of one's own law is comprehensible only with reference to shared social norms, values, and concepts."[46] She sees the traditional liberal view of the self as implying that the most perfectly autonomous man is the most perfectly isolated, and this she finds pathological.

Instead of developing autonomy through images of walls around one's property, as does the Western liberal tradition and as does United States constitutional law, Nedelsky suggests that "the most promising model, symbol, or metaphor for autonomy is not property, but childrearing. There we have encapsulated the emergence of autonomy through relationship with others . . . Interdependence [is] a constant component of autonomy."[47] And she goes on to examine how law and bureaucracies can foster autonomy within relationships between citizen and government. This does not entail extrapolating from intimate relations to large-scale ones; rather, the insights gained from experience with the context of child rearing allow us to recognize the relational aspects of autonomy. In work such as Nedelsky's we can see how feminist reconceptualizations of the self can lead to the rethinking of fundamental concepts even in terrains such as law, thought by many to be quite distant from such disturbances.

To argue for a view of the self as relational does not mean that women need to remain enmeshed in the ties by which we are constituted. Increasingly, women are breaking free from oppressive relationships with parents, with the communities in which we grew up, and with men—relationships in which we defined our selves through the traditional and often stifling expectations of others.[48] These quests for self have often involved wrenching instability and painful insecurity. But the quest has been for a new and more satisfactory relational self, not for the self-sufficient individual of liberal theory. Many might share the concerns expressed by Alison Jaggar that disconnecting ourselves from particular others, as ideals of individual autonomy seem to presuppose we should, might render us incapable of morality, rather than capable of it if, as so many feminists think, "an ineliminable part of morality consists in responding emotionally to particular others."[49]

I have examined three topics on which feminist philosophers and feminists in other fields are thinking anew bout where we should start and how we should focus our attention in ethics. Feminist reconceptualizations and recommendations concerning the relation between reason and emotion, the distinction between public and private, and the concept of the self are providing insights deeply challenging to standard moral theory. The implications of this work are that we need an almost total reconstruction of social and political and economic and legal theory in all their traditional forms as well as a reconstruction of moral theory and practice at more comprehensive, or fundamental, levels.

FOUR

Moral Theory from a Feminist Perspective

In previous chapters I have discussed the method by which feminist moral inquiry might best proceed, with special attention to concepts that feminists have begun to transform: reason and emotion, the public and the private, the concept of the self. I turn now to some recommendations that feminist moral theory might offer. But first a word about the search for theory.

The Need for Feminist Moral Theory

The claim that feminism requires a transformation of moral theory predictably encounters not only hostility but honest skepticism.[1] Skeptics wonder whether there is or can be such a thing as a distinctively feminist moral theory. They doubt that it could be more valid than, say, Marxist mathematics or Communist physics, since they imagine that the validity or truth of a theory should not depend on political outlook or gender. They may acknowledge that traditional principles of fairness or equality must be applied to women in ways that have not been applied in the past, but they disagree that the principles or the theories in which they are embedded need to be transformed. Many feminists respond that the likelihood of feminist moral theory being different from nonfeminist moral theory is at least as substantial as that Marxist social theory differs from the social theory of, say, traditional liberalism. And if feminism will change our views of almost everything, as many think it will, feminist moral theory might even be as different from nonfeminist moral theory as has all or most theory been different since Copernicus, Darwin, and Freud—who of course also built on their pasts.[2]

To those who draw analogies between moral theory and mathematics,[3] the suggestion that feminist moral theory might legitimately differ from nonfeminist moral theory would presumably be as suspect as the notion that there is a distinctively feminist mathematics. But to many of us, the analogy between moral theory and mathematics is much more suspect than the idea of feminist moral theory.

64

At the very least, we need theories to deal with what is already known about the differing experiences and approaches of women and men in dealing with moral problems. We already have a wealth of personal experience, of literary and reportorial accounts of women's experience, and of social scientific attention to the experience of women. And we already have evidence, from the work of Carol Gilligan and others, that girls and women tend to approach at least some moral problems in ways characteristically different from the ways boys and men do.[4]

In the 1960s and 1970s, the psychologist Lawrence Kohlberg concluded that in their moral development, children go through various stages during which they approach moral problems in characteristic ways.[5] From an early stage of worrying about whether they are likely to get caught and punished, they progress to a final stage, not reached by everyone, in which they decide what to do on the basis of universal moral principles and how to act out of respect for these principles. When further empirical studies were made using these stages as a basis of interpretation, some showed that girls do not progress as fast as boys.

Carol Gilligan, who had worked with Kohlberg, became suspicious of the claim that girls are less morally advanced than boys. She pointed out that the studies leading to Kohlberg's interpretation of moral development in terms of "stages" and to his conclusions about what to count as "progress" were based entirely on studies of boys. Kohlberg, following Piaget, had merely assumed the development of children could be understood by considering boys only. Gilligan found that girls and women seemed to approach moral problems differently and to speak in "a different voice." Whether it is a defective voice or just a different voice or perhaps even a better voice remains an open question.

Kohlberg's final stage bears a remarkable resemblance to Kantian morality. In the view of Gilligan and many feminist moral philosophers, when one listens to the moral reasoning of women, one can discern ways of interpreting moral problems and of organizing possible responses to them that are different from any of the established moral approaches, including Kohlberg's. Women seem to be more concerned with context, and we seem to rely less on abstract rules.

Some psychologists dispute the empirical claim that men and women score differently on Kohlberg's scale, showing that when education and occupation are similar, so are the scores.[6] But such findings fail to consider that the scale itself has been constructed from a masculine point of view, and that those who score equally with men may simply have been socialized to think the way men do.

Gilligan and various feminist moral theorists now speak of two main perspectives in the interpretation of moral problems: the "justice perspective" and the "care perspective." The justice perspective emphasizes universal moral principles and individual conscience. The care perspective pays more attention to people's needs and to the relations between actual people; it considers how these relations can be kept in good condition or repaired if damaged. On traditional moral theories, girls and women have been thought to be less morally advanced than boys and men; on feminist theories it might be boys and men who are morally slower because of their underdeveloped capacities for relatedness and for caring about others.[7]

Empirical studies have shown that females are significantly more inclined than males to cite compassion and sympathy as reasons for their moral positions.[8] We need theories to assess such differences as these and the others discussed, if they do indeed exist, and to consider whether and how, for instance, justice and care can be combined, or if not, whether and how they are incompatible. Feminist moral theorists are exploring these issues.

Gilligan finds that among the two-thirds of the men and women who focus on one perspective or the other, about half the women adopt the perspective of justice, and half the perspective of care; among the men who focus, nearly all focus on justice. She draws our attention to the fact that "if women were eliminated from the research sample, care focus in moral reasoning would virtually disappear."[9] Since women have been virtually ignored in the construction of traditional moral theory, it is not altogether surprising that moralities focusing on justice or abstract rules have often been imagined to be the only true moralities. Children, Gilligan and others find, seem to use both the approaches of justice and of care; the divergence develops as boys gradually give up "caring." Some girls join them. Whether this represents genuine moral development or learning the ways of male-dominated societies is obviously an important question; philosophical positions that merely assume the superiority of the moral thinking of men and of male experience fail to address it.

Also of interest are the observed differences of approach to moral problems evident when persons are dealing with an actual problem rather than thinking about a hypothetical one. The hypothetical problem studied by Kohlberg—whether Heinz should steal a drug to save his dying wife—is obviously a very different kind of problem from the real one faced by the women studied by Gilligan—whether or not to have an abortion. But even when two groups are asked about what seems to be the same problem, they may interpret it to a different degree as real or as hypothetical, and this difference too should be studied for its possible significance. In one study of college students facing an actual problem of civil disobedience (whether or not to participate in a sit-in) many used forms of reasoning rated higher on Kohlberg's scale in comparison with their reasoning about hypothetical dilemmas. On the other hand, many students whose actions were inconsistent with their ideologies used forms of reasoning rated lower on Kohlberg's scale for the actual problem compared with the hypothetical ones.[10]

Of course we need theory to understand whether the differences between women and men in approaching moral problems are historically and culturally determined and to what extent they result from more permanent aspects of femaleness and maleness.[11] This theory, while necessarily philosophical as well as largely empirical, will not be specifically moral. Still, even if such questions could be settled, we would need moral theory to evaluate the differences or lack of differences and to decide on the kind of moral theory compatible with feminist commitments to pay attention to the experience of women.

Traditionally, the experience of women has been located to a large extent in the context of the family. In recent centuries the family has been thought of as a private domain distinct not only from the public domain of the polis, but also from the domains of production and the marketplace. Women (and men) certainly need to develop moral inquiries appropriate to the context of mothering and of family relations, rather than accepting the application to this context of theories developed for the marketplace or the polis or dismissing family issues as outside morality because governed by "natural sentiments." We can certainly show that mothering requires moral decisions and guidelines and that these must often be different from those that now seem suitable for various other domains of activity. But we need to do more. We need to consider whether distinctively feminist moral theories, suitable for the contexts in which the experience of women has been or will continue to be located, are better moral theories than those already available and better for other domains as well.

Sara Ruddick was among the first of contemporary philosophers to discuss some of the considerations that arise in the context of mothering. She has argued that mothering calls forth "maternal thinking," which is different from the thinking arising in other contexts. "Maternal practice," she wrote, responds "to the historical reality of a biological child in a particular social world"; she sees humility and cheerfulness as values which emerge from the practice of mothering. These should not be confused with self-effacement and destructive denial, "their degenerative forms."[12]

If such valuations emerge from mothering, and if on reflection they are endorsed as evaluations appropriate to mothering, we can assert that the moral understanding of persons who mother, and not only their attitudes and activities, is different from that of persons who do not mother, because such values are the values of a distinct practice. And if we acknowledge that a mothering context is an appropriate one in which to explore moral values—an acknowledgment only prejudice could lead us to deny—then paying attention to this context, as feminist moral philosophy does, can lead to different moral theories than ignoring it.

Experience and Moral Inquiry

The experience of women so far has been distinctively different from the experience of men. We need a theory about how to count the experience of women. It is not obvious that it should count equally in the construction or validation of moral theory. Merely surveying the moral views of women is not necessarily going to lead to better moral theories. On the views of rationality that emerged in Greek thought and were developed in the Western philosophical tradition, Reason was associated with the public domain, from which women were largely excluded.[13] If the development of adequate moral theory would be best based on experience in the public domain, the experience of women would be less relevant to the development of adequate moral theory. But that the public domain is the appropriate locus for the development of moral theory is among the tacit assumptions of existing moral theory being effectively challenged by feminist scholars. We cannot escape the need for theory in confronting these issues.

We need to take a stand on what moral experience is. Moral experience, as I understand it, is the experience of consciously choosing, of voluntarily accepting or rejecting, of willingly approving or disapproving, of living with these choices, of acting and of living with these actions and their outcomes. Action and feeling are as much a part of experience as is perception. Then we need to take a stand on whether the moral experience of women is as valid a source or test of moral theory as is the experience of men—and to consider whether it may be more valid.

Engaging in the process of moral inquiry is surely as open to women as it is to men, though the domains where the process may be engaged in have been open to men and women in different ways. Women have had fewer occasions to experience for themselves the moral problems of governing, leading, exercising power over others (except children), and engaging in physically violent conflict. Men, on the other hand, have had fewer occasions for experiencing the moral problems of family life and of relations between adults and children. Though vast amounts of moral experience are open to all human beings who make the effort to become conscientious moral inquirers, the contexts in which experience is obtained may make a difference.

The insights offered by and the reliability of women's experience in engaging in the process of moral inquiry should be presumed to be as valid as in the case of men. To take a given moral theory such as a Kantian one and to decide that those who fail to develop toward it are deficient is obviously to impose a theory on experience, rather than letting experience affect the fate of theories, moral and other than moral. We can assert that as long as women and men experience different problems and as long as differences of approach to moral problems are apparent, moral theory ought to reflect the experience of women as fully as it reflects the experience of men. Men ought not to have the privileged position of having their experience count for more. If anything, their privileged position in society should make their experience more suspect rather than more worthy of counting, for they have good reasons to rationalize their privileged positions by moral arguments that will obscure or purport to justify these privileges.[14]

If the differing approaches to morality that seem to be displayed by women and men are the result of historical conditions, we could suppose that in nonsexist societies the differences would disappear, and at that point the experience of either gender would more adequately substitute for the experience of the other. But since we can hardly imagine what nonsexist society would be like, we can say that we need feminist moral theory to contribute to its development, and we need feminist moral theory to deal with the regions of experience that have been central to women, yet neglected by traditional moral theory.

If the differences between men and women in confronting moral problems are due to biological factors that will continue to provide women and men with different experiences, the experience of women should still count for at least as much as the experience of men. There is no justification on biological grounds for discounting the experience of women as deficient or underdeveloped. Biological "moral inferiority" makes no sense.

The available empirical evidence of differences in the ways women and men approach moral issues is sometimes thought to be based on report-age and interpretation rather than on something more "hard" and "scientific."[15] Clearly this evaluation does not undermine the claim that we need feminist moral theory. But even if the differences turn out to be insignificant, we will still need feminist moral theory to make the moral claim that women themselves are of equal worth as human beings. Moral equality has to be based on moral claims, and since the devaluation of women has been a constant in human society as so far developed and has been accepted by those holding a wide variety of traditional moral theories, feminist moral theory will continue to be needed to provide the basis for women's claims to equality.

Mothering and Markets

When we bring the experience of women fully into the domain of moral consciousness, we can see that the most central and fundamental social relation is that between mother or mothering person and child. It is mothering persons and children who turn biological entities into human social entities through their interactions. It is mothers and mothering persons who create children and construct with and for the child the human social reality of the child. The child's understanding of language and of symbols and of all that they create and make real occurs through cooperation between child and caretakers. Mothering persons and children thus produce and create the most basic elements of human culture. The development of language and the creation within and for each person of a human social reality thus seems utterly central to human society.

It is often argued that art and industry and government create new human reality while mothering merely reproduces human beings and their cultures and social structures. But in reality mothering persons change culture and social reality by creating the kinds of persons who can continue to transform themselves and their surroundings. And to create new and better persons is surely as creative as to construct new and better objects or institutions.

The familiar myth is that the original and creative achievements of the great men of history have been the result of the special talents within themselves which they developed. Or it has been thought that the bold and historic achievements of the masses have been the result of the social forces they brought into being. What is done in the sphere of government or production is seen as innovative, while what is done within the family is seen as the mere reproduction of people and forms. But just as bodies do not spring into being unaided and fully formed, neither do imaginations, personalities, or minds. New persons are created within families, in relations between mothering persons and children. And these relations are central not only to existing society but to its development.

In contrast, contractual relations, instead of being central or fundamental to society and morality, appear to be limited relations appropriate only for quite particular regions of human activity.[16] The relation of exchange between buyer and seller has often been taken as the model of all human interactions. Most of the social contract tradition has seen this relation as fundamental to law and political authority as well as to economic activity. And various contemporary moral philosophers believe that even morality itself should be based on the contractual relation.[17] The marketplace relation has become so firmly entrenched in our normative theories that it is rarely questioned as a proper foundation for recommendations extending far beyond the marketplace itself. Much moral thinking, then, is built on the concept of rational economic man. Relations between human beings are seen as justified, when they serve the self-interested goals of rational contractors.

In the society imagined in the model based on assumptions about rational economic man, connections between people become no more than instrumental. Nancy Hartsock effectively characterizes the worldview of these assumptions, and she shows how misguided it is to suppose that the relation between buyer and seller can serve as a model for all human relations: "The paradigmatic connections between people," on this view of the social world, "are instrumental or extrinsic and conflictual, and in a world populated by these isolated individuals, relations of competition and domination come to be substitutes for a more substantial and encompassing community."[18]

If instead we recognized the centrality of the relation between mothering person and child, the competition and desire for domination often thought of as characteristic of "human nature" would appear as a particular and limited connection suitable only, if at all, for a restricted marketplace. Such a relation of conflict and competition could be seen to be unacceptable for establishing the social trust on which public institutions must rest or for upholding the bonds on which caring, regard, friendship, or love, must be based.

A feminist approach to moral theory leads us to ask whether morality should not make room first of all for the human experience reflected in the social bond between mothering person and child and for the human projects of nurturing and of growth apparent for both persons in the relation. In comparison with this, the transactions of the marketplace seem peripheral, the authority of weapons and the laws they uphold beside the point. Clearly, the social map would be fundamentally altered by adoption of the point of view of feminist morality. Instead of seeing the relation between mothering person and child as peripheral and anomalous, and rational exchange as central, we might reverse the location of the "heart" or "foundation" or "core" of society. Relations between mothering persons and the future shapers of social reality would seem central, while the transient exchanges of rational calculators would seem relatively trivial. Social relations would be seen as dynamic rather than as fixed-point exchanges. And assumptions that human beings are equally capable of entering or not entering into the contractual relations taken to characterize social relations generally would be seen for the distortions they are. Though human mothers can, in an ultimate existentialist sense, do other than give birth, their choices to do so or not are usually highly constrained. And children, even human children, cannot choose at all whether to be born.

Perhaps no human relations should be thought of as paradigmatic for all the others. Relations between mothering persons and children can become oppressive for both, and relations between equals who can enter or not enter into agreements may seem attractive in contrast. But no mapping of the social and moral landscape can possibly be satisfactory if it does not adequately take into account and provide appropriate guidance for relations between mothering persons and children.

Suggestions have been made by some feminists that friendship rather than mothering should be the central category to be contrasted with rational contracting.[19] On the one hand this is appealing, since for many, friendship is a more satisfactory relationship, because based on choice, than are many family relationships. On the other hand, it weakens the contrast, since many friendships approach contractual relations in ways that the relation between mother and infant cannot. And we should not suppose that morality is somehow more relevant to satisfactory, chosen relationships than to unsatisfactory ones not chosen. To do so is to assume what we may be trying to show to be problematic.

When some male philosophers turn to friendship in this way, more often it seems to be part of a tradition of denying the significance of whatever it is in which they cannot participate. Giving birth is the foremost example, as they focus on giving birth to works of the mind or products of industry while overlooking the giving of birth to actual children. When feminist philosophers (who can be male) turn to friendship it is because they are skeptical that such a relation as that between parent and child—one not chosen—is capable of grounding any morality. But the very fact that it is not chosen is part of what makes it so important as an alternative to be considered. It requires us not to ignore the biological component but then to consider whether various contexts of human experience previously thought of in terms of voluntarily chosen relations do not actually resemble more nearly, instead, the circumstances, clearly not made by choice, of the family. We need to decide what to do and what to try to feel in any of the circumstances we find ourselves in. And devising an ethical theory that enables us to see this in connection with family relationships may help us to deal with relations in the wider world, where the members of impoverished societies have not chosen their circumstances and where models of social contracts—or friendships—freely entered into seem to be of so little help in deciding what to do here and now.

Between the Self and the Universal

Feminist approaches to moral theory often direct our attention to the domain between the self (the ego, the self-interested individual) on the one hand, and the universal (everyone, others in general) on the other. Traditionally, ethics has attended to these abstract or extreme alternatives but has neglected the intermediate region of family relations and relations of friendship, and felt sympathy and concern for particular other human beings. As Larry Blum has shown, "Contemporary moral philosophy in the Anglo-American tradition has paid little attention to [the] morally significant phenomena" of sympathy, compassion, human concern, and friendship.[20] The same is true of nonfeminist moral philosophy other than Anglo-American.

Standard moral philosophy has sometimes construed personal relationships as aspects of the self-interested feelings of individuals, as when a person might favor those he loves over those distant because it satisfies his own desires to do so. Or it has let others who are close stand in for the universal "other," as when the conflict between self and others might be resolved into something like "enlightened self-interest" or "acting out of respect for the moral law" and seeing this as what should guide us in our relations with those close, particular others with whom we interact.

Neither of these approaches is satisfactory. The region of "particular others" is a distinct domain where the "others" with whom we are interrelated are not valued merely in terms of our own interests and preferences, yet are not the "all others" of a universal point of view. They are particular flesh-and-blood others for whom we have actual feelings in our guts and in our skin, not the others of rational constructs and universal principles.

Relations can be evaluated as good or bad, and this can be a different question from how good or bad they are for the individuals in them. Evaluating relations as harmonious, say, or stressful will depend on aspects of what can be understood only if we look at relations between persons. To focus on either self-interested individuals or the totality of all persons is to miss the qualities of actual relations between actual human beings.

Owen Flanagan and Jonathan Adler provide useful criticism of what they see as Kohlberg's "adequacy thesis"—the assumption that the more formal the moral reasoning the better.[21] But they themselves continue to construe the tension in ethics as that between the particular self and the universal, ignoring the domain of particular others in relations with one another.

Mothering is, of course, not the only context in which the salient moral problems concern relations between particular others rather than conflicts between egoistic self and universal moral laws; all actual human contexts may be more like this than like those depicted by Hobbes or Kant. But the context of mothering may be the best in which to make explicit why familiar moral theories are so deficient in offering guidance for action and feeling. And the variety of contexts within mothering, with the different excellences appropriate for dealing with infants or with young children or with adolescents, provide rich sources of insight for moral inquiry.

The feelings so characteristic of mothering—that there are too many demands on us, that we cannot do everything we ought to do—are highly instructive.[22] They give rise to different problems from those of universal rule versus self-interest. They require us to weigh the claims of one self-other relation against the claims of other self-other relations, to try to bring about some harmony between them, to see the issues in an actual temporal context, and to act rather than merely reflect.

For instance, we have limited resources for caring. We cannot care for everyone or do everything that a caring approach suggests. We need moral guidelines for ordering our priorities. Though the hunger of our own children comes before the hunger of children we do not know, the hunger of children in Africa ought to come before some of the expensive amusements we may feel like providing for our own children. These are moral problems calling to some extent for principled answers. But we have to figure out what we ought to do in the actual context of buying groceries, cooking meals, refusing the requests of our children for the latest toy they have seen advertised on TV, and sending money to Oxfam. The context is one of real action, not of ideal thought.

Principles and Particulars

When we take the context of mothering as central for moral theory rather than as peripheral, we run the risk of excessively discounting other contexts. It is a commendable risk, given the enormously more prevalent one of excessively discounting mothering. But I think that the attack on principles has sometimes been carried too far by critics of traditional moral theory. Nel Noddings, for instance, writes that "To say, 'It is wrong to cause pain needlessly,' contributes nothing by way of knowledge and can hardly be thought likely to change the attitude or behavior of one who might ask, 'Why is it wrong?' . . . Ethical caring . . . depends not upon rule or principle" but upon the development of a self "in congruence with one's best remembrance of caring and being cared-for."[23]

We should not forget that an absence of principles can be an invitation to capriciousness. Caring may be a weak defense against arbitrary decisions, and the person cared for may find the relation more satisfactory in various respects if both persons, but especially the person caring, are guided to some extent by principles concerning obligations and rights. To argue that no two cases are ever alike is to invite moral chaos. Furthermore, for one person to be in a position of caretaker means that that person has the power to withhold care, leaving the other without it. The person cared for is usually in a position of vulnerability. The moral significance of this needs to be addressed along with other aspects of the caring relation. Principles may remind a giver of care to avoid being capricious or domineering. While most of the moral problems involved in mothering contexts may deal with issues above and beyond the moral minimums that can be covered by principles concerning rights and obligations, that does not mean that these minimums can be dispensed with altogether.

Noddings's discussion is unsatisfactory also in dealing with certain types of questions, including those about economic justice. Such issues cry out for relevant principles. Though caring may be needed to motivate us to act on such principles, the principles are not expendable. Noddings questions the concern people may have for starving persons in distant countries, because she sees universal love and universal justice as masculine illusions. She refrains from judging that the rich deserve less or the poor more, because giving care to individuals cannot yield such judgments. But this may amount to taking a specific economic stratification as given, rather than as the appropriate object of critical scrutiny that it should be. It may lead to accepting that the rich will care for the rich, and the poor for the poor, with the gap between them, however unjustifiably wide, remaining what it is. Some important moral issues seem beyond the reach of an ethic of caring, once caring leads us, perhaps through empathy, to be concerned with them.

On ethical views that renounce all principles as excessively abstract, we might have few arguments to uphold the equality of women. After all, as parents can care for children recognized as weaker, less knowledgeable, less capable, and with appropriately restricted rights, so men could care for women deemed inferior in every way. On a view that ethics could satisfactorily be founded on caring alone, men could care for women considered undeserving of equal rights in all the significant areas in which women have been struggling to have our equality recognized. So an ethic of care, essential as a component of morality and perhaps even as a framework, seems deficient if taken as an exclusive preoccupation or one which fails to make room for justice.

The aspect of the attack on principles that seems entirely correct is the view that not all ethical problems can be solved by appeal to one or a very few simple principles. It is often argued that all more particular moral rules or principles can be derived from such underlying ones as the Categorical Imperative or the Principle of Utility, and that these can be applied to all moral problems. The call for an ethic of care may be a call, in which I join, for a more pluralistic view of ethics, recognizing that we need a division of moral labor employing different moral approaches for different domains, at least for the time being. Satisfactory intermediate principles for areas such as those of international affairs or family relations cannot be derived from simple universal principles but only in conjunction with experience within the domains in question.

Attention to particular others will always require us to respect the particularity of the context and to arrive at solutions to moral problems which will not give moral principles more weight than their due. This is true for what has been thought of as the public realm as well as for what has been thought of as the private one. But we will continue to need some principles. We will need principles concerning relations, not only concerning the actions of individuals, as we will need evaluations of kinds of relations, not only of the character traits of individuals.

Knowledge or Action

A shortcoming of most standard moral theory is that it construes ethics too much in terms of knowledge, or of trying to get a true picture about what we ought to do. This traditional tendency has been carried on in recent years both by those who deny that ethics can amount to knowledge and by those who assert that indeed ethics is capable of acquiring and accumulating knowledge.[24]

Construing ethics as primarily a matter of knowledge lets us lose touch with the issue of motivation and with the connection in ethics between thought and action. It leaves unaddressed the question, Even if I know what I ought to do, why should I do it? It assumes that knowledge will motivate action, but as soon as we recognize a capacity of the will to defy the dictates of reason or the counsels of knowledge, we are left with the gap between knowledge and action unfilled by theories that see ethics as a branch of objective knowledge. A recognition such as Sara Ruddick and others provide—that thought arises out of practice—can mitigate this difficulty. But we may wish not to limit the concept of thought to what interests produce.

In recognizing the component of feeling and relatedness between self and particular others, we address motivation as an inherent part of the inquiry. Caring between parent and child is a good example. We should not glamorize parental care. Many mothers and fathers exercise power over children in ways characteristic of domination; others fail to care adequately for their children. But when the relation between mothering person and child is as it should be, the caretaker does not care for the child (nor the child for the caretaker) because of universal moral rules. The love and concern one feels for the child already motivate much of what one does and much of what one concludes one ought to do. This is not to say that morality is irrelevant. One must still decide what one ought to do. But the process of addressing the moral questions in mothering and of trying to arrive at answers one can find acceptable involves acting and feeling, not just thinking. And neither egoism nor a morality of universal rules will be of much help.

If we pay attention to the region of particular others in actual contexts, problems of motivation are likely to be incorporated into the inquiry. Ethics will be seen as a question of action and feeling: How ought I to act and to try to feel toward these particular others, and how ought they to act and to try to feel toward me in view of the relation we are in? Answers are sought not in moral judgments comparable to the true statements of a branch of science but in recommendations about how to act and to try to feel and in deciding whether to accept or reject (in action and feeling) these recommendations. Accepting and rejecting are appropriately connected with the actual experience of acting and feeling.

Furthermore, we focus on relations between persons rather than construing moral problems simply as issues for us as isolated individuals making decisions among a range of options. We are partly constituted by the relations we are in, and we cannot adequately understand our moral situation only in terms of individuals and their problems. We need to find moral guidance for the evaluation and shaping of relations.

A number of nonfeminist moral philosophers have expressed objections to the claims of a universal, impersonal moral standpoint. They have pointed out that considerations of what is best from an impersonal standpoint seem to rule out much that seems morally permissible and important to us. As Michael Slote summarizes these positions, "Common sense . . . presumably permits each agent to give some preference to his own concerns, projects, and commitments even when that prevents him from producing the objectively best state(s) of affairs he is capable of bringing about and thus from acting as impersonal benevolence would prefer."[25]

While these discussions have offered useful criticism of an ethic of universal rules, especially utilitarian rules, they have done so largely in terms of individual preferences. Conceptually, they have not moved far beyond traditional arguments between the defenders of egoistic claims versus the defenders of universal claims. The alternatives to impersonal benevolence are seen as the concerns, projects, or commitments of individuals as separate entities. Slote himself discusses our preferences for benefiting others as well as ourselves, but he still interprets the problem in terms of the preferences of ourselves as theoretically isolable individuals. And all such discussions have been confined to the realm of possible moral knowledge without addressing the problem of whether moral knowledge would translate into moral practice.

A feminist focus on evaluating and guiding relations among persons would be quite different from these discussions of the preferences of either individuals in isolation or of all persons in general. And it would move beyond the mere picturing of moral issues.

Considerable philosophical attention has been paid in recent years to the notions of virtue and vice, as distinct from those of the right and the good and their contraries. In virtue theory, in contrast to theories about objective moral knowledge, motivation may be built into moral precepts, since the precepts of virtue theory concern the kinds of persons we ought to admire and the traits of character that ought to be cultivated.[26] The virtues are usually seen as arising in or as connected to various practices, which are practices composed of actions. Here the connection between morality and action is not lost. But the practices to which attention has so far been paid by nonfeminist virtue theorists have not included the practice of mothering. Attention to the practices involved in bringing up children might greatly improve these theories. Further, all such theories need to address the problem of finding grounds on which to decide how existing practices ought to be changed. If one holds that imagined alternatives can arise from within a practice, it is not clear how such a position differs from, or whether it should rather resemble, a theory that appeals to some point of view outside any given practice from which to evaluate the practice.

We should be careful not to confine moral inquiry to anything that can only be conducted within an existing social practice.[27] The history of existing social practices is overwhelmingly patriarchal, and even human mothering, engaged in primarily by women, is suspect as an existing practice because of the extent to which it is embedded in male-dominated cultures and societies. The practice of moral inquiry itself is practice enough within which to define the virtues and vices, and this practice includes theories about relatively independent moral principles and values.

The contexts to which feminist moral theory pays attention are especially suitable for illustrating our claims about moral inquiry and for developing methods of moral inquiry that will be conducive not only to moral knowledge or understanding, but to the moral action of which morality itself must be composed or in which, at the very least, morality must be reflected.

Noddings does not lose sight of the issue of motivation. She offers a helpful account of how children learn to be moral and of how mothering persons shape this learning. But the conclusion need not be that moral principles and rules have little significance for morality. Rather we can see how action and feeling ought to inform the choice of principles as well as of practices and projects. Caring should not replace thought, nor should thought be a mere instrument of caring. Reflective choice and caring action are both needed for the development of adequate moralities.

Birth and Valuing

To a large extent the activity of mothering is as open to men as to women. Possibly fathers could come to be as emotionally close, or as close through caretaking, to children as mothers are. The experience of relatedness, of responsibility for the growth and empowerment of new life, and of responsiveness to particular others will have to be incorporated into moral theory if moral theory is to be adequate. At present in this domain it is primarily the experience of women (and of children) which has not been sufficiently reflected in moral theory and which ought to be so reflected. But this is not to say that it must remain experience available mainly to women. If men were to come to share fully and equitably in the care of all persons who need care—especially children, the sick, the old—the moral values that now arise for women in the context of caring might well arise as fully for men.

There are some experiences, however, that are open to women and not open to men: menstruating, having an abortion, giving birth, suckling. We need to consider their possible significance or lack of significance for moral experience and theory. Here I will consider only one kind of experience not open to men but of great importance to women: the experience of giving birth or of deciding not to while being capable of doing so, or of identifying, as a woman, with those who give birth.

Birthing, of course, is a social as well as a personal or biological event. It takes place in a social context structured by attitudes and arrangements which deeply affect how women experience it—whether it will be accepted as "natural," whether it will be welcomed and celebrated, or whether it will be fraught with fear or shame. But I wish in this brief discussion to focus on the conscious awareness women can have of what we are doing in giving birth, on the specifically personal and biological aspects of human birthing, and on the possible significance of these for moral experience.

Women are the persons who create other human beings. Women are responsible for the existence of new persons in ways far more fundamental than men are. We have in the past needed to call attention to the extent to which women do not control our capacity to give birth and to this extent are not responsible for its results. We have been under extreme economic and social pressure to engage in sexual intercourse, to marry, to have children. Legal permission to undergo abortion is a restricted and still threatened capacity. When the choice not to give birth requires grave risk to life, health, or well-being, or requires suicide, we should be careful not to misrepresent the situation of women when we speak of a woman's "choice" to become a mother, or of how she "could have done other" than have a child, or that "since she chose to become a mother, she is responsible for her child," and so forth. Still, in an ultimate sense, women are responsible for giving birth, and choices concerning it are increasingly uncoerced.

It does not follow at all that because women are responsible for creating human beings we should be held responsible by society for caring for them, either alone, primarily, or even at all. The two kinds of responsibility should not be confused. Women have every reason to be angry at men who refuse to take responsibility for their share of the events of pregnancy and birth or for the care children require. Because we have for so long wanted to increase the extent to which men would recognize their responsibilities for causing pregnancy and would share in the long years of care needed to bring the child of a mother and a father to independence, we have tended to emphasize the ways in which the responsibilities for creating a new human being are equal between women and men. The fact remains that it is women and not men who give birth to children. Men produce sperm and women produce babies, and the difference is very great. Excellent arguments can be made that boys and men suffer "womb envy", for indeed, men lack a wondrous capacity which women possess. To overcome the pernicious aspects of the womb envy she describes, Eva Kittay argues that boys should be taught that their "procreative contribution" is of equal importance. But while boys should certainly be told the truth, the truth may remain that, as she elsewhere states, "there is the . . . awesome quality of creation itself—the transmutation performed by the parturient woman."[28]

Of all the human capacities, it is probably the capacity to create new human beings that is most worth celebrating. It is to be expected that a woman would care and feel concern for a child she has created as the child grows and develops and as she feels responsible for having given the child life through giving birth. But it is more than what we might expect. It is, perhaps, justifiable in certain ways unique to women.

It might be thought that responsibility for the life of the child also lies with those who refrain from infanticide, and infanticide is as open to men as to women. But the killing of a child once the child has been born and is capable of life with different caretakers than the person who is responsible for having given birth to the child would be a quite different experience, and I am concerned in this discussion with the possible moral significance of creating life in the first place.

As suggested by Marcia Baron in correspondence, it might also be thought that those, including the father, who refrain from killing the mother, or from forcing her to have an abortion, are also responsible in some much more distant way for not preventing the birth of the child. But unless the distinctions between suicide and murder, and between having an abortion and forcing a woman to have an abortion against her will, are collapsed completely, the issues would be very different. To refrain from murdering a woman is not at all the same as deciding not to kill oneself. And to decide not to force someone else to have an abortion is very different from deciding not to have an abortion when one could. The person capable of giving birth who decides not to prevent the birth is the person responsible, in the sense of 'responsible' I am discussing, for creating another human being. And to give life is not the same as to refrain from ending it.

Whether there is or is not a significant difference between killing a person or letting that person die, where the person already has life, is yet another question. If one wishes to draw an analogy between taking life and giving life, the analogy, if it can be drawn at all, might be between the question of killing or letting die, on the one hand, and "natural" or "induced" childbirth on the other.

Perhaps there is a tendency to want to approve of or to justify what one has decided or done with respect to giving life. In giving birth to a particular child, perhaps women have a natural tendency to approve of the birth, to believe that the child ought to have been born. Perhaps this inclines women who give birth and those who identify with such women to believe whatever may follow from this, such as that the child is entitled to care, and that feelings of love for the child are appropriate and justified. The conscious awareness that one has created a new human being may provide women with an inclination to value the child and to have hope for the child's future. If in her view the child ought to have been born, a woman may feel that the world ought to be such as to be hospitable to the child. And if the child ought to have been born, the child ought to grow into an admirable human adult. The child's life has, and should continue to have, value that is recognized.

Consider next the phenomenon of sacrifice. In giving birth, women suffer severe pain for the sake of new life. Having suffered for the child in giving the child life, women may have a natural tendency to value what pain has been endured for. As often pointed out in connection with war, there is a tendency in people to feel that because sacrifices have been made, the sacrifice should have been "worth it," and, if necessary, other things ought to be done so that the sacrifice "shall not have been in vain." There may be comparable tendencies for those who have suffered to give birth to hold that the pain was for the good reason of creating a new life that is valuable and that will be valued.

Certainly this is not to say that there is anything good or noble about suffering or that merely because people want to believe that what they suffered for was worthwhile, it was. A vast amount of human suffering has been in vain and should have been avoided. The point is that once suffering has already occurred and the "price" (if we resort to such calculations) has already been paid, it will be worse if the result is a further cost, and better if the result is a clear benefit that can make the price, when it was necessary for the result, validly "worth it." The suffering of the mother who has given birth will more easily have been truly worthwhile if the child's life has value. The chance for the suffering that has already occurred to be outweighed by future happiness is much greater if the child is valued by the society and the family into which it is born. To say that the mother's suffering has been worthwhile because the child is a valuable and valued human being can be a valid judgment. If her suffering has yielded nothing but further suffering and a being of no value, it may truly have been in vain. Anyone could agree with these judgments. But the person who has already undergone the suffering has a special reason to recognize that the child is valuable and to want the child to be valued so that the suffering she has already borne will have been truly worthwhile.

These arguments can be repeated for the burdens of work and anxiety normally expended in bringing up a child. Those who have already borne these burdens have special reasons to see the resulting grown human being for whom they were necessary as valuable and as valued. Traditionally, the burden of childbirth borne by women has been added to very greatly by the burdens of child rearing. But of course the burdens of child rearing could easily be shared fully by men, as they have been by women other than natural mothers, and the extent of these cares may greatly outweigh the suffering of childbirth itself. This does not mean that giving birth is incidental.

In exploring the values involved in birth and mothering, we need to develop views which do not exclude women who do not give birth.[29] For some women, a decision against bearing children is easy, for others it is consuming. The decision is often affected by a tendency to value the potential child to a degree comparable to that experienced by potential mothers. Knowing how much care the child would deserve and how much care she would want to give the child, a woman who relinquishes the prospect of motherhood often recognizes how much she is giving up. For such reasons the choice may be very difficult, and a woman can feel overwhelming ambivalence about pursuing a career that is hostile to women who try to combine it with motherhood.

Since men, then, do not give birth, and do not experience the responsibility for, the pain in, or the momentousness of childbirth, they lack the particular motives to value the child that may rest on this capacity and this fact. Of course it is open to men to identify with women far more than they have in the past. And of course many other motives to value a child are open to both parents, to caretakers of either gender and to those who are not parents, but the motives discussed, and others arising from giving birth, may be morally significant. Perhaps the decisions and sacrifices involved in bringing up a child are more affecting than those normally experienced in giving birth to a child. So the possibility for men to acquire such motives through child care may outweigh any long-term differences in motivation between women and men. But it might yet remain that the person responsible for giving birth would continue to have a greater sense of responsibility for how the child develops and stronger feelings of care and concern for the child.

That adoptive parents can feel as great concern for and attachment to their children as can biological parents may indicate that the biological components in valuing children are relatively modest in importance. But to the extent that biological components are significant, as according to some theories they must be, they affect women and men in different ways.

Morality and Human Tendencies

So far I have been describing possible feelings rather than attaching any moral value to them. That children are valued does not mean they are valuable, and if mothers have a natural tendency to value children, it does not follow that we ought to. But if feelings are taken to be relevant to moral theory, the feelings of valuing the child, like the feelings of empathy for other persons in pain, may be of moral significance.

To the extent that a moral theory takes natural male tendencies into account, it would at least be reasonable to take natural female tendencies into account. Traditional moral theories often assume that people are motivated by the pursuit of self-interest or by a desire to satisfy their preferences, and then many such theories go on to suppose that it is legitimate for individuals to maximize self-interest, or satisfy their preferences, within certain constraints based on the equal rights of others. If it can be shown that the tendency to want to pursue individual self-interest is a stronger tendency among men than among women, this would certainly be relevant to an evaluation of such theory. And if it could be shown that a tendency to value children and to desire to foster the developing capabilities of the particular others for whom we care is a stronger tendency among women than among men, this too would be relevant in evaluating moral theories.

It is still different to assert that women have a tendency to value children and that we ought to. Noddings speaks often of the "natural" caring of mothers for children.[30] I do not intend to deal here with the disputed empirical question of whether there is or is not a strong natural tendency for mothers to love our children. Sara Ruddick's rich description of the ambivalent feelings mothers experience may be more relevant: "What we are pleased to call 'mother-love' is intermixed with hate, sorrow, impatience, resentment, and despair; thought-provoking ambivalence is a hallmark of mothering."[31] And I am not claiming that natural mothers have more talent for or greater skills in raising children than have others, including men.

What I am exploring, rather, are the possible "reasons" for mothers to value children, reasons that might be different for mothers and potential mothers than they would be for anyone else asking the question, Why should we value human beings? And it does seem that certain possible reasons for valuing actual living human beings are present for mothers, and for those who identify with mothers, in ways that are different from what they would be for others. The reason, if it is one, that the child should be valued because I have suffered to give the child life is different from the reason, if it is one, that the child should be valued because someone unlike me suffered to give the child life. And both these reasons are different from the reason, if it is one, that the child should be valued because the continued existence of the child satisfies a preference of a parent or because the child is a bearer of universal rights or has the capacity to experience pleasure.

Many moral theories, and fields dependent on them, employ such assumptions as that increasing the utility of individuals is a good thing to do. But if one asks *why* it is a good thing to increase utility, or satisfy desire, or produce pleasure, or *why* doing so counts as a good reason for something, the question is very difficult to answer. It is often taken as a basic assumption for which no *further* reason can be given. It may rest (unsatisfactorily) on some such claim as that people seek pleasure; or it may rest on the claim that we can recognize pleasure as having intrinsic value. But if women start with different assumptions and recognize different values as much weightier, that would certainly be of importance to ethics.

We might take it as one of our assumptions that the survival of children has priority over most other moral considerations. A number of feminists have independently declared their rejection of the Abraham myth.[32] We do not approve the sacrifice of actual children out of religious duty or moral abstraction: reasons to value the actual life of the born seem better reasons than reasons justifying the sacrifice of such life.[33] This outlook can be especially poignant in the context of struggles to achieve greater justice for oppressed groups. Women are sometimes criticized by more militant group members for a reluctance to sacrifice the well-being of children to the needs of the movement; they may respond that it is the children the movement is for, not the reverse. Feminist positions may reflect an accordance of priority to caring for particular others over abstract principle. From the perspective of much moral theory, a tendency to take such a stand is a deficiency of women. But from a perspective of what is needed for twenty-first century global responsibility, it may suggest a superior morality.

It is of utmost importance to create good relations of care and concern and trust between ourselves and our children, and to create the cultural expressions, social arrangements, and environmental conditions in which children will be valued and well cared for. All these are more important than maximizing individual utilities or fulfilling purely abstract moral norms. The moral theories compatible with these starting positions are likely to be very different from traditional and contemporary nonfeminist moral theories.

In discussing ways in which a feminist approach to morality differs from a Kantian one, Annette Baier writes, "Where Kant concludes—'so much the worse for women,' we can conclude—'so much the worse for the male fixation on the special skill of drafting legislation, for the bureaucratic mentality of rule worship, and for the male exaggeration of the importance of independence over mutual interdependence."[34] Only feminist moral theory can offer satisfactory evaluations of such suggestions because only feminist moral theory can adequately reflect the alternatives to traditional and nonfeminist moral theory that the experience of women requires.

Traditional moral theory provides us with two alternatives: survival of self or duty to all mankind. We see the central priority of survival of the self powerfully argued in Hobbes, and we see the priority of obligation to the universal persuasively argued in Kant. These are the positions which have preoccupied much of the debate in traditional and nonfeminist moral theory ever since.

Feminist moral theory, in contrast, will, I believe, develop around the priority of the flourishing of children in favorable environments. The flourishing of children requires survival, but not of any self in isolation—whether of child or caretaker—and not at the sacrifice of any self. It does concern obligation to humankind, but not to an abstract universal. It should not pit the well-being of one's own children against the well-being of others, justifying conflict and favoritism. On the other hand, it can recognize that if the children who depend on or are touched by our care do not flourish, we have not contributed what we should have to the flourishing of children.

How New Is Feminist Inquiry?

Is there anything really new about feminist moral inquiry, and will the theory that results be different from nonfeminist moral theory? The argument that there is nothing significantly new here asserts that if one looks at other parts of the various traditions in ethics than the ones on which I have focused, one can already find what feminists are saying and that what feminists are now proposing has been said before (and, it may be implied, said better). On the split between reason and emotion and the devaluation of emotion, for instance, it has been argued that Aristotle's emphasis on habit and practice in the development of morality, rather than on mere rational assent, is close to what feminists are arguing. Or it is claimed that Hume's reliance on emotion—on fellow-feeling and not being indifferent to the pain of others—as the foundation of morality already provides what feminists seek.

On the public/private distinction and the devaluation of the household, it can be pointed out that there is another tradition than the one I will emphasize: the tradition of Machiavelli, according to which one can be guided by morality in one's private dealings with family and friends, but in public, political life, "dirty hands" are inevitable and morality irrelevant. "You must realize this," Machiavelli said, "that a prince, and especially a new prince, cannot observe all those things which give men a reputation for virtue, because in order to maintain his state he is often forced to act in defiance of good faith, of charity, of kindness, of religion."[35] Isn't this, some ask, close to what feminists are saying?

Finally, on the concept of the self, feminists certainly have not been the first to criticize the atomistic, isolated self of liberal political and of much moral theory. Communitarians have long since done so. Marxists have said that the atomistic, individualistic self is not the human self but the bourgeois self. They have argued that the egoistic drives that such theorists as Hobbes and Locke assumed to be inherent in human nature are not inherent but rather are promoted by capitalism and transcendable through socialism. The self of liberal theory is thus defective, on the Marxist view, and should be replaced by a conception of the self as socially constituted. So again, it is argued that what feminists are asserting is a version of such critiques rather than anything new.

My response is that none of the nonfeminist theorists cited as having said before, or said better, what feminists are saying, has paid remotely adequate attention to the experience of women. They have not considered their alternatives from the points of view of women, and they have not listened to the voices of women expressing our thoughts, our feelings, our concerns. And these omissions make a difference.

For instance, the activity of mothering has been almost totally absent in all nonfeminist moral theorizing. Until Sara Ruddick wrote her paper "Maternal Thinking," there had been virtually no philosophical recognition that mothers *think*, that there are characteristic standards for *reasoning* in this activity, and that one can discern *moral values* being striven for and expressed in this practice.[36] On the few occasions in which mothering had been noticed, it had been evaluated in terms of the aims and projects of men, as with Locke and Rousseau, or its values had been seen as threatening to the "higher" values sought by men, as with Hegel. The whole area of relations between parents and children was characteristically conceptualized as belonging to the natural, empirical given, rather than to the domain of morality. But how could this be? The practice of mothering involves almost constant moral concern and deliberation. To characterize this large domain of human experience as irrelevant to the construction of moral theory is highly unlikely to have had no significant distorting effect on the shaping of moral theory.

Nor has there been any remotely adequate attention to other aspects of women's experience, such as friendship among women or life in women's communities. Or to the enormous *problems* women face *as women:* the problems of domestic violence, for instance, or of rape.[37] If "humanity" is recognized as including women on a par with men, then thinking about domestic violence should occupy as much theoretical space as should thinking about the kinds of personal security—the freedom to travel the highway unattacked, for instance, or the security of one's personal property—to which so much legal and political and moral theory has been devoted.[38] So even though there is, of course, a background on which feminists can draw, when feminists pay attention in *central* ways to the experience of women, we are doing something which has not been done before.

Moralities that do take adequate account of the experience of women will be unlike any traditional moralities, or their nonfeminist critiques, for they will combine theory and practice for an enormous but almost wholly neglected range of human experience. The virtues and practices and feelings upheld by the ethics of Aristotle and Hume uphold traditions mired in patriarchy. The "dirty hands" of men in public life can be matched by the moral impurities of domestic privilege and tyranny. If we look at Marxist criticisms of the tradition of liberal individualism, we find that they too accept a gender division of labor in the household as "natural," and they too pay almost no attention to the experience of women as women rather than as workers or nonworkers. Activity is divided between production and reproduction, and it is production only that is seen as transformative. And the "social self" of most communitarians, while offering helpful criticisms of the atomistic self of the liberal tradition, is still not the "relational self" of feminist theory. It provides a weak basis for oppressed members of actual communities to break away from and out of the traditions that contribute so much to their oppression.

We can conclude, I think, that feminist inquiry is offering something quite new and that feminist morality *is* different from prefeminist and nonfeminist morality. Even if the theories feminists will come to espouse turn out to resemble traditional theories—this may be unlikely, but even if it should be the case—the theories would be different in the sense that they would have been applied to and tested in a whole new and very large domain of human experience—the experience of women. These theories would have been developed on the basis of this whole new domain of experience and would have to have been found satisfactory for it. If a traditional theory does turn out to meet these requirements, it will be different from what it was before in having been seen to be applicable to all this new territory, and it could be judged to be, itself, feminist theory as well as traditional theory.

A primary aim of feminism is to end the oppression of women. This involves upsetting the primacy of the male in thought and in society. All agree that the achievement of such an objective would have to count as enormous change. Surely the changes in moral theory will have to be comparably profound.

Shaping Feminist Culture

The power to shape consciousness is an overwhelming one, ruling out alternative conceptions and perceptions, crushing aspirations unacceptable to it, and leaving us devoid of the words with which to express even our skepticism, and certainly our anguish and our opposition. What could be more total than the power to control the very terms with which we think, the language through which we try to grasp reality, the images with which we see or block out features of our surroundings and of ourselves, and the awareness we need to try to guide the trajectories of our lives? The culture of a society has such power.

I suggested in the first chapter that for the revolutionary feminist transformations of society that are occurring and will continue, culture is relatively more important than for other revolutions. I included in culture a wide range of thoughts and feelings and symbols and images. In this chapter I will look more closely at the production of culture and its existing institutions, and I will show how the institutions conflict with feminist values and should be transformed. I will consider, too, how feminist culture attuned to feminist morality can further develop.

Culture and Consciousness

I mean by the term 'culture' something distinguishable from social structure. The social structure of a society is in possession of other forms of power than the power to shape consciousness: the state has power to coerce through law and the use of force, the economy to determine outcomes through investments, wages, profits, and contracts. Culture is more dependent on symbols and meanings for its influence. On some views, culture may envelop the social structure or be indistinguishable from it; on others, culture serves as reinforcement, or exists as reflection only, of the social structure. On still other views, culture may guide social structure or evaluate it or lead it. I will not deal extensively with these issues but will proceed from the view that culture ought to evaluate and guide social structure; my concern will be how this can and ought to be done.

In contemporary society culture has to do with the making and receiving of symbolic messages, images, ideas. It includes both the popular culture of the mass media and the high culture of art museums and literature. It includes the creation and imparting of knowledge in schools, colleges, and universities. And culture includes the social and material realities in which and by which it is created and transmitted: TV networks and broadcasting studios and television sets, newspaper chains and printing presses, movie studios and theatres, university and school buildings and laboratories, and the salaries and fees of those who work in "the culture industry" and related activities.

Culture has receivers as well as senders, consumers as well as producers, readers as well as authors; and often what recipients make of or how they use a cultural object is different from what its senders intend. Some critics emphasize this difference, others find it easily exaggerated; most could agree that in exploring culture, especially in considering the ways we should shape it, attention needs to be focused on interactions, relationships, communication, not on objects and their properties in isolation.

Expression and Imagination

Much of what occurs in the domain of culture requires a focus on categories relatively unfamiliar to dominant philosophical traditions and to the social sciences. I will deal with the ways we express our experiences, our relations with others, our thoughts and feelings, and will explore alternatives to those ways. There will thus be a focus on expression and imagination of a kind that fits awkwardly with the philosophical analyses and theories that flow out of the scientific and the western liberal traditions and that can be found in Anglo-American philosophy. For my purposes, a relatively uncritical discussion of expression and imagination, especially in the experiences of women, will yield enough understanding of these concepts to be able to proceed with the inquiry and suggestions I undertake.

Much recent work in philosophy has taken the category of "action" as central, and has tried to analyze and to understand it. This has been an improvement over focusing almost exclusively on the "behavior" dear to the sciences. But perhaps we need to give a much more prominent place in our inquiries than we have so far to the category of "expression."[1]

What are we expressing when we raise our arm? An intention to signal someone to call on us? A desire to stretch? A plan to reach something on a shelf? To express something to someone requires a recipient of our message, but not all expression has an audience, and certainly not all expression is understood by its recipients.

When a baby smiles, she is expressing a feeling of well-being or delight. When a mother smiles back, she expresses a mutual relation of caring. Only by the artificial frameworks of science would it seem appropriate to reduce the smile of the baby and the smile of the mother to bits of behavior about which we could know only what a third person, an observer, could see or infer. And even to think in terms of action seems more artificial and less basic than to think in terms of expression. An action is by definition purposive, but it is doubtful that babies have purposes or that adults have them much of the time they do or express many things. Certainly some of the things we do are actions, but not all and perhaps not some of the most significant.

Expression can be a shared phenomenon. The concept of action still attaches to individuals in isolation, although some of us have argued for acceptance of notions of group action and collective or corporate responsibility.[2] Expression is less limited: we can speak of the expression of trust or mutuality or conflict as something existing in a relation between persons. As we have seen, much feminist concern focuses on relations between persons rather than, as does so much traditional theory and nonfeminist inquiry, on individuals and their characteristics or actions. Perhaps we should think of such felt relationships as those expressed between mothering person and child as the fundamental fabric of society, rather than supposing that individuals acting compose society. And we might think that experience of and in such relationships should be central to our development of morality and culture and that understanding expression is essential to understanding culture.

We might think, as well, that imagination is a human faculty or capacity to which far more attention needs to be paid in philosophical thought and that what we come to mean by it will be different from traditional interpretations.[3] It has often been seen as a capacity to entertain mental pictures and images. We may find it to be more concerned with alternative feelings and especially relationships than with alternative pictures.

The faculty of reason and the sense of sight have been the privileged concerns of philosophy throughout most of its long history. Many feminists have questioned the suppression or exclusion of other aspects of experience, deploring the habit of disparaging emotion and ignoring moral feelings.[4] Many, too, have questioned the way male attempts to be rational divide things into opposing and hierarchically ordered categories: mind/body, reason/emotion, subject/object, man/nature, and of course male/female.

Such alternatives as affirmation and negation are powerful tools of logical thinking suitable for some issues, and the dualism of true and false is often needed to make sense of thoughts and actions. But such categories are unsuited to deal with much human experience, including experience of change. Reason can recognize the existing world and its negation. "The king rules" may state a fact. "The king does not rule" *may* express a refusal to accept the existing social reality as well as a logical possibility. But if we think in historical terms, a simple negation expresses an impoverished set of alternatives.

If we think, instead, in terms of human imagination, we see that the alternatives to any existing reality are multiple yet that mere logical possibilities are not what we seek. We seek different realities, not total reversals. As Foucault suggests, "There is no binary division to be made between what one says and what one does not say; we must try to determine the different ways of not saying such things . . . There [are] not one but many silences, and they are an integral part of the strategies that underlie and permeate discourses."[5]

We are constituted in large part by our relations with other persons. Change for human beings is not a negation of existing reality so much as the strengthening of some relations and the weakening of others. "Clean" breaks are rare; even if we decide to "end" a relationship, historical and emotional aspects of it will linger. The tie will loosen rather than cease to exist. The language of "is" and "is not" seems clumsy rather than perceptive in describing the ever-changing relationships that connect us to others, not only in personal bonds but in the political and social ties that compose human reality as well. And at the level of historical change, the strengthening and weakening of ties may be more salient than the denial of existing reality.

For very many women and for some men, changing our lives has constituted significant social change in gender relationships. Imagination plays a major role in such change and culture a primary role in nourishing imagination.

Consider a woman involved in such change. She imagines her life as other than it is, especially as she sees culturally presented alternatives.[6] But the alternatives she imagines are multiple, not the simple negation of what is, and they are not clearly distinct. The relationships in which she finds herself are transformed by other relationships, and these processes are many rather than simple dualistic denials of those that exist. And the futures she imagines for herself, for her children, and for the world are as varied as the stories she hears or tells, to herself or others, and as varied as the images she entertains or expresses.

To deal with culture and the social transformations I am exploring, the notions of expression and imagination will often be involved. Human experience should be understood to include these as centrally as it includes the reasoning and observation on which Western philosophy has been built and as centrally as the action on which moral evaluation has focused.

The Philosophical Evaluation of Culture

What arrangements concerning the culture that has such power as the power to shape consciousness would be justifiable? How should the institutions which produce culture and shape consciousness through the mass media be constituted? What would cultural practices have to be like to be legitimate? What values should be sought in the making and receiving of the works of culture? What obligations and rights do those engaged in the production of culture have? What rights and obligations do the "consumers" of cultural "products" have, and what mistakes may we be making in thinking of them as consumers of commodities? Should all or most people participate in the shaping of the culture that surrounds us and that shapes the world of our children and grandchildren, and what forms should this participation take? Ought a more participatory and less elitist culture be a goal to be sought, or should "quality" be the higher goal? What sort of arrangements for the creation and acceptance of culture would be agreeable from a feminist point of view, and how should they be brought about?

These are all urgent and extraordinarily important questions.[7] Philosophers have not paid even remotely adequate attention to them. The tradition of liberal political thought has laid a firm foundation for expression unhampered by certain forms of interference; for "free thought and inquiry" without restrictions imposed by religious authorities and for "free speech" not hampered or controlled by government. Support of such fundamental rights as those guaranteed in the First Amendment to the Constitution of the United States have been given eloquent philosophical formulation by John Stuart Mill. And contemporary philosophers have considered certain complex and often technical problems within the range of liberal rights to free expression.[8] But philosophers in the liberal tradition have been almost blind to the problems of the control of culture by economic forces and interests and to the ways in which such control undermines free expression and restricts effective expression to those already in possession of economic power and of gender and racial advantage. Contemporary Anglo-American philosophers have been for the most part silent about the role of the mass media in affecting consciousness and thus society, about what the relation ought to be between the culture and the economy, about what arrangements for the production of such powerful cultural shapings of persons and of reality would be legitimate.

Though there have been important discussions of the media among those influenced by the Frankfurt school and by the writings of Adorno, Horkheimer, Marcuse, and others, these discussions have mainly been useful in dealing with questions of causality.[9] They help us understand how the media in capitalist societies reinforce the hold of capitalism on the popular imagination and divert the attention of oppressed groups from an accurate perception of their actual conditions and interests. Such analyses provide the bases for significant empirical studies of the processes by which consciousness is shaped and misshaped.[10] But we still need to deal far more than contemporary philosophy has with the prescriptive questions of what roles culture and especially the media ought to play in a free and decent and feminist society and what institutions for the production of culture would be acceptable. We need to deal with these questions from where we are here and now, considering feasible proposals that do not require the total transformation of the economic system or of society and culture all at once.

Many engaged in cultural studies dispute the view that the consumers of popular culture are stupid and passive, mere recipients of whatever the culture industry foists on them. In her summary of a representative sample of writers making this argument, Meaghan Morris says they hold that "consumers are not 'cultural dopes,' but active, critical users of mass culture; consumption practices cannot be derived from or reduced to a mirror of production; consumer practice is 'far more than just economic activity: it is also about dreams and consolation, communication and confrontation, image and identity.'" But Morris goes on to question the critical force of most of the populism these writers study; she raises doubts about the separation of production and consumption. What their thesis amounts to, she suggests, is this: "People in modern mediatized societies are complex and contradictory, mass cultural texts are complex and contradictory, therefore people using them produce complex and contradictory culture."[11]

We can agree with those Morris describes that some elements in popular culture encourage people to criticize society, to imagine better alternatives, and to experience genuine pleasure. But whether these elements are substantial or only minimal, we can surely argue that different arrangements for the production of culture could substantially enhance these possibilities.

A feminist morality for which the flourishing of children would be central could never agree that the enormous influence on children's development wielded by the mass media should be a mere commercial instrument, used in whichever ways will serve the economic interests of the producers of entertainment. Nor could a reasonable view of how culture should shape consciousness rest content with the wholesale ceding of that capacity to those whose primary aim is economic advantage.

The Liberal Position

When we try to think of a short list of universal human rights to which all can agree that all are entitled, it seems likely that freedom of expression should be near the top of the list. The Western liberal conception of freedom of expression contains much that is valid and indispensable for an adequate view of what free expression requires and of what we should do to encourage it. It also contains serious deficiencies, especially as it has been developed and as it now prevails in the United States. This view of freedom of expression has given us a cultural marketplace in which culture other than education is produced almost entirely for the purpose of economic gain and a supposedly "free market of ideas" which is very largely dominated by economic power. It has given us a mass media culture that reinforces, with ever more sophisticated and insistent techniques, the corporate values of a male-dominated economic system, turning the society as a whole into one permeated to unprecedented degrees by the commercial and gendered values of the marketplace.[12] The culture of the marketplace has often reinforced sexual and racial stereotypes, presenting women's bodies as objects to be bought and sold and used and discarded; it has made violence and domination sexually charged and appealing, and in its portrayals of social realities has often distorted and obscured them in damaging ways. Liberal mass culture has failed to provide a culture capable of offering some balance to or critical evaluation of the overwhelming promotion, glorification, and enhancement of commerce.

Contemporary popular culture in the United States employs massive resources to draw persons into its orbit, and it is extraordinarily successful in achieving this result. Reports show that high school students spend three to five times as much time watching television as doing homework. American children grow up watching four to seven hours of almost completely commercial television each day. Books addressed to concerned parents counsel them on the importance of limiting their children's television viewing and promoting activities more conducive to healthy development.[13] But many parents are unable to exercise such control; parents in the television programs themselves are ridiculed for trying to. And many parents do not find the reasons to curb their childrens' television viewing persuasive enough to warrant the effort and conflict involved in doing so.

Program content is determined almost entirely by economic considerations. The means to economic gain for broadcasters are increased ratings and thus higher advertising revenues, and if the way to achieve these is to provide ever more violent and brutal programs, and programs in which violence is increasingly sexualized, these are the programs that will be shown, however threatening to the women and men who will be victims of such violence and brutality. At the same time, "economic censorship" limits treatment of controversial topics.[14]

In the United States enormous sums of money are spent to fund advertising and the vast array of talent and cultural production harnessed to its demands.[15] The forces in the media promoting economic gain through advertising are controlling, and advertising, with its objectification of women, permeates public space through billboards and radio and inner perceptions through television and magazine images. The average American is subjected to five thousand advertising "messages" a day, and the number is growing.[16] It is hardly surprising that the consciousness of most Americans is swamped by this massive quantity of propaganda for commercialism. A culture not dominated by commercial interests has become, for most Americans, unimaginable.

Meanwhile, some popular and academic writers dismiss critics of commercial mass culture as elitist and as devoted only to a "high culture" in which their influence will be accorded the esteem they think it deserves. An example of this sort of argument is given by Herbert Gans in *Popular Culture and High Culture*. He ridicules the "anticommercial bias with which many scholars look at culture," suggesting that such critics only esteem culture that is "created by unpaid folk and by 'serious' artists who do not appear to think about earning a living."[17] The fact that "high culture" in the United States is also largely a commercial enterprise undercuts, he says, the persuasiveness of criticism of "mass culture" as an industry organized for profit. In characteristic ways, Gans's argument misses the point. What it shows is that there is even less of a ballast against the commercialization of everything in our society than some earlier critics of mass culture such as Dwight MacDonald and Leo Lowenthal supposed. It does not address at all the position for which contemporary critics can argue: that neither high culture *nor* popular culture should be dominated by commercial interests. Of course those working in the media have to earn a living. But they should be able to do so within arrangements that provide a decent level of artistic independence and intellectual integrity.

Commercialized culture presents itself and is often accepted as the only alternative to control by such forces as those of the religious right, or of government. Though we have seen a remarkable freeing of culture from governmental control in what used to be the Soviet Union and in Eastern Europe, the spectre of governmental control of culture is still vivid and is intolerable to anyone who values free expression. The commercialized culture of the West often claims to be the only alternative to these forms of unacceptable control. But it is of course not the only alternative, and it is only a failure of imagination and thought that keeps us from focusing on far better arrangements for making and receiving culture than those which now prevail.

Some critics think that the shift from words to images as the currency of culture is so complete that Americans are losing their power to think coherently.[18] To these critics, the content of programs may be less significant than the overwhelming impact of the discontinuity of television and of the cultural shift from word to image as the prevailing form of representation. On the other hand, if an abstracted reason divorced from human feeling is a dubious basis for morality, and if morality should to an important extent be based on empathetic feeling for others with whom we can identify and whose stories can move us, then the images television can provide could be promising rather than deplorable. Perhaps the problem now is more the messages than the medium. On both views, however, the quantity of viewing may be a serious problem. Dialogue with actual others rather than mere passive reception of either words or images is an intrinsic aspect of satisfactory moral and intellectual development.

The shopping mall culture should not be the only alternative to limiting freedom of expression. One can imagine, for instance, a culture combining the best elements of feminist moral inquiry with the possibilities that the media can provide of enlarging communication, heightening empathetic moral understanding, and thoughtfully discussing moral and intellectual issues. The glimpses available in contemporary programming of such possibilities illustrate what popular culture might do. But the institutions that now produce what some call our "televisual reality" will have to be fundamentally transformed.

The Marketplace and Social Change

Can the changes needed occur within the marketplace? When enough recipients of advertising or program images or enough potential buyers of videos or movie tickets "demand" nonsexist or nonracist cultural messages, a shift in this direction will take place. The expression of interest on the part of the audience in exploring such topics as violence against women and the sexual abuse of children, and in seeing films made by black directors—these have opened up possibilities for the commercial production of television programs and films with messages disturbing to viewers content with the status quo. Thus does the marketplace often respond to what audiences "want." Nevertheless, the cultural influences persuading audiences to want what will support the interests of already dominant groups often overwhelm such progress as might otherwise occur.

There have been many studies of the pervasive denigration of women in advertising images, in music videos, in television programming, in movies.[19] There is also by now evidence of some, if sporadic, change.[20] When women, acting independently or in groups, protest a particular advertisement, advertisers sometimes do change their images if they deem it in their economic interest to do so. On the other hand, if their target audience includes enough men for whom a sexist message will be appealing, that message will be favored. The same holds for all the other cultural products—the programs, the records, the videos, the movies, the books—tied to a system subservient to commercial domination. After two decades of complaints about sexism in television programming, almost no programs designed for and preferred by girls are offered on network television. The explanation is that girls are willing to watch programs directed at boys, but boys are not willing to watch programs directed at girls; the networks are unwilling to initiate change because the size of the audience for a program's commercials determines the content of programs.[21]

That some progress is possible even within a commercialized culture in no way indicates what might be possible in a culture liberated from commercial control. There are sound reasons for feminists to strive to free culture from the grip of commercial interests and to expect that the contribution such a liberated culture might make to feminist goals would be much more promising than anything possible within the culture of the marketplace.

In the meantime there are fertile grounds for despair about the grip of commercialism on culture and consciousness. The role of mass media culture has a bearing on how poorly American students are doing in comparison with students in other countries in learning the basics of writing, of reading, and of mathematics.[22] Some social critics fear that we are being "entertained to death" or that we are addicted to "the plug-in drug" of television. Some speculate that the complete domination of the culture of the United States by the interests, techniques, and approaches of advertising are leading citizens to lose touch with reality.[23] Television determines the agenda of political debate: what it fails to attend to goes largely unnoticed.[24] And any alternatives to the corporate worldviews of fast cars and quick remedies and magical cosmetics are, it may be thought, increasingly invisible in the media and thus absent from the minds of American viewers.

Mark Crispin Miller voices his pessimism:

> By the late Seventies . . . there were virtually no more public outcries from a critical intelligentsia, but only TV's triumphal flow . . . Whereas the earlier critics could track the flagrant spread of advertising and its media through the cities and the countryside, and even into common consciousness, one could not now discern TV so clearly (if at all), because it was no longer a mere stain or imposition on some preexistent cultural environment, but had itself become the environment. Its aim was to *be everywhere* . . . and this aim had suddenly been realized . . .
>
> TV ceaselessly disrupts itself, not only through the sheer multiplicity of its offerings in the age of satellite and cable, but as a strategy to keep the viewer semihypnotized. Through its monotonous aesthetic of incessant change, TV may make actual change unrecognizable . . . TV preempts derision by itself evincing endless irony . . . Thus TV co-opts that smirking disbelief which so annoyed the business titans of the Thirties . . . TV protects its ads from mockery by doing all the mocking, thereby posing as an ally to the incredulous spectator . . . Thus TV has turned the cultural atmosphere into one big ad . . . [25]

Grounds for Hope

Those of us who have lived through and participated in the women's movements of recent decades may be encouraged to take a less despairing view of the grip of the male-dominated commercial media on consciousness. We can remember or we hear about the years when virtually everything in the culture and virtually all aspects of the society worked together to shape the consciousness of women into the forms of subservience, stunted aspirations, self-doubt, and acceptance of inequality. And yet we have lived to see very substantial change. What this suggests to us is that the more the power to shape consciousness overwhelms the views we would otherwise have, the more these subversive glimpses can open our eyes to the hidden reality. Those who have experienced periods in which an injustice was most successfully hidden from what can be thought of as public awareness may also have experienced the power of a few words or images to make visible the invisible. And once those who wish to see have seen, even if only once, they may see again and not forget, and the injustice will never again be quite invisible to them. Even when the dominant forces controlling culture successfully relegate expression to quiet or hidden avenues, the symbols and expressions of protest can circulate in furtive conversations and concealed gestures.

Angela Davis, describing the people's art that emerged from the history of militant labor struggles and the protests of African-Americans, of women and peace activists, speaks of the cultural nourishment such people's art has provided for political action: "Black people were able to create with their music an aesthetic community of resistance, which in turn encouraged and nurtured a political community of active struggle for freedom."[26] Others agree that smaller-scale, popular, and participatory art forms can counter the influences of mainstream or mass media culture, promoting political movements to change society. Also worth considering is the process of transforming mainstream or mass media culture from within, subverting its racism, its sexism, its homophobia; many creative and responsible people have been striving to do this. Subverting the *commercialism* of mainstream and media culture from within may be a different and more difficult task, but it is not impossible. As talented people organize and demand cultural independence they can make gains in attaining it. And they can find allies among their audiences.

Television viewers sometimes experience the "conversion" of seeing for the first time how they have been used to further the economic gains of advertisers as they boost the ratings of one show or another. Women are often startled to realize how the advertising images we may have thought of as benign or attractive have contributed to oppressive aspects of our lives: an excessive concern about appearance, a fear that only female passivity is acceptable, an assumption that male dominance is inevitable. And when women understand how these damaging images are brought about by the economic interests of advertisers and corporations, anger at the culture of the media grows. As viewers come to see through the images by which they are surrounded, they find these images to be suspect rather than affecting. Learning to hold the messages of advertisements against rather than to the benefit of their senders, these viewers may never again be as naive or as receptive of the commercialized and masculinized images of media culture.

The more one has been deceived, the greater one's resentment on the discovery. When many viewers come to feel they have been deceived by the very structure of media culture, the possibilities for a transformation of that structure are promising. Already there has been a significant decline in network viewing. There is speculation that large numbers of people seek a more participatory and nourishing culture than viewing commercial television can provide.[27]

Without denying the very great power of the media to shape consciousness and thus to wield power, we need to acknowledge that it is *only* a power to affect our thoughts and emotions, a power against which we are not without at least potential resources. It is not a power to kill, imprison, or deprive of sustenance, at least not directly. And of course the power of the media can be used to foster liberation rather than control.

We need theories of social change that will allow us to account for the role that elements of culture play in encouraging or impeding social progress. At present, liberal theories characteristically pay too little attention to the realities of economic power and how it is institutionalized. With respect to the media, such theories of social change show inadequate concern for such contemporary trends as the ever-increasing commercialization of the media, the increasing concentration and corporate direction of media enterprises, and the subordination of genuinely cultural values to commercial interests in capitalist cultures.[28]

On the other hand, Marxist theories of social change give an inadequate account of how such phenomena as transformed consciousness can effect social change. The salient example of the development of the women's movements in the United States suggests that economic domination and the cultural structures that sustain it are more porous than they look. A given set of realities about social situations can be given new and different interpretations, and such transformed interpretations can themselves effect social change. A consciousness-raising group can confront media dominance. Even without distinctively different economic factors bringing such changes about, changed interpretations can develop through shared expressions of changed ideas. As women come to see their situation *as* oppressive, they strive to alter it, and the process seems to require a theory of social change that acknowledges an independent role for such cultural factors as images, interpretations, dialogue, and conscious awareness, and even for these to develop independently of the factors that would be attended to as providing causal explanations of them and their effects.[29]

Though the power to determine what TV culture will portray may seem overwhelming, it is vulnerable to transformations in consciousness cultivated elsewhere. And the revolution the women's movements are bringing about shows us how culture can be changed by nonviolent means, including such largely cultural methods of change as symbolic protests and actions, "guerrilla theatre," speakouts, and dialogue.[30] It also shows us how cultural change can effect change in the political and economic structure of society so often claimed by nonfeminist theory to be primary. While many feminists accept such views as that culture reflects changes elsewhere more than it causes them and that economic factors are the primary determinants of social reality, others acknowledge the capacity of consciousness and culture to shape society at least somewhat independently. The history of the women's movements seems to validate this view, as do some political events. An adequate account of the revolutions in Eastern Europe in 1989 must include attention to the part played by music and the arts. That popular music had broken down barriers which politicians could no longer maintain may have been an important factor.[31] That one of the most influential leaders in these developments was a playwright and another a conductor of an orchestra does not seem accidental.

Once we acknowledge how large a role culture can play in social change we can consider the kind of feminist society we might aspire to build. It might be one in which culture would have a primary role in shaping both the present and future course of the society. But to be acceptable, the structure of cultural production itself would have to be very different from what it is at present anywhere in the world, but especially in the United States, where commercial domination has become the most extreme.

The Transformation of the University

When one searches for free expression in the United States that does provide critical evaluation of existing arrangements, and substantive discussion of possible alternatives to them the university is often the best place to find it, and in many regions the only place.

Universities and colleges have undergone substantial overturning of their traditional outlooks and offerings. Women's studies courses, along with courses in Black studies and the studies of various minority and non-Western cultures, are now part of the curriculum across the country. Women's studies programs have become an established part of academic life, supported by budgets and upheld by faculty lines. It is hoped the wholesale forgetting of women's pasts and of earlier waves of feminism that occurred in previous periods can be forestalled. The historian Linda Gordon writes of the work of the first wave of women's historians in the late 19th and early 20th centuries: "I respond with a cold sweat when I remember how completely this first wave of history was suppressed. When I became a feminist and began, with a group of historians turned feminist, to find out something about women's situation in the past, I discovered these books, dusty, in the Widener library stacks, untouched for decades."[32] This was a common experience across all fields; those of us who were students before the rise of the recent women's movements had encountered nothing whatsoever about previous feminist work.

By now nearly every academic field has felt the force of feminist criticism of its gender biases. Most fields have undergone a profound transformation, as feminist insights and theories have required fundamental rethinking of assumptions, approaches, and topics of investigation.[33] The changes I am dealing with in this book requiring rethinkings of moral and social theory are illustrative. Comparable changes in other fields are often as upsetting of established views.

Among the most significant factors in the social changes brought about by the women's movements have been the altered perceptions contributed by the academic study of women and by feminist inquiry in the various academic fields of knowledge. Courses and readings dealing with the experiences of African American women, Latinas, lesbian women, women in the developing countries, as well as white North American women, have given whole generations of young women and legions of more mature women returning to college a transformed view of social reality. The gender domination of everyday life has become visible and has by now been investigated in almost all fields of what had been claimed to be impartial "knowledge."

The intensity of battles in the 1990s over multiculturalism and the broadening of the curriculum attests to the stakes involved in permitting or preventing critical views of American society from becoming prevalent in the university.[34] Conservatives charge that those striving for an antisexist, antiracist society are demanding conformity and "political correctness"; they deny that there is anything conformist in students being taught from canons of texts composed only of the work of and presenting only the views of Western white men. The rancor expressed by those opposing changes in the curriculum indicates how deeply conservatives and neoconservatives feel threatened by the academic independence of colleges and universities. Many conservative foundations have been generously funded to promote antiprogressive "research," and the reports and articles produced with their support have often been made influential by the commercial media. But many in the university have correctly seen the output from such sources as closer to ideological public relations than to what a genuinely independent view of society would provide. The independence that has been possible within the university has often permitted a critical view of American society to develop; though constantly and perhaps now increasingly under attack, such independence has not been defeated by the economic and political interests that strive to control it.

Comparatively, our institutions of higher education are less controlled by the government or by the economic sectors of the society than other institutions. Although often dependent to a very large extent on government funding and corporate gifts, they are protected at least partially by ideals of academic freedom.[35] And educational institutions at earlier levels are also to some extent independent. Although they serve corporate interests in an educated work force, and although schools are all too thoroughly influenced by the commercial values of the wider society, education is largely supported by public funds, and the goal of creating an educated citizenry still guides much that occurs in the classroom.

Perhaps those unaccustomed to seeing beyond the framework provided by the Western liberal tradition of freedom of expression can use the university as an example of the ways in which institutions for the production of other forms of culture, including mass media culture, could be comparably independent of, rather than subservient to, commercial interests and control. And perhaps they can learn from these observations that the alternative to government control is not necessarily commercial control but freedom from both kinds of outside pressure. There are obviously other values than commercial ones to be served by educational systems at all levels, and certainly there are other values that could be served by our cultural and media enterprises. We should proceed to delineate how these values should be understood and pursued. In the sector in which the mass media now affect the society, we could begin to offer at least possibilities of the independence and free expression that we can sometimes see in universities.

In asking for cultural independence, I have been accused by Alasdair MacIntyre and others of being ahistorical, of assuming there could be "purely external critics" who could escape existing beliefs, conventions, and institutions.[36] On the contrary, I am comparing the possibilities for independence in existing institutions—for instance, the pursuit of knowledge in the university—with the production of culture in the television industry. Since the pursuit of knowledge has through protracted struggles since the seventeenth century become relatively free from outside control by church, state, and corporation, it is not unreasonable to aim at some comparable independence for other forms of culture.

The Value of Free Expression

Freedom of expression requires more than the absence of interference.[37] Although the dangers of censorship and of chilling threats of interference are not behind us, especially from religious fundamentalists and in parts of the world without First Amendment traditions or their equivalent, there are issues concerning freedom of expression that have not yet begun to be addressed adequately, even in philosophical discussions of ideal societies. Theorists should consider how concepts of free expression need to be transformed to be suitable for the realities of a mass media culture.

In a media culture, the materials of expression are not only a voice, as the still dominant legal model of the orator in the public square assumes, but television studios, air waves, transmission facilities, and the like. Should these be available only to those already in command of large economic resources? It was certainly not the intent of the framers of our concepts of democracy and free expression that only those already powerful should be heard. And it is certainly not acceptable from a feminist point of view that those now in control of economic power should dominate the culture.

Elsewhere I have argued that we need a massive effort, comparable to that which brought about our system of public education, to publicly fund the production of noncommercial culture, including mass culture. Noncommercial culture should be as technically sophisticated, imaginative, and exciting as current commercial culture. Some such production should aim to reach large audiences, but instead of serving above all the values of commerce, it should serve the values of delight, well-being, aesthetic worth, and enhanced awareness—the values that feminists and creative people of various racial and class and ethnic and other groups, freed from the pressures imposed by the marketplace, would choose. If a given cultural production turns out to be economically successful, that should be an incidental bonus, not the primary objective of the production. And such production should be protected from government control by standards of artistic freedom comparable to those of academic freedom.

Of course those who create media and other culture need income and economic resources, just as those who teach in universities and schools do. But they need not be driven by the imperatives of accumulating capital and of maximizing profit. Private broadcasters and newspaper publishers can continue to turn out their products, just as private schools and colleges have continued to exist. But we need to supplement them with noncommercial alternatives, as we have supplemented private educational institutions with public ones on a truly massive scale. Public broadcasting should then be not a shoestring operation, as it is now, for very limited audiences, but a range of channels and stations offering highly popular programs as well as more specialized ones, all for the sake of cultural expression rather than commercial gain. And public funding, perhaps largely local but also national, for the production of documentary and other films, of drama and musical performances, of a wide range of cultural experiences, should be routine rather than exceptional. There should also be noncommercial sources of support for the tasks of the press: gathering the news and informing readers and viewers of what they need to know to be effective citizens and responsible participants in the shaping of culture. That newspapers and television news programs now often put the demands of commercial gain ahead of the goals of informing the public is a clear distortion of the work that ought to be done by the press in a democratic society.

There remains the question of whether the transition to a more independent and responsible culture should be brought about by further restraints on commercial excesses, as are now being considered with respect to the outrageous exploitation of children on commercial television programming designed explicitly to cause children to buy products, or whether it should be brought about by empowering voices that would provide alternatives to such excesses.[38]

John Stuart Mill believed that persons genuinely enabled to experience both admirable and unworthy cultural expressions—whatever we take these to be—will generally choose the admirable. If we share that belief, then of course we will advocate an empowerment of those not now able to provide noncommercial programs and productions. We will advocate empowering more expression rather than restricting the commercial production of media junk. We will choose, that is, the route of Mill, suitably repaved, rather than the route suggested by Plato's banishment of the poets, as updated by Alexander Nehamas.[39]

But even if we are highly skeptical of Mill's optimistic view, we still have good reasons not to choose the avenue of control until the test of empowering alternatives has been made. It certainly has not yet been made in the United States. And until the so-called consumers of the media have failed the test, there are good reasons to not even try to surmount the obstacles to the Platonic route that the First Amendment presents. The First Amendment makes restrictions on expression, even on commercial speech, difficult to uphold. But nothing in it prevents greatly increased support for noncommercial speech. As has been proposed, a tax on commercial broadcasting could well fund greatly increased offerings on noncommercial public channels. Other methods of financing would not be hard to devise.[40]

Feminists creating culture should express the values to which we give priority, not accede in the priority of commercial interests in culture. Because the struggles to free thought and expression from religious authority and from state control have often been successful, we have reason to hope that the liberation of culture from commercial domination is not an impossible goal.

Society and the Future

From the longer-range perspective of a feminist society, however, the concentration of cultural expression in the forms of the mass media, whether commercial or not, would be dubious. The sexism and racism and elitism that still taint the university might comparably color noncommercial media enterprises. A feminist objective for cultural expression might be more participatory, localized cultural expression supported by audiences no longer greatly attached to the mass media. We should try to imagine the sort of culture that women might create as we freely express ourselves and attend closely to other women. Models of smaller groups sharing in the making of cultural products, such as theatre or singing groups, local bands and craft collectives, may indicate more satisfying ways to create culture than further imitation, even in less commercial forms, of the heavily promoted star whose image is manufactured to serve the interests of his backers. The importation of the star system into the university in recent decades can serve as warning rather than model.

Still, we will probably continue to have and to want some cultural productions that can be shared rapidly by large numbers and that will still be mass media phenomena rather than small localized ones. No doubt tension between mass media and more participatory cultural forms may continue indefinitely. We will need to design institutions for the mass media as well as encourage culture not dependent on the media. For instance, panels of peers could determine which programs are aired or which newspaper ventures funded. Some decisions, between qualified persons or groups, could be made at random, by lot.

A media culture is a culture in which the mass media are the dominant feature; the United States at present has a media culture. A media society would be a society in which the influence of the media would be the dominant influence. The United States is not yet a media society, because commercial interests are still the dominant ones, and the media are their means to uphold this dominance. If the media somehow turned against business at this stage in our social development, business would win. But this may not always be the case. Although business interests are also probably dominant in the political process, it is not clear that if government turned against the business domination of the media, business would win. It is possible that the government, or more likely the public at large, led perhaps by women's groups and by persons working in the media themselves, could gradually liberate culture from outside domination.

If widespread acceptance of either public funding at adequate levels or adequate support by readers and viewers made it possible for the media and the press to gather and honestly present the news and to create excellent popular and serious entertainment, we could have the basis for the critical evaluation of the social structure that we now often lack. Such a genuinely free culture might then exert more influence in shaping consciousness and attitudes and thus society than the traditional sources of power such as government or the economy. And if processes for these and other kinds of cultural production were genuinely participatory and free of gender or racial or class domination, we might achieve greater gains toward the goal of a society feminists could accept than could be achieved by striving to change economic or governmental arrangements more directly.

A society shaped by a genuinely free culture would come closer than any we now know to being a society where decisions are made as a result of competing ideas, not force; of free expression and discussion, not raw power. The faculties of imagination, reason, and feeling would shape the future through cooperative production. The word and the image rather than the sword and the dollar would rule. But it would be the word and the image freed of their role in the service of religious institutions, of state power, of corporate interest, or, finally, of gender or racial advantage.

A feminist program for social transformation should focus special attention on the importance of a changed culture in achieving a justifiable society.[41] A feminist view of acceptable social arrangements should advocate ones which give priority to the possibilities of a free culture shaping a society in which the traditional forms of domination have been overcome and in which the power to shape consciousness belongs not to those with military or political or economic might, or racial or gender privilege, but to people responsible for choosing our own futures.

SIX

Preconceptions of Birth and Death

What sorts of changed preconceptions and perceptions, images and ideas, might we have as we begin to experience the world with a feminist approach to living in it, and how might we begin to express this in our culture? In this chapter I will look at preconceptions and ideas concerning birth and life and death, and how they affect prevailing views of political life and society. How, I will ask, might existing preconceptions be reformulated?

I try here to think anew about human birth, about the creation of human life, and about the experience of those who create human life. I argue that giving birth to human beings should not be thought to be any more "essentially natural," however that is conceptualized, than is human death. I suggest that human birth, like human death, should be understood to be central to whatever is thought to be distinctively human and that the tradition of describing birth as a natural event has served the normative purpose of discounting the value of women's experiences and activities. My discussion is often about images and associations, the preconceptual stuff philosophy should not ignore. I try to show how preconceptions shape our conceptions of birth and death, and how the standard conceptions are awry.[1]

Man and Nature

In recent years a number of feminists have successfully challenged the division characteristic of much thought—the division between "man" and "nature."[2] These feminists have criticized the preoccupations of male theorists with the domination and control of nature, which has usually been conceptualized as female, and they have speculated that the thinking of women may be more apt to seek harmony between people and our environment. Feminist theories of human progress in actual conditions should, it has been suggested, overcome the dualisms of mind and body, human and natural.

While sharing the ecological concerns in many of these views and without falling back on distinctions between man and nature as they have been formulated in the traditions of men's thought, I nevertheless assume that we can recognize some aspects of our experience as distinctively human. Perhaps what is distinctively human should be thought of in terms of the capacities for choice, for conscious awareness, and for imaginative representation. In any case, I will in this chapter take some such characteristics for the distinctively human as given, and contrast the ways in which death and birth have been traditionally interpreted. It is on the contrast between death and birth that I wish to concentrate, not the question of what, if anything, is distinctively human. I am particularly interested in arguing that a human being giving birth is engaged in as distinctively human an event as a human being dying. And to the extent that we continue to acknowledge a realm such as that of "the natural," human birth should not be thought to belong to it any more than does human death.[3]

The normative stance that nature should be cherished rather than exploited is one to which I, with most feminists, subscribe. But we should recognize that it does not require a denial of the distinctly human. Human choice, consciousness, and imagination may not be reduced satisfactorily to natural processes, as presently construed. And only human beings as distinct from other animals have the capacity to adopt a moral position of respect for nature. What my argument in this chapter implies is that the choices, conscious experiences, and imaginative lives of women are at least as central for the concept of the distinctively human as are those of men. Instead of incorporating "man" into the domain of "nature and women," we should, I suggest, incorporate women into the domain of the fully human, and advocate respect for nonhuman nature as well as for human beings. And we should interpret giving birth as a central event in human experience.

There are ways in which both birth and death have been thought of as divine rather than as either human or natural events: God giveth and God taketh away. But the distinction with which I will examine views of birth and death is that between the human and the natural once it has been acknowledged that there is more (or less) to both the human and the natural than the hand of God. I will thus not try to cover views of childbirth, or of death, that can be thought of as primarily religious.

When it has been thought of as other than a manifestation of the will of God, human birth has almost always been represented as a natural, biological event, rather than as a distinctively human one. Philosophers and the creators of masculine culture throughout the ages have presented human death as distinctively human. We should recognize giving birth as no less so.

The contrast between the humanness ascribed to death and denied to birth has had vast implications for conceptions of political life and society. In the male realm of the polis, it is assumed that men risk death for the sake of human progress; in the female realm of the household, on the other hand, it is assumed that the species is merely reproduced. Clearly, in overcoming male dominance, it will not be enough for women to be permitted to enter the "public" arena, where men are willing to cause death for their beliefs. Birth and the "private" world of mothering will have to be reconceptualized and accorded the evaluations they deserve.

The Aspect of Choice

Let us begin with the recognition that the capacity to choose (however this is further construed) is an important part of what it is to be distinctively human. And let us contrast how this capacity to choose has been emphasized with respect to death but denied with respect to birth. Human beings, we have often been reminded, can choose what to die for. We can overcome our fears and die courageously. We can die for noble causes and die heroically.[4] We can die out of loyalty, out of duty, out of commitment. We can die for a better future, for ourselves, for our children, for humankind. We can die to give birth to nations, or democracy, to put an end to tyranny, or war. We can die for God, for civilization, for justice, for freedom. Nonhuman animals can die for none of these; that human beings can do so is an important part of and perhaps essential to what it is to be human.

Contrast all this, now, with what has been said about human birth. Birth is spoken of as a natural, biological process. That women give birth is said to make us "essentially" close to nature, resembling other mammals in this crucial aspect of our lives. Human mothering is seen as a kind of extension of the "natural," biological event of childbirth. It is thought that women engage in the activity of mothering because we have given birth and that mothering should be incorporated into the framework of the "natural."

Until recently, childbirth has been something that has for the most part happened to women, rather than being something chosen by women. Adrienne Rich makes a concise statement:

> For most women actual childbirth has involved no choice whatever, and very little consciousness. Since prehistoric times, the anticipa-

114

tion of labor has been associated with fear, physical anguish or death, a stream of superstitions, misinformation, theological and medical theories—in short, all we have been taught we should feel, from willing victimization to ecstatic fulfillment.[5]

For most women most of the time, then, giving birth has represented most starkly women's lack of choice, our vulnerability to the forces of nature and male domination. With little chance to avoid pregnancy and few means of abortion, women have experienced childbirth as something almost entirely outside our control.

But even in the most extreme situations, giving birth is not wholly outside the control of women. A human female can decide not to create another human being, even if to avoid doing so entails great risk. Women throughout history have attempted to end our pregnancies, often endangering our health and lives.[6] A woman ultimately has the capacity to refuse to yield to the forces of nature and the demands of men, for these cannot prevent her from attempting abortion or killing herself if no other means of ending her pregnancy is successful. Thus any woman, unlike any nonhuman animal, can intentionally avoid creating another human being. Through contraception and more recently legal abortion, most women in the West now have a large measure of choice over whether or not to give birth.

Alison Jaggar has pointed out a possible paradox in the argument here: If it is supposed that what makes a human birth essentially human is that one can choose to die rather than give birth, once again it is the willingness to die that defines the essentially human.[7] I do not mean to suggest that it is the woman's willingness to die that makes giving birth essentially human, but rather that the conscious choice women can make of whether to give birth or to try not to is one of the characteristics of human birth that distinguishes it from animal birth. When less dangerous methods of avoiding or ending a pregnancy are available, there is nothing especially human about risking death to do so; what makes human birth *human* is that women can decide whether or not to try to end our pregnancies, that we can be conscious of the process in which we are involved, and that we can represent the surrounding decisions and events in symbolic and imaginative ways.

If a woman chooses to try to become pregnant or to continue with a pregnancy, she makes a choice that only a conscious human being can make, and the resulting birth is radically unlike the natural event of nonhuman birth. To construe human birth as primarily biological is as mis-

leading as to construe human life and human death as primarily biological. Of course they are all also biological, but this is only their primary
attribute in certain restricted contexts, such as a medical context, or from
only one among many points of view, such as that of biology. To the extent that we recognize that there is more to human life and more to human death than can be comprehended through a biological framework,
so should we recognize that there is more to human birth. If anything,
giving birth is more human, because we *can* choose to avoid it, whereas
death, eventually, is inevitable.

No one can possibly justify being born, nor should anyone ever be
asked to. The questions "What right do you have to have come into existence?" or "Why should you have been born?" make no sense asked of
the child. Any argument that a child should not have been born can only
be addressed to the child's parents or to those in a position, through
social policies of various kinds, to have increased or decreased the likelihood of this birth. But the questions "Why should you have a child?"
or "Why should you refrain from having a child?" make excellent sense
addressed to potential mothers. The rarity with which these questions
are seen to make human birth an event other than biological indicates
yet again how unaccustomed we are to viewing the world from the point
of view of women.

Men often imagine themselves to have come into existence full-blown,
as rationally self-interested entities in a "state of nature."[8] Sometimes they
remember that they were once children, and they can think back to their
own childhoods or even imagine their own births. They recognize the
inappropriateness of being asked to justify their own existence. But they
rarely imagine the women who gave them existence being in a position
to determine whether to give them existence or not and to do so for reasons of which women can be conscious. To understand childbirth from
the point of view of women requires a shift of perspective that seems
highly unusual. And yet we can hardly hope to gain an adequate conception of human experience without exploring human life from the point
of view of those in a position to create it or not create it.

Questions of what to give birth for, like questions of what to die for or
what to live for, can be asked even when women have no more control
over childbirth than refusing to give birth at extreme risk to ourselves.

When women have more control over whether or not to give birth,
and when we have, as many of us now do, almost full control, the appropriateness of the questions is even more pronounced. Any woman can

ask herself: Why should I give birth? What should I create a child for? To what end should I give birth? In giving birth, to what shall I be giving human expression? The compendium of reasons for which men (and women) have wondered what to die for or live for can be matched by a new and even richer compendium of reasons for which women can give birth. Men (and women) can die out of loyalty, out of duty, out of commitment, and they can die for a better future. Women can give birth, or refuse to give birth, from all these motives and others. We can give birth so that a new human being can experience joy, so that humankind can continue to exist, so that the family of which we are a member can maintain itself, so that the social movement which gives us hope may have another potential adherent, so that the love we share with another may be shared with yet another. We can give birth to express our conceptions of our selves, of humanity, and of life. And so on endlessly. That women can give birth for reasons should make clear how very *unlike* a natural, biological event of human birth is.[9]

It is altogether likely that most women do not ask ourselves why we should give birth or what we should give birth for. But neither do most men (or women) ask themselves what they should die for, or even what they should live for. Most deaths are not the result of such deliberations; neither is the conduct of most lives. Most deaths happen to people, and most people live their lives with little reflection about the ends to which they can devote themselves. Nevertheless, that a human being can choose what to die for and what to live for characterizes our concepts of being human and of dying a human death and living a human life. What we should open our eyes to, I am suggesting, is that women can choose what to give birth for or what to refuse to give birth for and that these options characterize human birth.

If it is inappropriate to ask what to give birth for, perhaps it is also inappropriate to ask what to die for. If we ought to give birth "as nature intends," to the extent that sense can be made of such a notion, and if birth should indeed be seen as "natural," then so perhaps should men live their lives and die "as nature intends," whatever that may mean. But if we recognize the appropriateness of asking for reasons to live or die one way or another, we ought to recognize reasons for giving birth. And the possibilities of deciding what to give birth for should characterize our concepts of woman and birth. These concepts should in turn be as much at the heart of our concept of being human as are our concepts of death and of living a distinctively human life. Perhaps they should be even more central.

SIX

The Aspect of Awareness

Consider now the aspect of human experience captured by the term 'conscious awareness'. To whatever extent other animal species may have a similar awareness, it pales beside the full human awareness of our own prospective deaths and of the meanings that can be attached to our deaths, an awareness heightened now by centuries of religious, literary, and philosophical attention. We are aware that we will die and that in a very real sense we die alone. We are aware that in death the selves we are as we contemplate our deaths will end. Compare this now with what is thought about birth. In men's traditional systems of thought it is usually seen in terms of "getting born," that is, of the starting of a man's life. From this point of view—the point of view of a person's own birth as an infant—it must be associated with an absence of conscious awareness, not only at the event but for some time afterwards. Since none of us can have been aware of our own births or can remember being born, thinking about our births, in contrast to thinking about our deaths, is thinking about a time before our own conscious awareness could have made sense to us. From the point of view of a man thinking about his birth and his death, there is a disanalogy.[10] Although we lose conscious awareness with death, and might lose it gradually, or before the death of our bodies, we can be aware now of what we will lose. In contrast, we could not have been aware at our births of what we would gain eventually in becoming aware. Death is seen as the ending of an awareness that is distinctively human and that has already existed. Hence a man contemplating his death will have no doubt that it will be a human death. He can, however, and often does, see his birth as a kind of natural event subsequent to which he developed the awareness that is essential to his humanity. Or if his religious images have led him to construe his humanity as commencing at conception, still, the event of his birth is probably construed as an event of the same type as the birth of other living creatures, part of God's plan perhaps, but not associated with a distinctively human consciousness.

Birth, then, from the point of view of the infant we once were, or of the observer of infants, is associated with the lack rather than the presence of consciousness. Death, in contrast, is what we are each approaching every day and what we can be conscious of approaching throughout our lives. Sometimes persons are conscious that they are dying; we can ask of another person, "Does he know he's dying?" But even when death is sudden

118

and unexpected, it is associated with the consciousness that it would come sooner or later.

If we think about birth from the point of view of the mother or potential mother, however, rather than from the point of view of a man observing an infant or thinking about the infant he once was, our conceptions of birth may be transformed. While it may be that women have often internalized the male point of view standard in the culture, we should not do so. A potential mother can be consciously aware at any time that she may be the creator of a new human being or that she may consciously seek to avoid becoming an actual mother. A pregnant woman is fully conscious for many months that she will give birth to another human being if she does not abort. She is conscious that she can prevent this birth, although perhaps at extreme cost to herself. And upon giving birth a woman will be conscious that she has brought into existence another human being. In Eva Kittay's words, there can be for women giving birth a "wonderful consciousness of one's connection with all of nature."[11] So while it is true that giving birth connects us to nature, we can have a distinctively human consciousness of this connection. The awareness that one is preparing for giving birth and then that one has given birth can be associated with consciousness as fully as can any contemplation of death. And in terms of overcoming one's own limitations and death, this awareness may far exceed anything available to men.

Consider, next, the "internal point of view" of which Thomas Nagel writes:

> In acting, we occupy the internal perspective . . . From the inside, when we act, alternative possibilities seem to lie open before us . . . From an external perspective . . . the agent and everything about him seems to be swallowed up by the circumstances of action; nothing of him is left to intervene in those circumstances . . . We may elaborate this external picture by reference to biological, psychological, and social factors in the formation of ourselves and other agents. But the picture doesn't have to be complete in order to be threatening.[12]

We cannot, Nagel continues, fully accept the picture provided from the external perspective because "the sense that we are the authors of our own actions is not just a feeling but a belief, and we can't come to regard it as a pure appearance without giving it up altogether."

Nagel thinks the problem of free will is at present insoluble, that neither the internal nor the external point of view concerning human action as so far understood is at all satisfactory. I agree. However, while almost everyone who considers an internal point of view epistemologically important recognizes that others as well as they themselves have an internal point of view and that the internal point of view cannot be given up without a problem for one's sense of conscious self, the concept of woman as mother has virtually omitted the internal point of view, as human mothers have been swallowed up into biological explanations and social descriptions. A woman giving birth is seldom thought of from an internal point of view. In a perceptive attempt to deal with the phenomenology of pregnancy from the subjective point of view of the mother, Iris Marion Young notes how pregnancy has been viewed: "Pregnancy does not belong to the woman herself. It either is a state of the developing foetus, for which the woman is a container; or it is an objective, observable process coming under scientific scrutiny; or it becomes objectified by the woman herself, as a 'condition' . . . Pregnancy omits subjectivity."[13] A person contemplating his death from his own inner perspective understands that it cannot be adequately described only from the perspective of an external observer. That giving birth cannot adequately be understood from an external point of view only is an unfamiliar cultural notion. Yet it is certainly true.[14]

It may be argued that a better analogy than that between birth and death is that between giving birth and taking life. But this places more importance on linguistic conventions than they deserve. Death has traditionally been conceptualized both in terms of the death a man is conscious of approaching and in terms of the death he might consciously inflict on others. Birth, in contrast, has seldom been conceptualized from the point of view of the person giving birth. And there are fundamental disanalogies between giving birth and taking life: for instance, we can take our own lives but we cannot give birth to ourselves; everyone who lives must have been given birth to, but not everyone who dies must have been killed. The proposed analogy does not address the question I am raising: From whose point of view should birth be conceptualized?

The Aspect of Imaginative Represenatation

Consider now how the capacity for imaginative representation has been developed with respect to death but stunted with respect to birth and mothering. Tales of battle and scenes of adventure make the risking of death central to the human imagination. That human beings can consciously choose death over surrender is at the heart of the image of "man." That human beings can "transcend" their deaths by the discoveries or achievements they leave behind is part of the awareness of human beings generally.

Images of birth, on the other hand, are traditionally images of natural events, if not of divine ones. Births are shrouded events, but they are presented as things that happen, arbitrarily or inevitably, without the conscious participation of the person giving birth. Only occasionally are they imagined to be glorious events, as when they are represented as the births of the sons or prophets of a male God, or the births of the heroes or adventurers who will fulfill the images familiar in representations of death.

Symbolic representations of giving birth, of creating new human persons through the distinctively human act of giving birth to a human being, are rare.[15] Imaginative representations of birth from the point of view of a woman contemplating it, or of a woman experiencing a pregnancy and consciously ending or continuing it, or of a woman giving birth— these are unfamiliar cultural constructions.[16] Even women who are writers and artists have rarely dealt with motherhood because it has seemed to lack value; we have often unconsciously assumed that to be serious writers and artists we must be outside rather than inside the framework of birth and mothering. The poet Adrienne Rich observed how, for many years, she did not write about her children or about mothering: "For me poetry was where I lived as no one's mother, where I existed as myself."[17]

Some feminists assert that men as a gender suffer from a preoccupation with death: To the extent that dominant forms of art and culture have been largely created by men, the prevalence of death as imaginative subject would be expected. The capacity for imaginative representation of most persons is enriched in some directions and impoverished in others, depending on the cultural resources available. We can recognize how underdeveloped are the subjects of giving birth and mothering as subjects of imaginative cultural representation. This in turn means that the capacities for symbolic consideration of birth and mothering that most persons have are likely to be unnecessarily limited. Associations between death and human imaginative representations are very strong. Associations between giving birth and human imaginative representations have been very weak. But the possibilities for the imaginative consideration of giving birth and for seeing the imaginative aspects of the activities of mothers are as limitless as they are for representations of death.

Rituals surrounding human death are multiple and varied. Ritual recreations of birth, as in *couvade* (the father simulating giving birth), initiation rites, or the rebirth of the boy as man are common in many cultures.

121

Restrictions on menstruating and pregnant women are common. But rituals celebrating the act of giving birth are rare.[19] Thus has culture limited the imaginative representation or celebration of birth. Some may believe that the precariousness of early human life—until recently—has contributed to the lack of celebration of birth itself, since if the infant may well die, one may hesitate to accord too much importance to its birth.[20] But if this were the major factor in the explanation, one would not expect *couvade* or most maternal restrictions either. With the decrease of infant mortality one could expect an increase of ritual and symbolic attention focused on birth. Without feminist awareness, however, the focus may be almost entirely on the child, as in christening rites, or on the father's role, rather than on the mother's giving birth.

In the region of experience involving the upbringing of children, the flourishing of human imagination is probably greater than in any other region of human experience. The caretakers of children suggest imaginative games and encourage the child's willingness to pretend. Children fill their worlds with imagined objects, events, and experiences. These scenes and stories build on each other yet remain fresh from day to day and year to year. The distinctively human symbolizing involved in the development of children's speech, images, and understanding is obvious. Yet representation of this experience in dominant cultural constructs often distorts the rich imaginative content of this domain and the contributions of mothers to it, reducing child care to an aspect of the "natural." Birth and the early upbringing of children are portrayed as a kind of prehuman period in the lives of men. Little children may move about the house, like dogs and cats; they need care, like flocks and gardens. But to the extent that little children are seen as already fully human, it has in male eyes been imagined to have resulted from what God rather than their mothers have given them or because of the potential within them to become, as if of their own efforts, "men." And human mothering, instead of being recognized as itself composed, to a very significant extent, of imaginative representation, has been imagined to be a biological process.

Feminist Critiques

It has been said repeatedly in masculine culture that it is the natural function of women to reproduce. The speakers usually go on to say that it is also the natural function of women to care for children.[21] Since engagement in the events of giving birth, nursing, and caring for children—events seen as natural and biological—consume so much of the lives of most women, we have been conceptualized as more deeply immersed in nature than men.

Feminists have made the valid point that men as well as women can be the caretakers of children and have shown how the concept of "natural," in the claim that women should be the ones to bring up children, has been twisted to serve the ideological purposes of men. Wanting to say that women ought to stay home and care for the children, or be forced to, some men have preferred to couch these prescriptions or threats in the more neutral language of what is "natural." Feminists have successfully challenged such misuse of the term.[22]

In proposing new interpretations of motherhood, some feminists have emphasized, with Plato, the irrelevance of whether one bears or begets. The fact that it is women who give birth should not be taken to imply that the whole of women's lives should be associated with motherhood, nor should it be used to justify excluding women from so-called male occupations. Other feminists have argued that women's reproductive biology is so fundamental a feature of the oppression of women that technological means should be developed to enable women to avoid having to give birth. Shulamith Firestone, writing early in the current wave of feminist thinking, called for birth to become something artificial, with infants being produced in a laboratory, so that women would no longer be defined by our biological function nor be tied to its consequences.[23] Most feminists have rejected artificial birthing as a solution to the "problem" of biology, preferring instead more natural birth processes and the social supports for bearing and rearing children that are now so inadequate.[24] In addition, recognizing the benefits for children and men as well as for women that genuinely equal participation by fathers in the care of children would bring, many feminists have sought ways to separate biological realities from the oppression of women. In doing so, the significance of the biological capacity of women to give birth has, I think, sometimes been underestimated.

There have been a number of studies of birthing as a social rather than a natural process. Brigitte Jordan's study of birthing practices in four cultures, using a biosocial framework for its descriptions, makes clear how inadequate it is to think of human birth as primarily biological.[25] Other studies have shown how the process of giving birth was taken over and controlled by men as male obstetrics in the seventeenth and eighteenth centuries replaced the art of birthing practiced by female midwives.[26] And studies have shown us how childbirth is still an event structured by social institutions controlled by men and still shaped by the ways in which men have molded the culture.[27] That women often lose our jobs when we give birth undermines our ability to control the way giving birth will affect our lives. That the culture portrays pregnancy and childbirth as processes that should lead women to become passive recipients of the advice and treatment of a male-dominated medical profession takes from women the power to determine even the aspect of our lives seen as most distinctively female.[28] And the ways in which male professionals have often been able to control, through the use of what has been claimed to be "knowledge," the activities of those, almost entirely women, engaged in child care, have by now been examined. To recognize childbirth as social, however, is not yet to acknowledge it as the fully human, as distinct from natural, event that it is. The labor of ants, for instance, can be described in social terms.

Alison Jaggar questions whether it makes sense to speak of the biological as distinct from the social in the case of human beings: "We cannot identify a clear, nonsocial sense of 'biology,' nor a clear, nonbiological sense of 'society.'" Even something like the smaller size of women, often thought of as a biological given, can be affected by a social organization in which "the nutrition of females is inferior because of their lower social status . . . Where human nature is concerned, there is no line between nature and culture."[29] Nevertheless, while it is clear that levels of technological development and forms of social organization deeply affect human biology and certainly affect human birth and the upbringing of children, I consider it useful to distinguish between the human and the natural, and between the distinctively human and the natural components of human reality. Experiences of choice, consciousness, and imaginative representation are distinctively human; that calcium is a component of human bones is not.

Many of the feminist arguments on various sides of these issues share with nonfeminist ones the assumption that birth is a "natural" process. Many of those who criticize the way childbirth has become a "culturally produced event" would like it to become more natural than it now is. They use the language of the "natural" to promote childbirth controlled by women to take the place of childbirth controlled by male institutions and male professions. But, for reasons I have suggested, the language of the "natural" can be misleading. Rather than accepting an incorporation of women into the domain of nature, a better argument might be that women, as distinctively human, should insist that childbirth be controlled by those who give birth and that nature should be respected rather than conquered.

In rejecting the separation of man and nature and the consignment of women to the latter category, many feminists have argued that men as well as women belong to a natural universe that should be treasured rather than dominated or exploited. Adrienne Rich and others effectively protest the way childbearing has been taken over by men who control women's bodies, and child rearing by male psychiatrists and other experts who cause women to feel incompetent even at what it is supposed to be "natural" for us to do. Rich and others are critical of man's view of himself as opposed to nature, and they advocate an assertion by women of our affinity with nature.

Quite possibly we should not think of nature in the causal, mechanistic, deterministic sense which depictions of it drawn from the sciences so often now present. Perhaps then it would be enough to think of women and men primarily as part of nature rather than emphasizing the differences between the human and the natural. But for the time being it seems important to stress that only human beings, as far as we can tell, can experience the capacities for choice, awareness, and imaginative representation, and to stress that women can experience these at least as fully as men can.

Women and Reproduction

Let us look at examples of writers who, though feminist, have viewed birth as a natural, biological event. Even Simone de Beauvoir, thoroughly aware of so many of the injustices suffered by women, and coming to these views so long before most others in the recent wave of feminist thought, wrote of human birthing as a natural, animal-like process. She concluded that woman "is more enslaved to the species than the male, her animality is more manifest." Sherry Ortner, in an important and much cited article, agreed: "It is simply a fact that proportionately more of a woman's body space, for a greater percentage of her lifetime, and at some—sometimes great—cost to her personal health, strength, and general stability, is taken up with the natural processes surrounding the reproduction of the species."[30]

These conceptions and their implications can of course be challenged. Giving birth to a human being is no more a natural process than is cultivating a wheat field or taming a wild horse. It only seems so if we have already at a prior stage of the conception denied the full humanity of the woman who gives birth. If we acknowledge her full humanity we must acknowledge the extent to which giving birth to a new human being is a human as distinct from a natural process. The term 'reproduction' is misleading, for it already assimilates human childbirth to the reproduction of animals. And human childbirth is radically different from the process by which animals produce repeated instances of their species.

Hannah Arendt sees reproduction as mere repetition.[31] Beauvoir shares this view. "On the biological level," she writes, "a species is maintained only by creating itself anew; but this creation results only in repeating the same Life in more individuals." To Beauvoir, man, in contrast with woman, much more frequently transcends, through action, the repeating of life, and "by this transcendence he creates values that deprive pure repetition of all value."[32] She thinks that for women to liberate ourselves from this confinement to mere repetition, we must be free to engage in the kind of action open to men, action that transcends biological reproduction.

In such passages, Beauvoir concedes what I take to be at issue: that human childbirth is primarily a biological event. If it is not primarily a biological event but a distinctively human event, then a woman, in choosing to give birth to a new human being, can engage in transcendence. No human person is a mere biological replica of any other. Every human person is a culturally created entity as well as a biological entity. To give birth to a new human being capable of contributing to the transformation of human culture is to transcend what existed before. And the activity of mothering, as it shapes a human child into a distinctive social person, is even more clearly capable of transcendence.

Beauvoir considers the view that "it is not in giving life but in risking life that man is raised above the animal; that is why superiority has been accorded in humanity not to the sex that brings forth but to that which kills."[33] She argues eloquently against the conclusion that women are inferior merely because we are more confined than men to the repetitive biological realm. But she does not dispute, as I am here doing, the conception of childbirth as essentially biological. Similarly, Ortner argues against the view that because we are "closer to nature," women should be deemed inferior, but she agrees that in fact women are more involved with "natural functions."[34]

Ortner concludes her essay by noting that "the whole scheme is a construct of culture rather than a fact of nature. Woman is not 'in reality' any closer to (or further form) nature than man—both have consciousness, both are mortal." But she continues to think "there are certainly reasons she appears that way." I am trying to show why women need not even appear to be closer to nature if we more adequately understand women and nature. A more satisfactory conception of human childbirth shows that women are not more involved than men in merely biological processes. Ortner declares that "ultimately, both men and women can and must be equally involved in projects of creativity and transcendence."[35] But she does not suggest that childbirth can be one such project of creativity and transcendence, which is the position I am advancing.

Elsewhere in her essay, Ortner writes of lactation and nursing as natural. But there is no reason to think of nursing as any more natural than, say, cutting down trees to make a clearing, or building shelter. How human beings locate and construct their dwellings are cultural matters; so are the practices surrounding nursing, such as how long children are nursed, whether wet nurses are used, whether nursing occurs openly or only "in private," and so forth. If men transcend the natural through their cultural practices and innovations, so do women transcend the natural through our practices and innovations through giving birth to and raising children.

Family and Polis

A long line of thinkers have associated the "public" sphere with the distinctively human, the "private" with the natural. They have represented the family as focused on particularistic and hence inferior concerns, often in conflict with the superior and more universal concerns of the public sphere.[36] In Ortner's formulation, "the family (and hence women) represents lower-level, socially fragmenting, particularistic sort[s] of concerns, as opposed to interfamilial relations representing higher-level integrative, universalistic sorts of concerns."[37]

It is easy enough, in questioning such an ordering of women and the family versus men and the polis, to rethink what is lower and what higher in such a contrast. One could describe family relations as rich, subtle, and capable of emotional sensitivity, compared to legal-political relations, which are rough, crude, and insensitive. One could think of family relations as higher in many respects, and what to conclude about the balance of both should be an open question. Though the two domains are different, and often focused on different concerns, it is clearly an unsatisfactory distortion of their reality to think of the public sphere as distinctively human and the sphere of mothering persons and children as involved in mere reproduction.

The claim that the family is particularistic while the polis deals with what is universal is questionable even in terms of existing institutions. And if the wall between the private and the public were dismantled in the ways many feminists advocate, support for the claim might erode.[38]

True, some public decisions involve large numbers of people in contrast to family decisions involving only a few. But consider a paradigm of the public sphere: a court of law. Here, typically, a single defendant is judged by a few individuals, and no case is quite like any other. It may be true that universal legal norms and requirements are being applied to this case, but so too can universal norms and requirements be applied in a family: parents may decide they ought to educate their child a certain way because they believe all parents ought to do so. Particular adolescents may seek independence from parental control; this is a universal of human development for which general norms can be sought. That no set of universal norms is adequate for the particular moral problems that arise in a given family can be matched by the recognition that no set of universal laws can truly do justice to all the particular aspects of a given court case. That state power is involved in a court of law can be matched by the acknowledgment that state power determines permissible family structure and greatly affects relations among family members. That individual personalities must be accommodated in family interactions can be matched by a recognition of how significantly individual personalities of lawyers, judges, jury members, defendants, and plaintiffs affect the outcomes of court decisions. And so on.

Finally, in a hierarchically organized society, the supposedly private decisions of powerful persons and families can affect the employment and well-being of countless others. Though we may continue to need different norms for different domains of human life, we should resist the terms on which conceptual claims have been built by male-dominated society. Among the concepts most clearly in need of reconceptualization are those of public and private, with their varying but characteristic associations with male and female, and of giving birth with the private and humanly insignificant.

The concepts have had different associations with men and women at different periods of history. The Greek polis was a male domain; women were confined to the household. But before the rise of liberal democracy, the family, with its clearly designated male ruler, was often seen as a model for the wider society. With the Lockean renunciation of political patriarchy, the family was relegated to a peripheral status outside of and irrelevant to the political organization of "free and equal men." Since then, liberal concessions toward equality for women have usually expected women to enter a political sphere structured by concepts designed for a male polis. Some feminists are now reversing these expectations and are suggesting that the postpatriarchal family and its norms be considered highly relevant as a model for much more than the family. Perhaps the postpatriarchal family should even be a model for much in political life.

From the time of the ancient Greeks it has been held that man transcends his animal, material nature while engaged in the public life of the polis, while those immersed in the daily tasks of the private household are engaged in the mere maintenance of man's material nature. We can dispute this contrast. Human beings engaged in giving birth and in bringing up children are as capable of transcending what already exists as are most of those in government or the arts and sciences. Creating new human persons and new human personalities with new thoughts and attitudes is as creative an activity as humans are involved in anywhere. And the norms for this activity may be a better source of recommendations for actions in various other domains than are many of the norms of what has traditionally been thought to constitute morality. At least, many feminists now believe, an ethic of care must be taken as seriously as an ethic of justice.

In claiming that women, in giving birth and rearing children, can indeed engage in transcendence and in the distinctively human and cultural activities of moving beyond mere repetition, we need of course to be on guard against misuses of such arguments. There will predictably be those who will say that since childbirth and child care are such admirable activities, women should have no complaints about being confined to them. But from recognizing that birth should be at the heart of our conceptions of life and from celebrating the wondrousness of empowering a child to live a good human life, it absolutely does not follow that women should be confined to rearing children or encouraged to accept the leadership of men in any domain. What is more plausibly implied is that the world should be organized to be hospitable to children and conductive to the flourishing of all persons, and that men, having failed to bring about such a condition, should have their leadership replaced or supplemented by those who may, with different perspectives, methods, and abilities, do better.

Changes are taking place such that more fathers share in parenting, and more mothers share in work outside the home. There are on independent grounds excellent and obvious reasons why forms of transcendence and cultural activity other than giving birth and mothering should be fully open to women. And there may be very good reasons why child care should be fully shared by men and why men should participate in decisions concerning the creating of new persons. The point is that adequate conceptualizations of childbirth and child care would recognize and appreciate their distinctively human features.

We might speculate that for such reconceputalization of childbirth and child care to be accepted on a broad scale, men may have to engage in domestic life as fully as women, and women in the political structuring of society as fully as men. But those willing to explore feminist perspectives need not wait for such a social transformation before changing our own conceptions of birth and of family life and of the implications of these for political theory.

Marxist Categories

The Marxist view of childbirth and child rearing has been essentially similar to the other views we have been examining. The traditional Marxist conception sees childbirth as an entirely biological process. And then, as Alison Jaggar notes, the implication is that "women, who are primarily procreative laborers, are biologically determined to a greater extent than men are." Moreover, traditional Marxists have extended the biological view of childbirth to the raising of children. "Marx and Engels," Jaggar writes, "clearly believe that the division of labor within the family is natural because it is biologically determined, 'based on a purely physiological foundation.'"[39]

Marxist analyses divide social activity into those activities connected with production and those connected with reproduction. In industrialized society, in the view of traditional Marxists, work in the factory or on the farm belong to the sphere of production; childbirth and housework belong to the sphere of reproduction. Production transforms the human environment, making raw materials into machines and finished products; reproduction merely repeats the bringing into existence of biological human entities.[40]

Socialist feminists have objected. Some have pointed out that childbirth and child rearing and housework in general contribute very significantly to production. They have tried to understand the economic value and effects of the work of "servicing" existing workers through cooking, cleaning, and so forth, and of "producing" new workers.[41]

Ann Ferguson and Nancy Folbre have focused on what they call "sex-affective production," or the production of that which is required for bearing and rearing children and for "the fulfillment of human needs for affection, nurturance, and sexual expression." They discuss the ways women have been oppressed by the division of labor in which "most of

[the] responsibilities and requirements" of sex-affective production "are met by women." The gender identity into which women are socialized "keeps them willing to give more than they receive from men in nurturance and sexual satisfaction." And the division of labor by which the burdens of sex-affective production fall mainly on women "is not a neutral one, assigning 'separate but equal' roles. It is an oppressive one, based upon inequality and reinforced by social relation[s] of domination."[42]

Alison Jaggar and William McBride have noted the serious ambiguities in the categories of production and reproduction; they have concluded that the distinction distorts the reality of women's work and serves largely to obscure the way women's labor is exploited by men. They propose that "procreation and nurturing are production in the broadest Marxist sense of being necessary to human life and they are increasingly productive in the capitalist sense of falling within the market." In their view, procreative and nurturing activities are "just as fully forms of human labor" as are the activities involved in agriculture or manufacturing.[43]

While these views represent highly important theoretical advances over those which relegate childbirth and child care to a realm of biological reproduction, they do not capture the reality of childbirth and child care. Either they subordinate relations between mothering persons and children to the wider conception of economic production, or they employ concepts developed for a realm quite foreign to birth and nurturance. Since Marxist concepts of production have been developed for a context that is overwhelmingly economic, it may be almost as inappropriate to think of childbirth and child rearing as forms of "production" as it is to think of them as forms of mere "reproduction." Giving birth and bringing up children may be closer to artistic expression than it is to the production of material objects. Both can involve very hard work, but the desire to give expression to human value may be paramount, and much of the activity of mothering can be more expressive than productive. Not everything that human beings do is best thought of as a form of labor. We seem to need to continue our quest for a way of conceptualizing childbirth and child care, a way that will adequately reflect and guide the experience of women.

O'Brien's Contribution

One of the most interesting attempts to rethink birth has been made by Mary O'Brien. In an eloquent book, she has analyzed women's consciousness of the process of birth, showing how it must differ in significant ways from the consciousness men have of reproduction.[44] She criticizes the failures of Arendt, Beauvoir, and others to value women's reproductive labor. She emphasizes that such labor is transformative, on a par with the transformative labor of production central to Marxist theory. She perceives the deficiencies of Marxist theories in their handling of the domain of reproduction and calls attention to the need for feminist theory concerning birth.

Her own speculations concerning the origins of patriarchy are suggestive. For men, she points out, awareness of paternity can rest only on a theory about reproduction, whereas women can directly experience genetic continuity. In her analysis, the male "alienates" his seed in the procreative process. To compensate for his inability to produce a child, he acts to assure his own paternity of a given child. And to establish the right to appropriate as his a child that has been produced, he bands together with other men to form the social framework that will keep women in a private sphere and assure his access to the means of reproductive labor.

O'Brien believes that the development of the technology by which women can control our own reproductive processes is what Hegel calls a world historical event. It can be expected to alter drastically the consciousness of women and relations between women and men: "The freedom for women to choose parenthood is a historical development as significant as the discovery of physiological paternity. Both create a transformation in human consciousness of human relations with the natural world which must, as it were, be re-negotiated." O'Brien's account should be examined by all who attempt to rethink the concepts of birth and motherhood. She observes that paternity is a more social than biological phenomenon: "The appropriation of the child defies the uncertainty of paternity, yet it cannot do so in biological terms. It must do so in social and ideological terms . . . The appropriation of the child cannot be made without the cooperation of other men."[45]

Her analysis, however, seems to me too narrowly focused on the moment of birth. Giving birth can be relatively less important in a woman's life and in shaping her consciousness than the succeeding years of rearing her child. The characteristics of female consciousness may arise more from the whole process of bringing an infant into the world and then nurturing it to adulthood than from the process of reproduction seen as ending with birth. And since O'Brien wishes to contrast reproduction with production as analyzed by Marx, what counts as reproduction should include rather than exclude the upbringing of children. But then it is not true that only women can engage in reproduction, since men can share in the upbringing and daily care of children. Hence O'Brien's formulation in which "only women perform reproductive labour"[46] is unsatisfactory.

Furthermore, the concept of reproduction is unfortunate. It suggests repetition, copying, producing more of the same. But since each new generation of human persons is as different, in terms of the social reality each incorporates, as is each stage of the economic reality changed over the generations by the labor of production, the contrast should not be in terms of production versus reproduction. It would be more helpful to draw the distinction in terms of such notions as economic production and the creation of social persons, or in terms of shaping the environment and shaping new persons, and transforming both. As O'Brien formulates the issues, the focus is on reproduction, or the process of giving birth to infants, and the labor involved. As I try to reconceptualize birth, I see in the event of giving birth not only the fruit of a woman's labor but also of her consciousness and, in addition, the first stage of bringing the infant to autonomous personhood. *In both giving birth and mothering, the woman expresses the kind of woman she chooses to be.*

As men come to care for children, they may experience much of the genetic continuity for which O'Brien thinks they go to such lengths to compensate. To "see oneself" in one's child, in the shape of a hand or tilt of an eyebrow, reminds one of this continuity. It may remind a father that the child is his as well as the mother's. (The mother, after all, may sometimes worry also: infants are occasionally exchanged, and the one she holds in her arms may possibly not be the one to which she has given birth.) A father's awareness of genetic continuity would, at least to some extent, overcome the male discontinuity between copulation and birth. Even more to the point, perhaps, a shared contribution by the father in the care of the child can overshadow the "separation" in which the mother but not the father actually "creates" the infant. Fathers as well as mothers can perform the transformative labor of bringing infants to grown personhood. And adoptive parents as well as genetic parents can experience a kind of continuity.

Whether to create an infant remains the mother's and not the father's ultimate decision, since after conception the potential mother has the capacity to do so and the potential father does not. From this perspective, the questions that should be asked concern what should be asked of the mother and what can be expected for the child and for the person she or he will become. Although men can participate in discussing these issues, the power to give birth remains the mother's, and the right to use or to refrain from using this power ought to be hers, at least until male dominance has been safely overcome. And human birth should be celebrated above human death. But just as women should increasingly be recognized as having the capacities to engage in a full range of activities outside the household, the abilities of men to participate in various aspects of birth and nearly all aspects of child care should also be acknowledged.

For Mary O'Brien, the technology allowing women's control over reproduction can be expected to transform history.[47] The feminist revolution she believes to be occurring will in her view drastically alter human society by breaking down the distinction between public and private. But we might also note, I think, that changed conceptions of birth and the upbringing of children and changed conceptions of the appropriate participation of men and women in these activities could, if acted upon, have brought about many of the anticipated changes even without the technology. Arguments for such changes should therefore depend less on scientific advances and more on conceptions of giving birth and of mothering as central human activities rather than as merely natural, biological events.

Various feminists express worries all should share that the new technology surrounding late twentieth-century childbirth will be used to uphold male dominance rather than to liberate women. Such techniques as *in vitro* fertilization and embryo transfer can deprive women of grounds we have had from which to demand consideration.[48] It is clear that who controls the technology can often be more important than the technology itself. In trying to deal with conceptions of childbirth and child care, I am not suggesting that changed conceptions alone can lead to changed configurations of power in the traditional sense. I am only trying to deal with the ideas that I take to be one necessary component in a change of such power relations.

Women and Male Dominance

To cite the work of women, including feminist women, to illustrate the misconceptions that women are more involved than men in the primarily biological is not to accuse such women of collaboration with patriarchal ways but to substantiate the depth of the traditional distortions. That even so powerful an intellect as Hannah Arendt's moved so little distance beyond the mistaken view that the birthing and upbringing of children are essentially natural processes drenched in immanence, as distinct from the transcendence of the work performed in the polis, deepens our awareness of how subservient vast stretches of our thinking are to these faulty conceptual assumptions. That even Beauvoir, so perceptive of the domination of women by men in so many ways, should share the mistaken construing of birth and child care as inherently natural reminds us of how gendered are the underlying assumptions with which we must begin and from which we can of course not break free all at once. And that even the more recent thinking of many feminists retains the traditional and dubious conceptualization of human childbirth as reproduction makes it clear that to overthrow the conceptions of male dominance is a monumental task.

Not only has the dominant culture denigrated the giving of birth; it venerates intellectual and artistic creation, which it takes to be a form of giving birth, and it associates this kind of creation with the male. The capacity to "give birth to" wisdom, knowledge, and art has long been set beside the mere bodily capacity to give birth to infants. Such metaphors of creativity suggest that men too can give birth; and they may fix the association of the term 'male' with the former and "higher" type of creativity and the term 'female' with mere propagation of the species.

As Nancy Hartsock recounts the early history of such associations, "the real activity of reproduction is thus replaced by the mental activity of achieving wisdom and immorality." Writing of Plato's *Symposium,* whose account of paternity can be seen also in Pythagoras and in Aristotle, she traces the development of the attitude that "there is an opposition of creativity to fertility—the one a male capacity, the other a female property." Whereas for the Homeric warrior-hero, immortality was to be achieved by dying a glorious death in battle, for Plato, "immortality can now be achieved by begetting immoral children in the forms of art, poetry, and philosophy."[49] Men, thus, are imagined to be able to give birth by themselves to what is truly valuable; women give birth only to flesh.

How can we possibly free ourselves from the assumptions and fundamental concepts of male dominance? To nearly all feminists, male dominance is not inevitable. We do not know whether a tendency to wish to dominate is or is not present in males, or possibly in all persons, but even if it is, that by no means suggests that culture and society need reflect and reinforce this tendency rather than curb it. Society now curbs many "natural" tendencies: people wear eyeglasses, for instance.[50] Society counteracts innumerable tendencies toward disease and disability. Further, it establishes norms that routinely conflict with tendencies thought to be "natural." It establishes what to hold concerning what belongs to whom, and it curbs tendencies to take from others what does not, according to given social rules, belong to one. That such rules concerning property have usually been highly unjust does not change the fact that they do restrain various tendencies. And they can be made more just. A society could well curb tendencies in men as a group to try to dominate women as a group, and culture could lead the way.

It is increasingly becoming clear that in trying to overcome the long history of male dominance, we need to overthrow traditional ways of thinking as well as traditional ways of acting. Among the views that need to be turned around, as I have tried to show, are those that see human childbirth as primarily natural or biological. Also in need of transformation are views that see women as inevitably vulnerable to domination and views that political life must always be organized around men's conceptions of power.

Women's Understanding

Some anthropologists have speculated about a time in human history that can be called prepatriarchal.[51] Mary O'Brien argues that after men discovered their role in paternity, a "genderic struggle" must have occured that was protracted and bitter.[52] Only after such a lengthy contest was the female gender subordinated. If we look to images of a future in which male dominance is finally overthrown, the images will seem less distant and less utopian if we successfully reconceptualize giving birth and creating new persons.

Goddess-cults have at times been prominent, and their images may help us to free ourselves from the patriarchal images with which we have all grown up. One of the fascinations of trying to imagine prepatriarchal society, whether or not it in fact existed, is that it opens the imagination to alternative conceptions. Attention to the goddess worship characteristic of some cultures can alter our perspective and allow us to envision a social order totally unknown to us. Adrienne Rich writes that "the images of the prepatriarchal goddess-cults did one thing; they told women that power, awesomeness, and centrality were theirs . . . ; the female was primary." But this power was not the power to cause others to submit to one's will, the power that led men to seek hierarchical control and then contractual restraints between men of equal power. It was the power to create and to transform. Rich writes: "Not power *over others,* but transforming power, was the truly significant and essential power, and this, in prepatriarchal society, women knew for their own."[53]

Women today need to recognize as our own the extraordinary human power to transform mere genetic material into new human persons. But women would do well, I am arguing, to recognize this power as a human rather than natural power, such as when human death is distinguished from a natural event and when human art and culture are seen as distinctively human.

Not only would giving birth not have to be a source of oppression in a society that appropriately valued women and children, but the capacity of women to give birth and to nurture and empower could be the basis for new and more humanly promising conceptions than the ones that now prevail of power, empowerment, and growth. Patterns of activity to express these conceptions have begun to be imagined by various feminist writers.[54] Instead of organizing human life in terms of anticipated male tendencies toward aggression, competition, and efforts to overpower, and in terms of institutions to contain male desires to dominate by balancing and equalizing the power to bend others to one's will, one might try to organize human life to nurture and express creativity, cooperation, and imagination, with the point of view of those who give birth and nurture taken as primary. Instead of starting with assumptions of isolated, self-seeking individuals accommodating to one another's competitive desires, or of contending economic classes overcoming their conflicts, one might, by starting with the assumptions of life-giving, nurturing beings, imagine entirely different ways of organizing society than are familiar to us.[55]

To imagine and to strive for a culture and a society in which male dominance has been overcome, those who give birth and nurture need to affirm our own points of view, and to discover the outlines, the shapes, the details, and the meanings our own points of view can yield. Only when the conscious experience of mothers, potential mothers, and mothering persons are taken fully into account can we possibly develop understanding that may someday merit the description "human." And only when human birth and mothering are appreciated as the fully human achievements they are can we expect that human death will less often be pointless, debased, and needlessly early.

SEVEN

Gender and Violence

Whether from a willingness to court death or a tendency to cause it, man can be recognized as having displayed it in all its purported glory and actual gore. Social organization has accordingly been structured around causing or avoiding death. Masculine aggression and defense have determined the boundaries of societies and their survival, masculine combat has been the activity for which societies have prepared and on which they have been judged, and the handling of men's violence against men has structured law and political organization.

Feminists are raising questions about all of these social realities and are considering how they should be transformed. Suppose the kinds of persons who create life, rather than men, were to organize society along lines reflective of our points of view. Could society then better deal with the problems of aggression and violence? How does culture now heighten and reinforce male aggression rather than redirect or curb it, and how should this change?

The Natural and the Cultural

Many studies show a greater tendency towards aggression among males than among females.[1] These findings are across species as well as across cultures. Whether or not empirical claims of the kind these studies make stand up to further feminist scrutiny, they are not necessary to the arguments I am exploring in this chapter. The questions I raise concern how society should be organized to deal with the tendencies of men toward aggression and violence, whether these tendencies are "natural" or "precultural" or the results of variable cultural and social factors.[2] Traditional claims have been made that because of natural or precultural tendencies toward aggression, an organization of society in which the aggressive dominate is inevitable. An alternative view holds that whatever the natural tendencies toward aggression or violence, culture and social organization can affect and modify them. Law now attempts to curb such violence to individuals as occurs in murder, assault, and battery, whether it results from biological drives or not. Political organization now attempts to alter the outcome of "might makes right" by giving each citizen an equal vote. To a significant extent, such arrangements do succeed in redirecting or curbing natural or precultural tendencies. And we should ask whether a different organization of society and the world than any with which we are now familiar might be superior in handling the problems of aggression and violence.

In exploring the links between gender and violence, a prime candidate for consideration can be found in the cultural construction of sexuality. How does culture now associate male sexuality with violence and domination, and how could it transform these associations so that male sexuality would be better linked with mutuality and cooperation rather than with conquest and violence? To what extent would this lead to less violent societies and a more peaceful world?

Catherine MacKinnon's views on the entanglements of sexuality with force and violence are among the most stark. It is her claim that feminist inquiries into the realities of rape, battery, sexual harassment, incest, sexual abuse of children, prostitution, and pornography indicate that the mechanism of sexual arousal for men is force. Sexuality as understood at present is defined by and for men:

> What is sexual is what gives a man an erection. Whatever it takes to make a penis shudder and stiffen with the experience of its potency is what sexuality means culturally. Whatever else does this, fear does, hostility does, hatred does, the helplessness of a child or a student or an infantilized or restrained or vulnerable woman does, revulsion does, death does. Hierarchy . . . does. What is understood as violation, conventionally penetration and intercourse, defines the paradigmatic sexual encounter.

In short, "male sexuality is apparently activated by violence against women and expresses itself in violence against women to a significant extent." And the connections go both ways: "Stated in boldest terms, sexuality is violent, so perhaps violence is sexual." Sexuality is a form of power:

> Gender, as socially constructed, embodies it, not the reverse. Women and men are divided by gender, made into the sexes as we know them, by the social requirements of its dominant form, heterosexuality, which institutionalizes male sexual dominance and female sexual submission. If this is true, sexuality is the linchpin of gender inequality.[3]

For MacKinnon, the cause of women's subordination lies in sexuality. Other feminists are skeptical of the primacy of sexuality in causing oppression, including that of women, for male aggression is directed at males even in the absence of females. The causes of women's subordination may lie in aggression and its many different manifestations as well as in sexuality. Though sexuality has often been enlisted to serve male aggression, women's efforts at liberation may need to address, as well, aspects of violence relating to how societies and the world are organized. Power is used against women and the racially and economically less powerful in multiple ways.

The shortcomings of Marxism, with its focus on economic causes and its reduction of other factors to economic ones, is mirrored in MacKinnon's focus on sexuality and her reduction of other aspects of relations between women and men to those of gendered sexuality. As I have said, I doubt that any single-cause theories of women's subordination can be adequate. I doubt that they can work better than such single-cause theories as those of Marx or Freud work for other liberatory purposes. Alas, there just may be no linchpins. This makes the task of overcoming oppression more complex theoretically but not necessarily more insurmountable in practice. A focus on experiment and experience and especially on the ways we can work to transform existing social realities shows us diverse areas in which progress toward liberation can occur.

Many feminists question the claim that male sexuality depends on the violation of women. There are men for whom sexual arousal is entirely compatible with, or heightened by, mutuality and tenderness, rather than hostility and force.[4] While for some men sexuality is connected with domination, for others it is not, or not usually. And men as well as women can learn to change their experiencing of sexual arousal and its concomitants.

Those who criticize feminists as prudish and as opposed to sexuality itself miss the point of feminist analyses.[5] Feminists attack the linkage of male sexuality with violence and its resulting female devastation. Figures on the sexual abuse of girls are turning out to be horrendous.[6] Figures on domestic violence and rape are alarming, and increasing.[7] Many women experience sexual intercourse as violative because of the way male sexuality is now constructed.

The cultural construction of sexuality reflects or magnifies male tendencies toward aggression, but it could construct masculinity and the way sexuality is experienced by both men and women very differently. Mass culture, now enlisted in the service of economic gain, uses and strengthens sexualized male aggression.[8] The cultural enhancement of violence as sexualized and associated with male dominance and the objectification of women that psychologically contributes to male aggression occur routinely in pornography, in films, in television programs and music videos, and in advertising. In the U.S., pornography is a $10-billion-a-year business, advertising one thirteen times as large.[9] There is a vast cultural support system for the use of violence to preserve male dominance. It may take the form of verbal and psychological cruelty toward women, of sexual harassment in the workplace, of domestic violence, of rape. But nothing should prevent us from considering how culture could instead reinforce and enhance the sexualization of mutuality, care, empathy, and peacefulness. And nothing should keep us from considering how society could be reorganized to help bring this about. Culture can magnify the sexual appeal of men who care for children and who defuse conflicts. It can strengthen and help to be less fleeting the experience of sex as mutual giving. The associated feelings can then reduce the appeal of violence and domination.

There is little doubt that there are important connections between gender and violence, whether or not sexuality is at the core of these connections. Dominant cultural attitudes toward war and violence seem to be shaped in conjunction with the way men come to think of themselves as men and the way they feel about their masculinity.[10] Sometimes sexuality is powerfully linked with the idea of masculinity or is enlisted to further the project of "man." And sometimes men think of themselves as men in ways that exclude women more than they involve sexual interaction; sexuality may be seen as threatening because of the tenderness it promotes. In this perception of masculinity, what seems overriding is a longing to surmount death by acting heroically or a passionate desire to triumph over other men by a greater willingness to risk destruction.

Violence, War, and Politics

Feminists are beginning to explore the connections between gender and violence, war, and politics. We need to examine the moral acceptability of using violence to enforce law and order, to effect political change (as in terrorism and revolution), or to achieve personal gain (as in the legalized brutality of some sports). Only recently are scholars addressing issues of gender as they underlie questions about violence and war, and their studies have not yet received the needed funding or institutional support. Often the most that can be achieved at this stage is to suggest directions for the further inquiry that ought to be pursued. This chapter must often be based on the imaginative insight and speculation, but limited investigation, of feminist scholars, activists, and writers.

Societies have not in fact come about through voluntary and rational agreements among their members, as prevalent images of what are thought to be democratic societies sometimes suggest. They have come about largely through violent conflict. Contemporary nation-states maintain themselves through a willingness to use force against external opponents and to suppress internal challengers unwilling, in seeking change, to use procedures deemed legitimate by the existing state. What would a feminist morality have to say about a world system built so fundamentally on violence? And how could a feminist point of view possibly be adequate to meet the challenges of nations poised for armed conflict, seeking much of the time to impose their views on others? How can women and children not be mere pawns in this scenario?

In most or perhaps all of the societies we know much about, men have been the dominant gender.[11] Since the coming of settled agriculture, men have organized society in hierarchical ways such that some men have more power than others, and although the women attached to some men may have higher status than some men have, the women at any given level are subordinate to the man of that level. And all men are "united in their shared relationship of dominance over their women," as Heidi Hartmann puts it. In her view, men are dependent on each other to maintain that domination, and "all men, whatever their rank in the patriarchy, are bought off by being able to control at least some women."[12] Such a structure of domination is what is often meant by calling societies "patriarchal,"[13] as virtually all still are.

Let us look at some suggestions being made by contemporary feminists concerning the connections between gender structures and prevalent views of violence, war, politics, and society. The political scientist Judith Stiehm asks a series of what she calls "men questions":

> Why do men so routinely use violence in their relations with each other Why have men sought to depersonalize rather than eliminate violence? . . . Why have men kept weapons from women? . . . Western thought has described man as an egoistic, atomistic individual, or, if social, as economic exploiter or exploitee . . . What if political theorists had begun by constructing generic man based on all that they knew about women? Wouldn't we speak quite differently about human nature? . . . Why must the appeal to manhood be linked to the killing of others? . . . It is clear that the use of organized force,

whether that of the outlaw, the revolutionary or the government is a "man problem." Men do most of the violence and they do it mostly to men. Is this the result of a patriarchy that is particular and mutable? Can men be made less dangerous? . . . Can proof of manhood be detached from willingness to use force?[14]

In merely posing these questions, Stiehm reveals how fundamental, yet how neglected, is inquiry into the connections between gender and violence. Another political scientist, Nancy Hartsock, has been examining the way the conceptualization of politics for the last two thousand five hundred years has been an extension of the male barracks community of ancient warrior-heroes. Throughout this long history, although what it was that has been associated with the female has changed, politics has been constructed as a community of males united in opposition to such supposedly threatening and supposedly female forces as the Furies, Fortuna, Commerce and Credit, and finally Nature. In Hartsock's analysis,

> The barracks community imagery is clear in ancient Greek political thought, as the nature of the warrior-hero emerges in the *Iliad* and the *Odyssey* . . . The re-working of ancient (archaic) materials in fifth-century Athens makes important additions and helps to bring out the efforts at domestication of disorderly female forces which typify this period . . . One can follow these images from Athens down to the nineteenth and even twentieth century.[15]

By the eighteenth century, Hartsock indicates, the forces thought to be threatening the masculine world had changed into the forms of corruption and commerce. By the nineteenth century, the commercial figures of merchant and capitalist had become the locus of public, masculine achievement; Nature had become the female to be subdued. The extollers of capitalism saw the *virtu* of the entrepreneur as his industry; through his technology he would progressively triumph over the dangerous female forces of Nature. And Marx "presents the capitalist as the most powerful warrior-hero in history."

In considering future possible transformations, Hartsock observes that if her analysis of politics as an extension of the barracks community is correct, and if politics has been composed out of masculine fear of and hostility toward women, then those who favor the equal participation of women in the political community have two alternatives: either they can try to change the nature of the political community, or women must become warriors also.

Hartsock argues for the first alternative, which would require profound changes both in the conduct of politics and in how politics is understood. For instance, "If the community has been defined and constituted by its opposition to the natural world (conceptualized as female), the new community would have to profoundly alter its relation to nature." The changes necessary for a genuinely human community will have to be far greater than even the massive reorganization that takes place when one mode of production is superseded by another. The barracks community has continued to define political life and thought throughout several changes in the mode of production, which shows clearly that in itself a socialist transformation is insufficient. "The creation of a fully human community," Hartsock writes, "would require as a pre-condition that the barracks community face its fear of and hostility toward the female— both as external nature, and as the internal passions, needs, and even biology of individuals."[16]

It is no argument against views such as these that some women are as militaristic as some men, or that a few women who have become the leaders of nations have not significantly altered the policies of nations in relation to violence or war, or to the conduct of politics-as-masculine-combat. Lone women do not succeed in the male domain of political life unless they learn its ways and are willing to follow them. When we speculate about the characteristic features of what have been taken to be the masculine and public realms and those taken to be the feminine and private realms, the issues are not best considered in terms of exceptional cases.

The picture often presented in popular myths is that men use violence against other men to protect women and children from harm. Violence is then seen as a necessary evil, for the sake of peace and for the sake of women. But this is probably a false picture. It seems likely that in societies where a lot of violence is used against other men, a lot of violence is used against women *also*. And this relation may well hold when men are heavily involved in preparations for war rather than in more overt uses of violence, and it may well include psychological as well as physical forms of violence against women.

Domestic Violence and Peace

We need to consider whether a reduction in violence against women could lead to a reduction of violence against men. Barbara Roberts suggests that there seem to be definite links between violence against women and male violence in general, and understanding these would be of obvious value. Psychological patterns among men engaged in child abuse, wife abuse, and rape appear similar: "They deny culpability, blame the victim, are unfeeling about and deny the extent of harm and injury to their victims, and have callous and unrealistic attitudes about women."[17]

Finding out whether societies which successfully curb domestic violence are more likely to be peaceful toward their neighbors would be to a large extent a straightforward empirical question. It would be highly useful, and feasible, to have it answered. Many other questions concerning the relations between gender and war are far more conceptual and theoretical and more difficult to deal with. Yet even feasible inquiries concerning such relations have received little attention, even by most of those engaged in peace research. And the male-dominated peace movement has been slow to confront sexism in its own ranks. Violence against women, as in the rapes of several women at the Molesworth peace camp in England, has not received the attention it deserves.[18] Women's concerns have often been disparaged as unimportant, and men in the peace movement have often dismissed the efforts of feminists to trace the connections between the construction of male sexuality and the proneness of men to resort to violence.

Some feminists raise the question of what peace for women would consist in. While women are the victims of domestic violence, they experience little of the personal safety that has traditionally been associated with peace. Some feminists recommend that the term 'peace' be redefined so as to include the ending of domestic violence against women, but I continue to use the terms 'war' and 'peace' in connection with violence at an international or at least organized intergroup level, as in civil war. It also seems to me better to keep the meanings of 'peace' and 'justice' distinct, though the latter is a condition for the former. It should be noted that for many women, ending violence in the home is an even more immediate and pressing need than ending threats to international peace, but it is unclear that revising the meanings of words referring to the latter so that they include the former will contribute significantly to this objective. It is the connections between militarism and the abuse of women, however these are designated, which ought to be explored.

In the course of the proclaimed UN decade for women, through the three world conferences held respectively at Mexico City in 1975, at Copenhagen in 1980, and at Nairobi in 1985, the thinking about the relation between women and peace that was reflected in the conference documents underwent significant development. From merely recognizing that opportunities to take part in negotiations concerning peace should be open to women as well as to men, acknowledgment was given, by the time of the Nairobi conference, to the feminist argument that women may have a distinctive perspective and special contribution to make in framing issues concerning peace and in recommending solutions.[19] The tasks ahead should not merely be to fit women on a basis of equality into the international structures that have led to arms races and to conflicts between nations. Violence against women—what some call the war against women—should also be dealt with. And efforts should be made to develop specifically feminist and possibly better ways to avoid violence of all kinds and to resolve conflicts nonviolently.

Betty Reardon claims that sexism and the war system arise from the same set of authoritarian constructs.[20] A social order based on competition, authoritarianism, and unequally valued human beings, upheld by coercive force controlled by male elites, gives rise, in her view, to both sexism and the system of war. The profile of men who abuse women is similar to that of soldiers; some view the similarity as "deliberate and necessary." Military combat training uses woman hating as part of its method of turning men into soldiers, and the process in which a soldier must learn to dehumanize other people and make them into targets, to cut himself off from his own feelings of caring and connectedness, yields woman hating as a product.[21]

In discussing studies such as Gilligan's, which suggest that women and men approach moral problems differently, Barbara Roberts notes that male training to think abstractly, to strip problems from their contexts, to dissociate feeling from thinking, to rationalize (in both senses), "provides a moral and emotional insulation that makes violence more comfortable for the assailant, be he rapist, batterer, or soldier."[22]

Weaponry, War, and Sexual Associations

Let us look next at associations between weaponry and gender. At the symbolic level we can hardly fail to notice the visual associations between such weapons of war as missiles, guns, and shells on the one hand, and the phallus on the other. It is hard to believe that such associations have no effect on cultural attitudes.

Helen Caldicott writes as follows of the sexual aspects of nuclear weaponry:

> The hideous weapons of mass genocide may be symptoms of several male emotions, reflecting inadequate sexuality, a need continually to prove virility, and a primitive fascination with killing. I recently watched a filmed launching of an MX missile. It rose slowly from the ground, surrounded by smoke and flames, and elongated

into the air. It was a very sexual sight indeed; more so when armed with the ten warheads it will explode with the most almighty orgasm. The names used by the military are laden with psychosexual overtones: missile erector, thrust-to-weight ratio, soft laydown, deep penetration, hard line, and soft line. A McDonnell Douglas advertisement for a new weapons system proudly proclaims that it can "shoot down whatever's up, and blow up whatever's down."[23]

Carol Cohn, examining the language and imagery of "defense intellectuals," the men involved in planning nuclear weapons systems and developing strategic doctrines, finds their discussion laced with sexual imagery. They and the members of the military with whom they interact also use terms that domesticate the instruments of terror; missiles are "patted" appreciatively, and bombs are referred to as "RV's"—the usual acronym for recreational vehicle, here standing for reentry vehicle.[24]

In writing of the First World War, Paul Fussell claims that war was an erotic experience for men.[25] In an article examining women's attitudes toward the war, Claire Tylee notes that "more than one British writer expressed the 'vile attraction' of war in sexual imagery." She goes on to assert that "part of the repressed guilt associated with war neurosis seems to have stemmed from the ecstasy men felt in killing to save their own lives."[26] But popular images continue to heighten the associations between wartime violence and sexuality rather than help to change them. Examining a variety of contemporary war films, Tania Modleski notes how they show "the activities of breaking hearts and taking lives—that is, sexual domination and wartime aggression—to be so intertwined as to make it nearly impossible to speak of a 'displaced sexuality.' In fantasies of war, sexuality is manifested in violence, and violence carries an explosive sexual charge."[27]

Analogies between the penis and a weapon seem to be very deeply embedded in the male psyche. The word *vagina* is the Latin word for sheath or scabbard. It is a knife that has a sheath, a sword that has a scabbard; to conceptualize female genitals in this way presumes the conceptualization of the penis as a weapon. In at least one language, the polite term for the penis is the word for sword.[28]

Innumerable images of comic book adventurers and motion picture heroes portray their (metal) swords as arising from a penile location, or their guns as firing from a genital position. In fact, few images are as culturally familiar as that of the penis as weapon. It seems implausible that this would have no bearing on the emotional response of men towards "their" military weapons.

Consider, next, the ways in which sexual identity is connected to whether one is a protector or one of the protected. Women have been almost everywhere excluded from combat. Although many men do not themselves engage in combat or even take part in military service, they can identify sexually with those who are the protectors, supposedly, while women are everywhere seen as dependent on men for protection. But in modern war women, like men who do not themselves bear arms, are as vulnerable to bombings as are those with arms; the "protection" afforded may be mythical or worse than nothing. Nevertheless, masculine identity is tied to images of being a protector.

Social and parental attitudes toward aggressive behavior are quite different for boys and for girls, and the social construction of "manhood" is routinely connected with the willingness to use force or violence. To accuse a young man of "acting like a woman" can then undermine his hesitation to participate in violence and destruction. And to accuse a young woman of being "unfeminine" can damage her desire to cease being dependent on others for protection.

In trying to uncover the connections between gender and the militarization of society, Cynthia Enloe suggests that the military plays a central role in the ideology of patriarchy because the notion of combat is so fundamental to the notions of manhood and male superiority. According to prevalent myths, "to be a soldier means possibly to experience 'combat,' and only in combat lies the ultimate test of a man's masculinity." A drill sergeant disgustedly shouting "Woman!" at a resistant young male recruit is teaching him that "to be prepared for combat, to soldier, a man must be stripped of all his 'feminine' attributes."[29]

Men who have learned, from childhood and through military and other training, to reject whatever aspects of the feminine they suspect they may harbor within themselves are then, in the nuclear age, in a position comparable to that ascribed to a deity, in possession of that most ultimate and awesome power, the power to destroy the earth. As nuclear weapons aimed at enemies confront one another, the arms of "manhood" seem to have reached their ultimate absurdity. But can men who will feel themselves sexually disarmed without their weaponry recognize this?

The Masculine and the Heroic

Nancy Hartsock traces the ways in which "virility and violence are commonly linked together." She holds, with most feminists, that masculinity is a cultural construction, rather than a matter of hormones, since how the culture shapes differences between males and females into standards of masculine and feminine can vary greatly, and could be altogether different from traditional ways. What a culture considers "masculine" shapes what an individual man feels about his virility. Hartsock believes that masculinity "has been centrally structured by a linked fear of and fascination with the problems of death, mortality, and oblivion."[30] She examines how the Greek conception of the hero allowed men to believe they could overcome the meaninglessness of death; by dying gloriously in battle they would be remembered, they would achieve immortality. Heroic actions take place for the approval of an all-male community and provide a kind of birth that overcomes the defects of actual birth, which leads only to death. As James Redfield puts it, "To die for something is better than to die for nothing—and that is, after all, the alternative. In accepting death . . . the hero is in a sense rescued from mortality; he becomes godlike in status and immortal in memory."[31] In Hartsock's interpretation of this ideal, "Whereas the first birth, from the body of a woman, is a death sentence, the second, through the bodily might of the man himself, leads to immortality."[32]

The ideal of the hero is particularly clear in the *Iliad*. "Achilles as hero is best in war," Hartsock writes, and he is "the best of the Achaeans, because he is the best in war, which is the supreme, and even necessary, test of manhood."[33] But the ideal of the hero is still very much with us. Redfield in 1975 said that in describing the Homeric world, he has intended to praise it.[34] Ernest Becker, in a prizewinning book, asserts that "our central calling, our main task on this planet, is the heroic" and that society as a whole should be understood as a "vehicle" for heroism.[35] More dangerously, the talk of generals and politicians is laced with heroic aspirations. American leaders continued the war in Vietnam largely to avoid the "humiliation" of defeat, and to preserve national "honor." Among nuclear strategists, flirting with oblivion, facing coolly the possibility of nuclear war, gains a person respect.[36] In Hartsock's discussion of the *Iliad* and its ideological elements as reflected in contemporary attitudes among ruling groups of men, "rather than war being politics by other means, political action . . . is simply war by others means. Through this war, citizens, not-yet-citizens, and warriors attain and celebrate manhood."[37]

From a feminist point of view, the absurdity of aspects of these ideals should be apparent. To nurture children creatively so that they flourish and can lead ever more humanly fulfilling lives is to "die for nothing"? Nurturing children *may* require that one risk death, as many women have to do; giving birth to children also risks death. But mothering persons risk death to create and to preserve actual lives; they do not court violent conflict to attain glory or to achieve immortality. Bringing about the flourishing of human lives *may* require facing down violence with the courage of a warrior, and many women display such courage. But this is to defend the prospects of life, not to welcome combat as an occasion to prove one's manhood. When the willingness to court death risks the death of humanity, as it does in the nuclear age, human survival seems to require that the ideology of heroic man be replaced by feminist sanity.

Gender and the Valuing of Children

In chapter 4 I discussed some possible implications of the approaches women and men take toward mortality; how these approaches may or may not provide "good reasons" for moral positions is a matter of moral theory. But consider now the possible differences in the tendencies among women and men to regard particular children as valuable, and how this may affect their attitudes toward violence and war. Normally, we all agree in general terms that human beings have intrinsic value, that a human life has worth and is in some sense "supremely" valuable or "irreplaceable." But perhaps there are some not insignificant differences in the ways women and men regard particular, actual children.

Although men and women may share a desire or an instinctive tendency to wish to reproduce, such feelings might affect their attitudes toward a given child differently. In terms of biological capacity, a mother has a relatively greater stake in a child to which she has given birth. This child is about one-twentieth or one twenty-fifth of all the children she could possibly have, whereas biologically a man can potentially have hundreds or thousands of other children. In giving birth, a woman has already contributed a large amount of energy and effort toward the production of this particular child, while a man has biologically contributed only a few minutes. To the extent—which admittedly may be small—that such factors as these influence attitudes, the attitudes of the mother and the father toward the "worth" or "value" of a particular child might be different. The father might consider the child more easily replaceable in the sense that the father's biological contribution could so easily and so painlessly be repeated on another occasion or with another woman; for the mother to repeat her biological contribution would be highly exhausting and painful. The mother, having already contributed more than the father to the creation of this particular child, might value the result of her effort proportionately more. And her pride at what she has achieved in giving birth could be appropriately greater: she has indeed "accomplished" more than has the father.

So even if instincts or desires to reproduce oneself or one's genes or to create another human being are equally powerful in men and in women, from the father's biological standpoint a given child is more incidental and interchangeable: any child out of the potential thousands he might sire would do. For the mother, in contrast, if this particular child does not survive and grow, her chances for biological reproduction are reduced to a much greater degree.

Although it is not in fact likely that a given man will impregnate vast numbers of women, fantasy may enlarge the effect of this biological possibility. Images of the supposedly deserved rape of the women of one's opponents abound in military contexts.[38] Available prostitutes surrounding military bases and conceptions of the sexual rewards awaiting returning soldiers may all heighten the ways in which a man's drive to perpetuate his genes may extend itself promiscuously and to merely potential children, especially when associated with war and military action. In comparison, a woman's drive to perpetuate her genes may be expected to be far more focused on safeguarding the lives of actual, living children. Women are not likely to desire, even in fantasy, to have thousands of children. To give birth is exhilarating, but a woman seldom wishes to do so more than a few times.

It may offend many men—and women—to suggest that men may think of their children as replaceable. The years of child care in which men can share fully and the cultural norms and practices surrounding parenthood and childhood may be far more important in shaping attitudes than are biological realities about impregnation and birth. Still, we should be willing to examine the sorts of arguments here suggested that if anatomy is destiny, men may be "naturally" more indifferent to particular children than has been considered. Examining such issues would then appropriately be the beginning rather than the end of an argument about cultural norms and social structure. If we came to believe that men are genetically weak in the degree to which they value actual, living children, we could discuss what social arrangements and cultural influences ought to be like to counteract such "natural" weaknesses. Men could, for instance, be expected to do enough "caring service" to compensate for any "natural" indifference toward children and the infirm. Or the culture could sufficiently applaud male achievements in, for instance, mothering to overcome any genetic tendency men might have to devalue such activity.

To raise questions about genetic influences is not at all to succumb to biological determinism. Just because sociobiologists have largely been the ones to suggest these sorts of influences does not mean that we need to share any assumptions they may make that the influences are determinative. But while we discuss what morality ought to prescribe or what culture or political and social institutions ought to do to shape human behavior, we would do well to understand the human tendencies with which we are dealing. We should ask culture and our institutions to recommend actions and influence emotions and try to affect behavior in the light of what is possible and in the light of the biological as well as other conditions they confront. Where there are natural tendencies—of empathy, for instance—on which morality can build, morality would do well to recognize them. And if there are genetic influences leading women and men to have somewhat different attitudes toward the worth of a given child's life, we would do well to understand them. Recommendations for the kinds of cultural and social arrangements to bring about do not "arise from" any findings of biology or sociobiology or biopsychology, but such recommendations have a better chance of being morally valid if they are drawn with an awareness of what these findings suggest.

Mothering and Nonviolence

In understanding how gender affects participation in military activity, consider the place of mothering in society. Mothering is an activity conducted almost entirely by women, and it gives rise to attitudes and practices incompatible with militarism. Although a few men are gradually coming to participate more than in the past in the activity of caring for children and although they could share equally in this activity, mothering has for the most part been so associated with women and not with men that many people find it difficult even to imagine men engaged in "mothering."

As we have seen, Sara Ruddick analyzes the thinking that mothering promotes. "Maternal thinking," she holds, is distinctively different from some other ways of thinking; and it can be contrasted with, and seen as opposed to, ways of thinking conducive to militarism. Maternal thinking, as Ruddick defines it, could give rise to cultural norms and practices very different from those which prevail in patriarchal society:

> A mother caring for children engages in a discipline. She asks certain questions—those relevant to her aims—rather than others; she accepts certain criteria for the truth, adequacy, and relevance of proposed answers . . . The discipline of maternal thought, like other disciplines, establishes criteria for determining failure and success.[39]

In characterizing the thinking that arises in the practice of mothering, Ruddick identifies various demands to which maternal practice responds: demands to preserve the life of the child, to foster the growth of the child, and to have that growth shaped in an acceptable way. In Ruddick's view, "these three demands—for preservation, growth, and social acceptability—constitute maternal work: to be a mother is to be committed to meeting these demands."[40] Although some individual mothers may of course not actually participate in this work, the standards by which maternal practice is evaluated reflect the goals of meeting children's needs. And mothers typically recognize that these needs can conflict and that mothers must try to reconcile them.

There are characteristic defects of the virtues sought in mothering, Ruddick notes; for instance, a mother aiming at preserving the life of her child may be tempted to engage in excessive control. And mothers often, in fact, take on the values of the dominant culture. Nevertheless, Ruddick argues, the authentic characteristics of maternal thinking embody aims opposed to whatever human tendencies exist leading to military destruction and opposed to the thinking that arises in connection with military pursuits:

> When maternal thinking takes upon itself the critical perspective of a feminist standpoint, it reveals a contradiction between mothering and war. Mothering begins in birth and promises life; military thinking justifies organized, deliberate deaths. A mother preserves the bodies, nurtures the psychic growth, and disciplines the conscience of children; although the military trains its soldiers to survive the situations it puts them in, it also deliberately endangers their bodies, minds, and consciences in the name of victory and abstract causes. Mothers protect children who are at risk; the military risks the children mothers protect.[41]

We should not sentimentalize either mothers or soldiers, but we can observe these different and conflicting approaches.

Maternal life is rife with conflict. Conflict is part of everyday maternal reality, as children refuse their caretakers' demands and fight with each other. But maternal practice develops ways of dealing with conflict that are consistent with the goals of mothering. These ways do not seek to cause damage or destruction; they seek to achieve peace and to do so nonviolently. Certainly, some mothers are sometimes violent, but in their daily practice mothers uphold the standard of nonviolence. And given the temptations to resort to violence which the frustrations involved in mothering present, it is noteworthy that mothers succeed as often as they do in avoiding violence and in making peace.

A commitment to peacemaking, we should emphasize, is not at all the same as surrender, or complicity in being overpowered, or merely accepting a bargain between contending parties regardless of the merits of their positions. Ruddick traces parallels between mothers' peacemaking and the techniques of nonviolence advocated by Gandhi and Martin Luther King. Mothers, too, can be fully committed to opposing injustice and aggression, and to achieving their goals nonviolently. They seek a peace not of contending parties who then leave each other alone and go their separate ways but a peace with the human connections between persons restored or reconstituted.

The peacemaking of mothers is not yet in a position to bring about less militaristic public policies in most societies, but it is a potentially powerful source of influence for peace. For mothers' peacemaking to have a public impact, maternal practice will have to recognize its nonviolent components and extend them to wider domains. And feminist politics will have to achieve a social transformation in which maternal thinking, instead of being denigrated as it has been, will pervade much of society's thinking about politics and war.

Many feminists believe that it is not female biology or anatomy that gives rise to the nonviolence of mothers but engagement in the activity of caring for and raising children.[42] This activity is of course open to men as well as to women, and many feminists suppose that if men would take part equally and share fully in the activities of mothering and of caring for the sick and old and otherwise dependent, they might develop aims comparable to those of mothers in the preservation and growth of children and in the well-being of the dependent, and they might develop comparable tendencies toward nonviolence. Those feminists who think there may be a biological component to these tendencies are likely to share the view that mothering is highly important in shaping them.

We can add that the same standards of nonviolence that mothering suggests for settling conflicts to which military practice is now addressed would suggest, even more clearly, that nonviolent forms of upholding law and controlling violence within societies ought to be developed. There are many ways to restrain a violent child and to bring a child to control her own violence. There are better ways to restrain violent adults and to bring them to control their own violence than are characteristic of most "law-enforcement" practices in male-dominant society.

The Reality and the Hope

In estimating the prospects for nonviolence in the wider world, how much significance should we attach to feminist examinations of the practice of mothering? It should be emphasized that many feminist portrayals of mothering are not intended as descriptions of the actual ways in which most mothers behave but as discussions of the criteria and standards by which the practice is understood and evaluated. These criteria and standards can be compared to those by which other practices, such as those of military combat or of rational calculation in the marketplace, are understood and evaluated, which criteria and standards are often also quite remote from actual practice.

The problem of armed conflict and preparations for it are often presented to us in terms of threats posed by others. It is pointed out that it does little good for us to be peaceful when others cannot be counted on or when they give us grounds to fear that they do not desire peaceful relations with us. Peace, in this standard argument, can only be achieved by being "stronger."

What a feminist perspective may best contribute is motivation to encourage the defusing of confrontations, to value the risks of nonviolence and disarmament over those of preparing for conflict and accumulating weapons. As one feminist points out, "In relationship to men women have long practiced unilateral disarmament."[43] Yet women have been successful in achieving considerable change nonviolently. The suggestion that women should acquire guns to protect ourselves against domestic violence or rape is at best temporary strategy to call attention to the extent and seriousness of these problems and to the failure of other forms of "protection" as provided by existing legal arrangements. By and large, the efforts of the women's movement to bring about profound changes in society are pursued through organization, pressure, persuasion, and cultural transformations, almost never by violence. Men who maintain that only a greater capacity to inflict violence will provide a position from which they can negotiate honorably or effectively may suffer a characteristically masculine failure of imagination and of realism.

Women have long been active, and outstandingly so, in a wide variety of peace activities. Opinion polls regularly show women more opposed than men to increases in military expenditures and to the deployment of new weapons.[44] It is often asserted that when force is considered inescapably and genuinely necessary to defend the safety of children, women can be as resolute in using it as the situation requires. This is not inconsistent with findings that women tend to seek peace more consistently and patiently than do men nor that women may have more effective methods to suggest for the resolution of conflict without violence than has been recognized.

As defenders of nonviolent techniques repeatedly point out, nonviolent action is not surrender, and it does not accept defeat. Barbard Deming notes that the alternatives are not a mere appeal to conscience on the one hand or the use of violence on the other: "Nonviolent action does not have to beg others to 'be nice.'" It can resort to power, it can use physical force, as in blocking entrances and refusing compliance. What is distinctive is that those committed to disciplined nonviolence refuse to injure their opponents. In Deming's view we can put more pressure on the antagonist for whom we show human concern, for "we put upon him two pressures—the pressure of our defiance of him and the pressure of our respect for his life—and it happens that in combination these two pressures are uniquely effective."[45]

Deming is certain that with nonviolence, one will in the long run suffer fewer casualties. This may be difficult to understand, because if those seeking change are suffering casualties and their opponents are not, they may fail to recognize that the numbers of their casualties are lower than they would have been had they turned to violence. Nonviolence can inhibit the ability of one's opponent to hit back. In Deming's view, "There is simply no question that—in the long run—violent battle provokes a more violent response and brings greater casualties."[46]

The experience of women, especially of mothers, may be especially suitable for grounding the theory and practice of nonviolent resistance. A major hindrance to nonviolence may be social norms and psychological positions that make it difficult for men to renounce violence and still "feel like a man."

The process of overcoming the obstacles to nonviolence will be difficult. Ann Snitow reports on the findings of a study group dealing with the networks women often develop in traditional societies to deal with urgent problems. Peasant women, working women, colonized women, women in ghettoized racial groups have a long history of forming movements for survival, but these movements are often "like firestorms, changing and dissolving," and have little effect on the political structure of the group. Networks of women are often necessary to the survival of children, and thus of the groups of which they are part, but the "energy, loyalty, and passion" which women thus provide go unacknowledged by the group, which denies to women any "say in the group's public life, its historical consciousness." The group of feminists studying these women's networks agreed that "traditional women's concerns—for life, for the children, for peace—*should* be everyone's." They were divided on the question: "*How* can the caring that belongs to mother travel out to become the responsibility of everyone?" They agreed that "women's backs hold up the world," yet this passionate caring is taken for granted, too often even by women.⁴⁷ What must develop is a widespread feminist recognition that until women shape the wider culture and institutions surrounding the practices of mothering and care, traditional women's concerns will be undermined by traditional male hierarchy and conflict. What must develop also is a vast restructuring of society to reflect this recognition.

As Sara Ruddick examines traditional associations of men with war and women with peacefulness, she calls them "myths," while acknowledging that they have some basis. The facts these myths belie are that men are not as warlike as the myths suggest; many may resist participation in war and are even more ambivalent about fighting than women are about mothering. And many women encourage men to fight and support war with their comfort and admiration. Ruddick concludes that "a pure maternal peacefulness does not exist." Nevertheless, she argues, "maternal practice is a natural resource for peace politics," and the "passion of maternity can turn against the military cause that depends on it."⁴⁸

Barbara Omolade writes of the predicament that black women face most acutely: black women have cheered and dated black soldiers because black soldiers seemed able to be first-class citizens who could provide for their families. Black mothers encourage their sons to enlist in the military because the social system offers so few other chances for employment and self-sufficiency for black men. At the same time, blacks can recognize how their service in the military supports white domination over peoples of color throughout the world, how black men "were the cannon fodder for the whites against the Vietnamese."⁴⁹ Underneath the conflicts between resistance and collaboration, black women understand particularly sharply that only if black women and black children survive can either resist. And so, like women everywhere, black women collaborate if necessary and continue to struggle for a liberation that will make such collaboration unnecessary.

The project for feminists must be to develop the hope, which women and men can share, that nonviolence can eventually triumph. The aims of those who care for children and feel for the futures of particular, vulnerable bodies should become more salient in political life, while the power of those willing to use up those young bodies for the sake of their own interests or abstract principles should diminish. Even when the cause is just, nonviolent ways to fight for it should have priority.[50] And the fascination with armaments and firepower and military prowess and the technology of war and national strength should yield to a fascination with life.

Fascination with death has been tied in with the way gender has been constructed. Men have been persuaded to associate their manhood with their willingness to fight and to use violence and to die; women have been encouraged to admire such men as virile. Yet most men, including those in peace movements, have not paid sufficient attention to the connections between violence and gender. The task for feminism is to explore these connections so that peaceable human beings can reconstruct gender in ways that render both women and men adept at achieving peace, protecting lives, and improving the future of children.[51] Feminism can empower women to strive aggressively but nonviolently for a more peaceful and more equitable world and for less violent societies. It can also help men to feel strengthened rather than emasculated by their refusal to resort to violence even in defense of or to promote what they consider right.

When individual women ridicule rather than applaud the macho posturing of men, they contribute to the politics of peace. When groups of women change the cultural climate to one of support for negotiation over wielding military might, they expedite the process of overcoming violence. As Ynestra King, an influential activist in the women's peace movement and in the development of ecofeminism, argues, "to assess the *potentiality* of feminist peace politics, we must include all the activities undertaken by women that move the world toward peace in big or small ways, but mostly in small ways, on a local and often personal level." Feminism tries to remake politics. In King's words, feminists understand that "politics has more in common with art than with science [and] to oppose a culture and politics of death with a culture and politics of life is a requirement of our time."[52] She tries to foster the spontaneous emergence of love of life into the public arena. She finds this so commonsensical and yet utopian that it is not politics in the old sense but is what is needed to make possible the continuation of life on earth.

When we move away from considering the way violence has been used to organize societies and their boundaries and interactions, we may develop a very different view of what society should be like. Instead of aiming to create a pyramidal structure with law backed by force at its apex or a balance of power among states armed for violent conflict, we might see the creation and nurturing of the next generation as the most central task of society and the world. And devising environmental policies and family support programs and child care and educational practices worthy of this task might become central for the efforts and attention of society as a whole rather than, as at present, relatively peripheral.

EIGHT

Feminist Interpretations

of Liberty and Equality

In previous chapters, I have discussed how feminist rethinking can transform moral inquiry and the preconceptions about birth, life, death, and violence that shape social and political theory. I turn now to examine in their historical context some feminist reconceptualizations of political theory, focusing on the key concepts of liberty, or freedom, and equality.

One of the saddest realizations that women have had to come to is that repeatedly flowerings of feminist thought have been ploughed under by the dominant cultural-political order, leaving, at least until they have been unearthed again, hardly a trace. Feminist thinking certainly did not begin in the 1970s, but it is true that during the 1950s and 1960s, a book such as this one would not have been published, students did not have the opportunity to work in women's studies, and feminist views were almost never discussed either inside or outside academic circles. So I will begin my account of feminist views with the wave of the women's movement that started in the late 1960s and early 1970s in the United States.

The First Phase

In the early 1970s, women began to be aware of the degree to which we had been excluded from the liberal principles of freedom and equality that were said to guide the systems we lived in. Women saw clearly, often for the first time, that when Locke and Rousseau and the Founding Fathers proclaimed that all men are free and equal until they consent to put themselves under government, they meant all *men*—and *not* women. Of course they didn't really mean *all* men; earlier critiques had pointed out the property qualifications and racial exclusions contained in the liberal tradition and how these should be overcome. But there had been little explicit discussion of how all women were left out of the picture drawn by the principles of democracy and almost no discussion of why such omissions had *not* been corrected.[1] On the one hand, that women could now vote in most countries otherwise considered democratic was assumed to be evidence that women were adequately covered by the principles of freedom and equality. On the other hand, that women in Switzerland, for instance, could still not vote in 1970 was not even noticed as grounds for hesitating whether to classify Switzerland as a democracy. Whether principles of liberty and equality did or did not apply to women was simply not considered a topic of importance or interest.

As women began to look at all the ways we did not enjoy equality, glaring inequities leapt into view.[2] When women tried to enter the professions, we found the doors to medical school or law school either completely closed to us or open only a sliver. When we tried to advance in academic or business positions, we found blatant hostility or sturdy barriers. And at every level women were paid less, even for the same kind of work when we were permitted to do it, and especially for the kinds of work thought of as "women's work" to which we were largely confined. Or women were paid nothing at all for, and not even recognized as working at, the enormous amounts of labor involved in bringing up children and running a household.

In the United States, although women could vote, we had almost no representatives in Congress or in state legislatures; at the higher levels of government where policies were made and implemented, women were virtually absent. The leadership of every major institution in the society, whether corporate, cultural, governmental, or academic, was populated by what women would only later characterize as white males; so pervasive was the dominance of white males, it was ordinarily not noticed. Gradually women saw how unmistakably and routinely we were denied the equal opportunity proclaimed to be a fundamental value of liberal society.

In examining this lack of equality, women became aware, again often for the first time, of how inconsistent with any principle of equality was the most basic assumption made about how, as women, we should lead our lives. Women were expected to choose between parenthood and a career. Though it was standard for men to expect to enjoy both, women were not thought "entitled" to combine motherhood and a serious commitment to an occupation.

In the 1970s women began to apply notions of equality to personal life and to the household.[3] We demanded an end to the double standard with respect to sexuality, and we expressed our dissatisfaction with the unequal division of labor in the household. Though women have not succeeded in getting men to share equally in housework, particularly in child care, most women who wish to marry now aspire to what we think of as egalitarian marriages, and many men do somewhat more sharing in housework and child care than they used to. And women have increasingly become aware that if we really are to enjoy equal opportunities and equal respect, absolutely enormous changes are going to have to be made in the way societies structure occupations, public institutions, and the family.[4]

If we turn from equality to liberty, we can see, again, the implications of extending liberal principles to women. At first, women recognized, as we had not done before, the extent to which we were denied freedoms enjoyed by men. Laws often required wives, for instance, to live where our husbands chose or to work outside our homes only if our husbands agreed. Laws failed to recognize that women could be raped by their husbands; even when the spouses were estranged, women were often not protected. And the law's recognition of a "private" sphere into which the law should not intrude and in which a man's liberty should be supreme often amounted to a license for male heads of household to exercise near absolute rule over wives and children. Family violence was little discussed and often dismissed as the fault of its victims.

In the 1970s, women demanded that interferences with our liberty be made no greater than those of men and that failures to safeguard our liberty be corrected. Furthermore, we could see clearly how inadequate was the traditional distinction between the public and the private, and we could recognize the deficiencies of the liberal tradition's interpretation of freedom as negative liberty.

The conception of freedom as the absence of interference has been a central aspect of the liberal democratic tradition. Underlying this conception has been the assumption that a man could fend for himself if he were not assaulted or interfered with. He could make a living by growing produce or he could develop a trade, and if he had no land or skill, he could move to some unoccupied land and put his labor to use; he could, Locke suggested, go to America. He would be able to earn a living, acquire some property, and live his life, if only others would leave him alone and not force him to do what he did not want to do.

The conception of law in this picture included, of course, some restrictions on liberty, for legal prohibitions would curb the use of force to murder or steal. Such legal interferences, however, would be justified by the greater and superior liberty that would be made possible by law, as men were left alone, free from interference by their fellows, to add to their property and to live their lives in peace. And the free man would only submit to law to which he, as free and equal citizen, agreed.

Women were missing from this picture. A woman could not be the free and independent citizen provided by this conception of liberty, since she was not thought of as able in any comparable sense to fend for herself, and was not permitted, except in rare cases, to be other than dependent.

Behind the picture of free and equal self-sufficient citizens governing themselves have been actual families from whom these citizens received care and replenishment. But family members other than the male head of the household have been thought of as dependents, whose interests and needs were provided for by the head of the household, thanks to his concern for their welfare. The basic political unit has been, then, the single male or the male head-of-household rather than the individual person regardless of gender or economic status. As Susan Okin observes, "Behind the individualist rhetoric, it is clear that the family, and not the adult human individual, is the basic political unit of liberal as of non-liberal philosophers."[5]

Although the modern welfare state could potentially provide the rights to basic necessities that would enable all citizens to participate equally in political life, in fact welfare systems have perpetuated this history of tying concepts of citizenship and full political participation to economic independence of a kind rarely open to women; "dependents" and welfare recipients have been seen as occupying a "private" sphere that provides no basis for democratic self-government. As Carole Pateman writes,

> Welfare policies have reached across from public to private and helped uphold a patriarchal structure of familial life . . . Theoretically and historically, the central criterion for citizenship has been "independence," and the elements encompassed under the heading of independence have been based on masculine attributes and abilities. Men, but not women, have been seen as possessing the capacities required of "individuals," "workers" and "citizens." As a corollary, the meaning of "dependence" is associated with all that is womanly—and women's citizenship in the welfare state is full of paradoxes and contradictions.[6]

The conception of liberty as the right to be left alone was unsatisfactory for all who were not economically self-sufficient—nearly all women and many men. This could have been recognized at the time the concept was formulated and became entrenched in legal and political thought, but its inequity is even more glaring today. That liberty as an absence of interference continues to be the standard conception accepted by many contemporary philosophers and most economists is regrettable; it sharply limits the freedom of those not favored by existing economic, social, political, and legal arrangements. The assumption that a person not interfered with can adequately acquire what she needs to live is very often false in a modern industrialized society where land and economic resources are already appropriated and where owners feel no obligation to share what they have with those who have neither property nor the means to acquire it. Without the means to acquire what we need, noninterference does not amount to freedom. Anyone lacking what she needs to stay alive, and lacking what she needs to act at all, is of course not able to act freely.

That freedom as mere noninterference is not a satisfactory notion for all those who lack economic resources became especially clear for many in the women's movement. If one then remains within the liberal tradition at all, rather than moving on to, say, the Marxist tradition, one recognizes the need to think in terms of enabling rights to the means to be free. With an absence of interference, the man of property may be in a position to exercise his liberty, but to be well and *free* those without property need more than to be left alone with nothing.[7]

When political theorists argue that we need to distinguish liberty from the material resources that are the conditions of its exercise, that rights to liberty only assure the former, and that these have priority over any claim one may make upon the latter, we must protest. Such theoretical justifications of actual institutions and arrangements will leave those already privileged free of interference and in possession of the resources with which to act. But they will leave those unable to obtain such resources without a comparably strong claim to them. In order, however, for human beings in a developed, industrial society to be independent and for the members of groups previously excluded from such independence to attain it, human beings must be assured of much more than an absence of interference. We must be enabled to live and to act freely through having access to decent jobs, minimum incomes, adequate care for our children, and affordable housing and medical care.

The deficiencies in the concept of freedom as noninterference and the clear need for workers to have access to the means to live and act have been recognized in the Marxist tradition. These arguments took on new urgency for women struggling for independence. And feminists began to understand the degree to which the welfare state substituted dependence on the state for dependence on husbands rather than offering women, at even minimal levels, liberty and equality.[8]

The Second Phase

For many feminists, the framework of liberty and equality as I have sketched it, with its ties to the spheres of law and government, seemed too narrow. Women's *oppression* was not adequately expressed in the language and concepts of legal, or even moral, rights denied. And women's *liberation* would not be adequately striven for in the mere reforming of such liberal concepts as liberty. As many feminists saw it, the oppression of women stretched across the whole society in the most fundamental structuring of it in gender terms. And liberation would have to involve aspects of human experience for which the worldview of liberalism made little room.

Feminists of all kinds became more and more interested in trying to understand what was called the sex/gender structure of society which underlies all institutions, not just the legal or political. And we pursued explorations into gender identity and all it brings with it in terms of self-conceptions of superiority or inferiority. Society as a whole and everywhere and throughout history can be characterized as patriarchal, or phallocentric, or masculinist, as the depth and pervasiveness of gender domination in all its aspects become visible.[9]

Many feminists were drawn to socialist feminist analyses of the role of economic structures in the oppression of women, expanding in theoretically important ways conceptions such as exploitation and alienation. These analyses often illuminated gender relations more satisfactorily than could liberal principles of equality and liberty. Alison Jaggar, for instance, showed how the concept of alienation could make sense of the experience of women. Women, she writes, are in contemporary society "alienated in all aspects of their lives." Women's sexuality is developed for men's enjoyment rather than for women's, and thus "women's sexual situation resembles that of wage workers who are alienated from the process and product of their labor." Since men control the dominant images and theories of the culture, women are led to accept the male identification of women's selves with our bodies. Women come to be alienated from one another as we are made to compete for the sexual attention of men. Women are alienated as mothers, as we are unable to control the conditions of motherhood, but must raise our children within the structures of male dominance. And men and women are alienated from one another as they pursue their incompatible interests, "men in maintaining their dominance and women in resisting it."[10]

Many feminists showed how arrangements within the household perpetuated male domination. In the provision of housework and child care, in the domain of sexuality, and in the maintaining of relationships between family members and friends, women give more than we receive. Women's economic dependence, or relative dependence, contributes to conditions that enable men to exploit women in the personal domain and to leave men dominant beyond it. Affective energy in the household flows from women and to the advantage of men.[11]

Within the framework of law and legal institutions, many feminists came to recognize the deficiencies in claiming that differences between men and women are irrelevant and in expecting women to fit into categories constructed from the point of view of men. In an article entitled "Reconstructing Sexual Equality," which appeared in 1987, Christine Littleton shows how the concept of equality as it has been developed in the law has itself been enmeshed in the very gender system feminists are trying to overcome. When phallocratic standards are applied "equally" to men and to women, the results for women can be disastrously unequal. Differences between men and women need to be recognized, not denied. Women, not men, get pregnant. But it is only from the male point of view that pregnancy may seem to be best thought of as a "disability" similar to something males experience. Littleton writes that "what makes pregnancy a *disability* rather than, say, an additional ability, is the structure of work, not reproduction."[12] To escape the charge that women are being given favorable treatment in conflict with requirements for equality it should not be necessary, as assimilating women to male models of equality would require, to be able to demand pregnancy leaves in the workplace only when "comparable" disability leaves for men are already available.

Littleton argues that instead of denying differences, or locating the difference in women as compared to a male model, differences should be recognized but made socially "costless." Yes, women get pregnant and men don't, but women should not have to "pay" for such a difference in reduced chances for health benefits or occupational success. And the same can be said for other differences. "Differences," Littleton writes, "should not be permitted to make a difference in the lived-out equality of those persons."[13] And other feminist theorists are reconstructing other legal concepts, from sexual harassment to pornography to rape.[14]

In a more general context than this restricted legal one, Iris Young has been writing about gender and other differences. Instead of denying racial, cultural, sexual, and other differences, assimilating all to what has been a white, male, Western model of equality and liberty, or of classless society, we need theory that appreciates difference without devaluing it.[15]

Some feminists fear that to take differences between women and men as significant rather than as incidental is dangerous.[16] Especially those who have lived through historical periods in which women were urged or required to limit ourselves to the tasks of housework and mothering, because these were thought to be the "natural" functions of women, often fear any opening wedge acknowledging significant differences between women and men. Now that doors to careers and offices are at least partially open, these feminists emphasize that women can perform the tasks and fill the offices just as well as can men, and the fact that women are biologically or psychologically different is irrelevant.

We can be sure, however, that new attempts to keep women subordinate will not resemble past ones that have been discredited. The psychoanalytic claim that for women to have professional aspirations is "unfeminine" was not like the earlier, nineteenth-century "scientific" claim that exercise of the female brain would harm the female womb. Psychoanalytic theory was new theory that was effectively put to use to curtail the growth of female independence, which had made considerable progress in the 1920s.[17] It was able to set back women's gains in part because it was so hard to disprove. One can anticipate that new theories will arise to challenge recent feminist gains and that they will become popular among those eager to return women to their previous positions. But one can be confident that these new efforts will be different from those with which we are familiar. Perhaps they are likeliest in the region of sociobiology: here there can be little doubt that differences between males and females are significant, and those opposed to feminism often argue that these differences make male domination inevitable, or else acceptable because understandable in evolutionary terms.

To accept such inevitability or justifiability assuredly does not follow from a recognition of sociobiological differences. But feminists can argue against this fault of inference. We can find arguments that show how various differences give women advantages rather than disadvantages in achieving the goals women and men can set ourselves. Women may, for instance, have natural advantages in organizing society in ways that will be conducive to its well-being rather than to its destruction by violence.

Another reason feminist inquiry should not be deflected from exploring differences between women and men is that such a refusal is often disadvantageous to women. This has been demonstrated for legal contexts, but it can be shown in much wider contexts as well. Recent research indicates that girls and boys, even at a very early age, inhabit different linguistic "cultures." These differences are found within the same language, ethnic, and social groups.[18] And these patterns persist in the linguistic styles of women and men, so that communication between genders is sometimes thought of as analogous to cross-cultural communication; they share many of the same difficulties.[19] Women tend to be more concerned with intimacy, with negotiating relationships between persons in networks of connection. Men tend to be more concerned with independence, with asserting status and avoiding being put down in a hierarchically ordered and competitive social world. Perhaps these gender differences in linguistic patterns are the results of social patterns already in place; perhaps there are biological components to them.

Regardless of the origins of such differences, when they are ignored, women are often damaged. When they are overlooked, there is a tacit assumption that women can be or should become like men. The standard adopted has been and usually continues to be the male standard, and women are expected to adopt it, to change our behavior to conform to it, to "rise" to the male norm or linguistic pattern. Women's differences have been perceived as women's inferiorities, as women's deviances from the standard. But overcoming the consignment of women to an inferior status should not require women to accept the styles or behavior or norms of men. Feminists are increasingly asserting that differences between women and men are often real and should be respected, not ignored. Some such differences result from social practices which should be changed, usually by both men and women. If some differences, though significant, cannot or need not be changed, it should be made clear that difference does not imply inferiority.

In sum, feminists have applied principles of liberty and equality in ways that would include rather than exclude women, and in doing so have recognized the extent to which such principles themselves have been reflective of male dominance. Feminists have tried to reconstruct the concepts and principles involved in genuine human concern for equal freedom so as to reflect women's experience and aspirations as well as men's. And feminists have gone still further.

The Third Phase

Feminist theorists often now suggest that instead of seeing the world and society and everything in it from the point of view of men, or just correcting that view for bias, we ought to try seeing the world and society and everything in it from the points of view of women. Perhaps this view will only be a temporary stage to go through, a period in which we can all gain a correction across the board of the misleading views of the past. But we cannot know if it will be temporary. Perhaps the points of view of women will turn out to be genuinely better ones for gaining moral insight and social knowledge, and everyone will be able to recognize this.[20] The perspective of women should be considered not only as a corrective but as offering the possibility of an alternative worldview that may be better and truer.

Here as elsewhere, feminist transformations are suggesting new avenues for moral and social inquiry. Traditional moral theory is thought to be oriented around an ethic of justice. Formal principles or abstract rules of justice, autonomy, liberty, and equality are adopted, and moral problems are dealt with in terms of reasoning from such abstract principles; notions of social contract and individual rights are prominent. In the alternative approach being developed by a number of feminists, caring relationships between actual human persons are the basis for interpreting what a particular situation calls for in the way of responsible moral behavior; the reasoning involved is more apt to be narrative and contextual. Carol Gilligan sometimes referred to this alternative approach as a "morality of responsibility."[21] Sara Ruddick suggests it should be called a "morality of love" and thinks we can confront frankly the dangers of sentimentality that such a label may have.[22] But an "ethic of care" is the phrase which is gathering most support as a way of designating an alternative feminist moral outlook. While no label seems adequate yet, "care" seems to come closest, and to contrast well with traditional approaches based on rationality, rules, and the conceptualization of morality in terms of such public or political concerns as justice, or liberty, or equality.

We have seen how, in the domain of "particular others" central to the approach of many feminists, relationships are salient, while the "self" and "all others" of traditional moral and political theories seem artificial and problematic. Feminists are also questioning the contractual view of society so central to the liberal tradition, and underlying that still growing field of endeavor known as rational choice theory. From a feminist perspective, society as it exists, and certainly as it ought to exist, can be seen as noncontractual if it includes, as a reasonable view of it would, relationships within the family and between friends. At best, society may contain contractual enclaves, but they should probably be embedded in noncontractual relationships of trust and concern.

Most of those trying to clarify the alternative ethic of care question the individualistic assumptions of much moral theory. A relationships of care or trust between a mother and a child, for instance, cannot be understood in terms of the individual states of each taken in isolation.[23] And the values of relationships cannot be broken down into individual benefits and burdens; we need to assess the worth of relationships themselves. As Gilligan sees it, "Care is grounded in the assumption that self and other are interdependent . . . The self is by definition connected to others."[24] In their introduction to *Women and Moral Theory*, Kittay and Meyers draw the following contrast: "A morality of rights and abstract reason begins with a moral agent who is separate from others, and who independently elects moral principles to obey. In contrast, a morality of responsibility and care begins with a self who is enmeshed in a network of relations to others, and whose moral deliberation aims to maintain these relations."[25] Further, most of those pursuing the nonindividualistic aspects of feminist theory think that persons are not only deeply affected by their relations with others, but are at least partly or largely constituted by these relations, though we may seek to change them.

Liberty and Equality

What are the implications of such developments for our notions of liberty and equality? To begin with, to the extent that liberty and equality have been developed in contractual terms, they may be deficient for representing the moral considerations most fundamental from a feminist perspective. Liberty and equality may be highly important within certain regions of human interaction, but these regions themselves may be less extensive and less important than has been thought. To the extent that liberty and equality have been formulated in strictly individualistic terms, as in the liberal tradition, we can notice, again, how they fail to provide evaluation of or protection for the relationships that may be most central to our human well-being and to our abilities to lead our lives as we, together with those with whom we share our lives, choose.

Many feminists have been concerned with extending principles of liberty and equality to women and to what occurs within the household, so that, for instance, the physical safety of women and children would be protected against domestic violence the way the safety of men as they venture forth into public space has been protected by centuries of legal attention. And feminists emphasize the case for equality between women and men in, for instance, the division of labor needed within the household and in the care of children. These are extraordinarily important issues, and to suggest that liberty and equality are more limited concepts than the tradition of liberal political thought can acknowledge does not diminish at all the need to persist with these arguments and their implementation.

We can, however, understand the ways in which these are efforts to rectify certain serious defects in liberal thought and in existing societies, not ways to give adequate expression to the concerns we might take to be central to women in a society that had overcome male dominance. In postpatriarchal society, the moral minimums of personal safety against attack and of fairness in the division of labor might be relatively easy to achieve, and our efforts might be largely devoted to all the valued concerns over and above such minimums: to creating conditions that would be conducive to the flourishing of children, not just protection from injury. We would discuss the ways in which children can *best* grow and develop, sustained by loving relationships, not just by adults who respect the rights of a child not to be assaulted or killed. And in relations between women and men, we would seek the joy and laughter and affection and trust that such relationships can bring over and above the respect for each others' claims to equality.

To take an example: Even in patriarchal society, structured as it is to maintain domination and to take conflict as given, there are many pockets of cooperation. When several women, say, cooperate to provide an outing for their children, there may be minimal levels of a fair distribution of expenditures of money and time that will be met. But such cooperation is often characterized to a much greater extent by shared attention to and interest in aims over and above an equal distribution of burdens. The focus might be on what might make the outing enjoyable, interesting, aesthetically pleasing, an event to remember. This will not be just an attempt to achieve a utilitarian maximizing of individual utilities over and above what would be required by a nonutilitarian respect for rights to equality. It will be an attempt to realize various shared values. Attention might center on what will make the occasion harmonious, the outing one of shared joy, and conducive to the increased mutual understanding of the children and the adults. It is by no means to be conceded that this sort of perspective on what is important and what is trivial is suitable only for private outings among friends. Many feminists are now considering how a comparable focus may be suitable for social and political concerns at a much wider level.

The Perspective of Giving Birth

In chapter 6 I discussed outlooks toward birth and life and death that might differ between women and men in significant ways. Let's consider some implications of these possible differences for our concepts of equality and liberty.

Birth and death are obviously central events of human experience. They have been conceptualized, or misconceptualized, I believe, from a male rather than from a gender-neutral point of view. Death has been understood as an obviously human event, an event associated with what distinguishes us as human beings most clearly from animals. Because we can risk death and choose what to die for and be conscious that we will die, our deaths are distinctively human. We represent this consciousness and this choice in our art, literature, music, and theories of all kinds. Birth, in contrast, has been construed as a natural event, something that happens, and women, in giving birth, are thought of as doing something very similar to what nonhuman animals do when they give birth. This contrast results, I think, from seeing birth and death from the point of view of men. From this perspective, one sees birth in terms of getting born, in terms of one's own beginnings, or one sees it from the point of view of the observer.

All this changes if we see birth from the point of view of those who give birth. From the standpoint of conscious human subject, birth becomes as fully a human event as distinct from a natural one as is death. Women, unlike nonhuman animals, can be fully conscious that we may give birth, or that we have done so. We can give birth, or try to avoid doing so, for as many reasons as men can choose to die or to cause death. From the point of view of those who give birth, birth could be associated with imaginative human representation in art, literature, music, and all our theories, as fully as death has always been associated with such imaginative representation.

What might the implications be for equality and liberty? Many conceptions of equality are tied to empirical claims regarding death. Hobbes's view is perhaps the most notorious: all men are vulnerable to the swords of their fellows and hence must recognize each other as equals.[26] Others may argue for equality on the basis of an abstract moral principle rather than of any empirical description, but their justifications of such a principle often rest on such observations as that we are all not so different: we are all born, feel pain, and die. And as moral and political arguments are extended to women, it may be supposed that such characterizations apply equally to women.

But let us pause. From the point of view of those who give birth, all this changes. *We* give birth, and you do not. This *is* a radical difference, and the fact that you lack this capacity may distort your whole view of the social world. From the point of view of those who give birth, the social, political, economic, legal, educational, cultural, and familial realms should be organized to be, *first of all,* hospitable to children. From this perspective, it seems pathetic that, instead, these realms are seen as contracted for by men equally able to kill or harm one another, or arranged to promote the self-interest of agents in a marketplace, or aimed at satisfying the preferences of individuals conceptualized as existing in isolation from one another. Occasionally, for those who give birth, equality will be an important concept as we strive to treat children fairly and have them treat each other with respect. But it is normally greatly overshadowed by such other concerns as that the relationships between ourselves and our children and each other be trusting and considerate.

And liberty? From the point of view of those who give birth, it is absurd to assume that we are born free. We are born helpless infants, and will remain unfree for many years. We are only relatively free if those who have cared for us have empowered us to be so. From the point of view of those who give birth, the familial, cultural, educational, legal, economic, political, and social realms should be organized to assist children to develop in such a way that they will flourish, in harmony with others, growing in their capacity for free expression.

It is obvious that a world of militarized states and armed groups, geared to inflict death on each other's and their own people while they progressively despoil the environment, cannot provide such assistance. And to bring about the kind of world that will indeed allow its children to be free will require transformations far more fundamental than anything envisaged in the tradition that has given us the liberal concepts of liberty and equality.

These are dangerous thoughts. As long as the world is structured and thought of from the point of view of those who do not give birth, then, to have a fair chance in this world, women may need to emphasize how little difference it should make that women are those who bear rather than beget, as Plato put it. As long as the social world is structured by and for those who think of themselves as equally vulnerable to the sword of their fellows, or equal abstract rational beings, feminists need to keep in view how extraordinarily important rather than peripheral are the concepts of equality and liberty, both as traditionally understood and as reformed by feminist critiques.

When we dare to give voice, on the other hand, to how we think the world ought to be, we can imagine that whether one adopts the points of view of those who create human life or ignores these points of view may radically change one's perspective on what is most important. From a feminist perspective, the best that could be achieved by attending to the requirements of equality and liberty might fall far short of what an even adequate society needs to provide for the future of the world's children.

NINE

Democracy and the
Critique of Individualism

In discussing moral inquiry in chapter 2, I argued that there is no substitute for feminist inquiry and theory. I will now make the case in connection with social and political theory. To do so may be useful in seeing how key feminist approaches differ from those of democratic theorists who are closest to us in arguing for economic equality and the equality of women, but whose views show little evidence of having been affected by feminist theory. In this category are social and political thinkers who have been influenced by Marxist criticisms of the class structure underlying the liberal tradition and who are fully appreciative of the importance of the democratic political institutions and judicial protections of rights emphasized by that liberal tradition,[1] yet whose work still lacks feminist substance. Because C. B. Macpherson fits this description, I will use his work as a basis for drawing a contrast between feminist and nonfeminist (though allied) approaches and for discussing some feminist concerns that are not adequately dealt with in such a largely appealing theory of democracy.[2] And I will go on to consider various questions about individualism inadequately treated by both individualistic nonfeminist theories of democracy and by their communitarian critics.

In many ways feminists share the perceptions and concerns of such democratic theorists as Macpherson, but we find that their vision of a free, just, and democratic society leaves out much of what is needed for women to be full participants and equal members of such a society. More important, the issues are not primarily ones of omission, which might be handled by supplementing the proposals of these theorists. Current feminist inquiry raises questions about certain of the basic assumptions and categories of such theorists that are at least as fundamental as Macpherson's own doubts about the liberal tradition of possessive individualism.[3] Any feminist can greatly appreciate the contributions of various nonfeminist democratic theorists to the furthering of goals we share, but in this chapter I focus on a number of deep concerns about the adequacy of their criticisms of liberal theory and of their proposals for social change. As Anne Phillips has noted of many nonfeminist theorists of democracy, "In identifying politics with (a very particular definition of) the public sphere, they have made democracy coterminous with the activities that have been historically associated with men."[4] Such a deficiency may characterize, as well, nonfeminist theorists who understand that democratic theory must be a theory of society as well as of politics.

Democracy and Feminism

We can agree with Macpherson that for any theory of democracy to be adequate, it must be a theory of society, not only of political procedures. Macpherson argues for democracy as committed to maximizing the developmental powers of human beings, their powers to fully develop their human capacities; he well understands that for such democracy to exist, people must have access to what they need for human development. The principle that ought to guide democratic institutions, he asserts, is that everyone "ought to be able to make the most of himself, or make the best of himself." On this conception, developing one's capacities requires the capacity for materially productive labour, but it requires much more than that. It sees a human being as "essentially a doer, a creator, an exerter of energy, an actor."[5] And it is aware that human beings are not necessarily the insatiably possessive individuals of classical liberal theory.

Feminists can admire and share Macpherson's emphasis on the possibilities of increasing the developmental power of citizens, since this kind of power is not the zero-sum power over others of standard liberal theory but a kind of power such that more for any one person is compatible with more for any other. Macpherson acknowledges this may be an optimistic view of human beings, one which sees their contentiousness to a large extent as historically conditioned rather than essential. It is an optimism many feminists share.[6]

Democratic theorists influenced by the Marxist tradition characteristically have a fuller understanding of what it means to live as a free person than do theorists squarely in the liberal tradition. Macpherson, for one, argues eloquently that a person cannot be free without the means to live and work and act, and feminist views of liberation appreciate these understandings. The experience of most women makes clear how unsatisfactory is a conception of freedom that does not include access to the means to be free. Clearly, freedom from interference with our possession of property and our exercise of our rights cannot provide the liberation women seek if we have no property and are unable to acquire the means to live and to act and to feed our children.

Liberation is unmistakably connected with freedom, and so we can argue from one to the other in ways in which a separate concern with welfare or well-being may not allow. And liberation requires that the means to be free be understood as an aspect of *freedom,* not only of welfare or of various preconditions for the enjoyment of freedom. If freedom is separated from the means for its exercise, then, if freedom is thought to have priority over other considerations, as it is in many theories and judgments, it follows that the claims of those individuals lacking the resources to live and to act freely will always have to yield to the claims of those already in possession of such resources. The argument that the rights to freedom from interference of those with property must not be infringed on for the sake of the welfare of those without property has been the bulwark, lately in libertarian guise, upholding the advantages of the advantaged. Many women's experiences of lacking freedom can make a powerful contribution to arguments exposing the realities of who gains and who loses from such questionable construing of freedom. And in this, women's experience supports the insistence of Macpherson and related democratic theorists that for a society to be one worthy of the name "free," it must assure its citizens access to the means to live and to labor.

I have disagreed with Macpherson's acceptance at the more strictly definitional level of freedom as negative only, as freedom from interference, freedom from external impediments. Because he includes within the category of impediments the lack of resources needed to live and to act, he of course avoids the conclusion a libertarian reaches with this analysis, and he argues forcefully for overcoming the lacks that prevent so many in capitalist society from being free and full participants in democratic life. But it seems to me unduly awkward to construe such lacks as "impediments." I have found Gerald MacCallum's analysis persuasive: freedom is a triadic relation in which we are free *from* x *to do* y.[7] We should be as concerned with the capacities and enablements that make us free *to do* what we choose as with the interferences that restrain us. Though he fits his concerns into the language of interferences, Macpherson agrees, and in one sense it matters less how we describe interferences and capacities than what they amount to in terms of social theory. But in another sense the definitional issues are important.

Macpherson calls attention to the ways in which a person can be incapacitated. In his discussion of how power is to be measured in terms of the absence of impediments, he considers what are to count as impediments, and he specifies three types: (1) lack of adequate means of life, which includes the "material prerequisites for . . . taking part in the life of the community, whatever the level of its culture may be";[8] (2) lack of access to the means of labor; and (3) lack of protection against invasion by others. Since he thinks the third type of impediment can be removed by guaranteeing the civil liberties of traditional liberal theory, it is with the first two that he is primarily concerned. He answers the objection that if the development of human capacities is infinitely great, the task of removing obstacles to this development would be insuperable. He argues that the *material* prerequisites of such development are not infinitely great and are, in fact, within the capacity of democratic industrialized society to provide. As for the means of labor, the continuous transfer of powers from the nonowners of capital to owners that occurs in capitalist market societies can be overcome, so that gains in productivity and in leisure can be used to enable all members to develop their capacities.

With such criticisms as these of existing arrangements, arrangements which make it unduly difficult for so many women to acquire what we need to live and to develop, many feminists largely agree. Where a feminist might depart from such views is in assessing the major requirements for what would be considered absence of impediments and presence of empowerment. Macpherson sees the problems of existing systems that fail to offer the kind of democracy he advocates as problems caused by allowing unjustified and unnecessary interferences with persons' development. As we have seen, he writes of some having been stunted by "external impediments" that would be removed by the kind of society he advocates. The images he uses are always of inner capacities in place, though their development may be thwarted by external conditions. He fully recognizes that lack of access to the means to feed and shelter oneself will constitute such an external impediment. But he does not call attention to a range of problems needing to be addressed for women to be able to develop our capacities. And to construe the lacks he does focus on as "impediments" may further complicate the task of conceptualizing the components of freedom and democracy for women.

The Empowering of Women

Consider Sandra Bartky's discussion of a kind of disability that, at least under social conditions so far and in given societies, women are more apt to suffer than men: shame. Bartky considers the shame of embodiment attendant on women's sense of being a spectacle, of being continually on display, but she is concerned in this book with a less specific kind of shame. "This shame," she writes, "is manifest in a pervasive sense of personal inadequacy that, like the shame of embodiment, is profoundly disempowering; both reveal the 'generalized condition of dishonor' which is woman's lot in sexist society." She further characterizes this shame as "the distressed apprehension of the self as inadequate or diminished."[9]

In contrast with guilt, which one may feel for one's actions, shame is felt for shortcomings rather than wrongdoings, and for some, shame may be felt routinely rather than from a particular diminishment on a particular occasion. Shame, in Bartky's analysis, is a kind of psychic distress occasioned by the "apprehension of oneself as a lesser creature." She examines the "affective taste, the emotional coloration" of the traits that textbooks in the psychology of women report to be characteristic of women: lower self-esteem, less overall confidence, poorer self-concepts, measured by women's beliefs and dispositions. She cites a variety of empirical observations to confirm that women experience such disempowering feelings as shame more than men do. She concludes that "shame is not so much a particular feeling or emotion (though it involves specific feelings and emotions) as a pervasive affective attunement to the social environment" and that "women's shame is more than merely an effect of subordination but, within the larger universe of patriarchal social relations, a profound mode of disclosure both of self and situation." She goes on to probe with care and insight the ways in which this affective attunement is disempowering:

> The heightened self-consciousness that comes with emotions of self-assessment may become, in the shame of the oppressed, a stagnant self-obsession. Or shame may generate a rage whose expression is unconstructive, even self-destructive. In all these ways, shame is profoundly disempowering. The need for secrecy and concealment that figures so largely in the shame experience is disempowering as well, for it isolates the oppressed from one another and in this way works against the emergence of a sense of solidarity.[10]

What are the implications of these observations and reflections? Certainly such obstacles as a college climate in which instructors use sexist humor or a dismissive tone of voice toward women need to be removed.[11] Certainly the well-documented tendencies of men to interrupt women more than women interrupt men need to be made visible and corrected. Though these are not the external impediments noticed by Macpherson, perhaps they can be added to his list. But it seems inadequate to think here primarily in terms of the removal of external impediments, especially of the kind which Macpherson focuses on. Though removing an obstacle like the inability to find employment is certainly essential, it will not be nearly enough to enable women to achieve such inner empowerment as is provided by a sense of self-worth. The self-development of women involves changing the affective tastes, the emotional coloration, with which we experience the world, not only the outer obstacles in that experience. And doing so will require not that women learn to interrupt men as often as men interrupt women or that women become as aggressive, assertive, or overconfident as male norms prescribe for men but that women and men develop mutually respectful and shared practices of conversation and behavior and mutually considerate and caring emotional relations, and that these be supported by and reflected in the cultural expression that predominates.

Consider, next, a kind of transfer of power different from the one examined by many democratic theorists who, influenced by Marxist critiques, enlighten us on how the transfer of power from nonowners to owners of capital conflicts with the principles of democracy. Consider the transfer of power in what Ann Ferguson and Nancy Folbre call sex-affective production. In exploring the ways in which Marxist views of production and reproduction need to be reconceptualized from a feminist point of view, they focus their attention on the production of all that is required for childbearing, child rearing, and "the fulfillment of human needs for affection, nurturance, and sexual expression." They discuss the ways women have been oppressed by a division of labor that results in most of the requirements and responsibilities of sex-affective production being met by women. Women are socialized into a gender identity such that their sense of identity "keeps them willing to give more than they receive from men in nurturance and sexual satisfaction." [12] The division of labor providing that the burdens of sex-affective production fall more heavily on women than on men is not a neutral division that assigns separate but equal roles. It is a division that is based on inequality, that is upheld by social relations of domination, and that oppresses women.

Macpherson defines extractive power as a man's ability "to extract benefit from others." [13] If we accept that definition, it is clear that men have employed extractive power to exploit women, that women have had to enter into unequal relations with men in which we have routinely given more affection to men than we have received, and in which we have devoted far more time and energy than men, and far more of the caring concern that can drain its giver, to the mutual project of having and raising children. But again, it seems inadequate to think largely in terms of the removal of external impediments, especially of the kind focused on by Macpherson. Of course, without the means to live, women will be unable to achieve any measure of self-development. But the means are needed as fundamentally for the development of our children as for the development of ourselves, and they are needed in ways that contribute to rather than disrupt the relationships between us. So to overcome the imbalance in "sex-affective production" between them, relations between women and men will have to be completely reconstituted. Access to the means of labor in the sense in which many democratic theorists have called for it is an important component, but only a component. As has often been noted, even when women work at paid jobs outside the home as long and hard as men do, they routinely do a far larger share of the housework and child care. Not only do women have less actual leisure, but such concerns as whether a child is ill, or in danger, or whether outside child care arrangements are adequate are more frequently present in women's minds, and are more disempowering. And the new relationships between women and men will not be adequate if they merely bring women to be as concerned as men are with their own unique, essentially individualistic self-development. The relations will need to be ones of mutual caring and concern, as well as of respect and noninterference.

Without the insights of feminism, democratic theory, even when informed by the insights of Marxism, does not contribute to our understanding of how transforming gender relations may be at least as fundamental a project as transforming relations between the owners of capital and those who must sell their labor. Macpherson considers how the latter transformation might involve changed personalities and aspirations: "man as maximizing consumer" would be replaced by "man as exerter and developer of his human capacities."[14] But there is no indication of the sorts of comparable transformations that would be needed in gender characteristics and aims to overcome the oppression of women. Liberation from gender oppression may involve factors that can only be understood at the level of internal affect, self-perception, and their cultural expression, all of which Macpherson neglects.

Consciousness-raising

Macpherson briefly considers the question of "internalized impediments," the phenomenon of "men hugging their chains" or becoming "slaves of their own possessions." He acknowledges that his recommendations for judging how impediments are to be reduced has dealt entirely with external impediments. His response to possible criticism along these lines is to suggest that the impediments "were external before they were internalized," and to hope that the gradual reduction of external impediments will contribute to a reciprocal "breakthrough of consciousness."[15] But this can hardly be an adequate suggestion for handling the sorts of considerations a feminist view of the requirements for liberation brings to light. It has been no accident that repeatedly, and in one context after another, consciousness-raising has been the beginning of feminist action, not the byproduct. This does not mean that consciousness-raising is a solitary flash of awareness; though it can be that, it is typically a shared and participatory practice. But it involves changing internal ways of thinking and feeling. And what this changed consciousness first affects seem to be the internal springs of empowerment even before any external expression of resistance or exercise of power is possible, and certainly before the external impediments have actually been removed or even reduced. The power to give voice to one's aspirations to be heard is not so much the removal of an external impediment as the beginning of internal empowerment. The latter fits awkwardly into Macpherson's analysis, yet is an essential component of feminist theory and practice.

Truly democratic society, various theorists argue convincingly, will require equal access to the means of life and the means of labor, which will require an end to class inequalities. While feminists often share this view of one set of needed changes, they also point out that the end of class inequalities may leave gender inequalities relatively intact. That racial antagonisms may outflank a diminishment of class conflict has also been demonstrated.

Few accounts of how class inequalities might be overcome provide the insights needed to grasp the more cultural forms of capitalist hegemony—the ways, for instance, in which media images of the rich and famous and beautiful make aspirations, and false hopes of reaching them, into greater and more resilient obstacles than are usually recognized. This is an enormous topic to which social and political philosophers should pay far more attention than most have, especially those in the liberal tradition. And it seems even more clear in the case of gender inequalities than in the case of class inequalities that a focus on the external impediments Macpherson examines can hardly be adequate for understanding oppression and how it might be overcome.

What we can conclude, then, is that the range of what must be attended to in removing obstacles to self-development must be greatly expanded beyond those offered by nonfeminist democratic theorists. It must deal with many deprivations women suffer as women, not only as members of a class from whom power is extracted by the owners of capital. We can conclude, too, that revisions in nonfeminist views must go deeper still, so that attention is paid much more explicitly and fully to how the provision of internal empowerments is to proceed. The removal of external obstacles, even when the range of the latter has been expanded appropriately, is surely part of the process. But the process may be vitiated by inattention to other parts.

Feminism and Individualism

Let's turn now to another question: What kinds of beings are those for whom full development, making the best of themselves, is to be facilitated by democratic social arrangements? Macpherson and others argue convincingly that such persons need not be the insatiable consumers, the egoistic economic agents, of traditional liberal theory. But are these persons then seen in ways that coincide with feminist views of persons?

In his discussion of how our concepts of property ought to be revised, Macpherson argues for rights to property as rights of access to the means of life and labor, as rights not to be excluded. "The concept of property," he writes, "as solely private property, the right to exclude others from some use or benefit of something, which is already a concept of individual right to a revenue, will have to be broadened to include property as an individual right not to be excluded from the use or benefit of the accumulated productive resources of the whole society."[16] He recognizes the ways in which the productive resources of a society should be thought of as collective, socially achieved capacities to provide persons with what they need, not as the mere privately and individually owned results of individual efforts and transactions. But the rights of access to the means of life and labor which should, in his view, be assured by new conceptions of property and adequate understandings of the kinds of institutions needed for such rights to be protected in a truly democratic society remain, for Macpherson, individual rights. And the persons who are to be the bearers of these rights, while not merely consumers and egoists, are still individuals of a conceptually fairly isolated kind. Their self-development is not seen as intimately tied to the development of any other persons. Macpherson requires only that the development of any one individual not be at the *expense* of any other. The power of a person is measured by an absence of impediment to his own individual development. The classless society sought by Macpherson will free individuals from the impediments they now suffer as a result of their membership in an exploited class. But freed from class membership, they will not be defined, inherently, by any other social group or by ties to any other persons.

From the perspective of much feminist theory, this degree of individual isolation is questionable. Even if the oppression brought about by class divisions were a thing of the past and even if gender domination were overcome, we would still be persons with ties to other persons, and we would still be at least partly constituted by such connections. We would still be the daughter or son of given parents, and probably the mother or father of given children. We would still have racial or ethnic or linguistic or other ties that at least in part would make us the persons we would be. Though we often aspire to be free of the debilitating aspects of some group memberships and of various ties, we seldom aspire to be the unattached individuals of liberal theory. We recognize that in the case of some of our relationships, self-development of a separate kind may be less important than the development of the relationship and its members together; and that we often wish to evaluate relationships in ways that cannot be broken down into gains, or lack of expense, or losses, for the persons, as individuals, in the relationship.

Brian Barry has aptly characterized the essence of liberalism: it is "the vision of society as made up of independent, autonomous units who cooperate only when the terms of co-operation are such as to make it further the ends of each of the parties."[17] From a feminist view, such persons would be consigned to an impoverished social and political as well as family life. What often matters in relations between human beings, including relations at a social level, will involve aspects of human social reality which cannot even be discussed in the individualistic and self-interested or non-tuistic terms of the liberal tradition, even as reinterpreted by Macpherson.[18] Macpherson's individualism is the individualism of John Stuart Mill rather than that of Hobbes or Bentham. But it seems little touched by the kinds of feminist doubts to which I have referred.[19]

Of course the objection may be raised that intimate relations are irrelevant for the construction of democratic society or of the public institutions with which Macpherson and the traditions of political and social theory have been concerned. But this is where feminist theory may depart most significantly from traditional political and social theory, liberal and otherwise. Feminist theory insists on reconsidering the concept of the person who is to enter into the public life of government or economic activity. There are not two or three separate entities here, a public or a working person, and a private person; there is only one person, involved in and affected by both public and private social realities, however they are understood. And if we must rethink the liberal concept of person to acknowledge how artificial and male-biased is the individual of classical liberal theory, springing full-blown out of nowhere into a self-sufficiency from which he considers entering into social relations, then of course we must rethink the social and political theory built around this concept of person. And if we must rethink the concept of person selling his labor, recognizing that it too has been constructed without adequate regard for the labor of those who have created and brought up and continue to care for this worker, then again, we must rethink the social and political theory built around this concept of person.

Feminist theory asks why the relationships between persons in what has mistakenly been relegated to a private sphere beyond public concern should not be considered in the construction of broader social arrangements. Certainly we reject arguing from the patriarchal family to the patriarchal, monarch-headed society, or to a paternalistic workplace. Certainly we can agree that Locke's vision of public equality divorced from private patriarchy represented progress over Filmer's defense of public patriarchy, and that Marx's vision represented progress over Locke's. But if we look at the postpatriarchal relations of care and concern that we expect to be possible in family relationships or in relationships among friends, it is not unreasonable to suggest that some perhaps weaker but still analogous versions of these should characterize social relations generally. In place of the development of individual powers that at best do not *diminish* the powers of others—the sort of self-development at which many theorists of democracy would aim—we might aspire to the development of social *relations,* such as relations of trust, or relations of care and concern, of mutually appreciated expression, of shared enjoyment.[20] It is not at all utopian to consider the sorts of political and social institutions that can foster such relations, and they might be rather different from those that Macpherson would recommend, those that would, in his words, "maximize men's developmental powers."[21]

Macpherson does consider how "membership in a national or cultural community which has defined itself historically is part of what it means to be human" and how "the right to national self-determination may be humanly more important to its claimants than any of the individual rights" on the usual lists of human rights.[22] But he does not pursue this challenge to his own notions of individual self-development. He briefly considers how participatory democracy "brings with it a sense of community" and how "the enjoyment and development of one's capacities is to be done for the most part in conjunction with others, in some relation of community." But he immediately moves on to the vicious circle we seem to be in: "We cannot achieve more democratic participation without a prior change in social inequality and in consciousness [away from man as maximizing consumer], but we cannot achieve the changes in social inequality and consciousness without a prior increase in democratic participation." He then examines where loopholes may occur, and how roadblocks to participation may be reduced. No version of participatory democracy could develop or last, in his view, without a strong commitment to "the equal right of every man and woman to the full development and use of his or her capacities."[23] It is this conception of self-development that remains at the heart of Macpherson's hopes for the future.

For many democratic theorists, as for Macpherson as I interpret him, collective enterprises are valued only instrumentally, in terms of the contribution they make to individual self-development. If individual self-development includes a need or desire to work cooperatively with others, institutions should fully permit such activity. But there seems to be no way, on these scales, to appreciate the value of shared, relational activity in itself. Certainly a society should resist excessive collectivism. It should not promote shared feelings and activities at the expense of all privacy and unshared self-development. But we ought to be able to evaluate how a society is doing at both levels, that is, in terms of both (1) the fostering of social trust and shared concern for community projects, and (2) the fostering of individual self-development. Macpherson has a much more satisfactory view of the latter than has most of the liberal tradition, but his ontology and his ethics make little room for the former. Feminist conceptions of persons and of democracy lend themselves to avoiding this characteristic deficiency of nonfeminist theory.

Relationships and Shared Values

Let's consider these issues in a domain different from that of the family—the domain of expression. Clearly, the developmental power of someone who learns to play a musical instrument better, and to play more songs, can be increased without decreasing the developmental powers of anyone else, once the material needs for the expression—the instrument, the leisure, the music lessons—have been made possible. Macpherson would emphasize that for many activities, providing such material means would not be especially difficult, and that persons can gain great satisfaction from such pursuits in place of the market contests requiring that for some to be winners, others must be losers. But now consider the difference between playing music as an expression of individual achievement and playing music as a social, shared activity. On Macpherson's view of self-development, there is no reason to value an experience of shared enjoyment, as when those who listen to a song are moved by it or join in the singing, as contrasted with the experience of an individual who demonstrates to his own satisfaction, based on his own criteria, that he has achieved a certain level of excellence. But while we may hesitate to subscribe to any general claim that shared aesthetic experiences are always or even in general to be preferred to individual ones, it does seem that social arrangements which foster interpersonal, intergroup, and intercultural aesthetic experiences may be worth striving for, and that they cannot be evaluated in terms that measure only the development of expressive monads. This is not to deny that much artistic creation is a lonely task; the point here is about the wide range of cultural experience engaged in by anyone or everyone. And even if it is not intuitively clear whether shared cultural experiences that foster relationships of trust or concern between persons or more purely individualistic cultural experiences are of greater value, we can recognize that the former can have value not reducible to the latter. Not all shared cultural experiences are morally admirable: many express nationalistic xenophobia or racist intolerance or sexist reaction. But many others express care and concern between persons, thus nourishing the bases for social trust. It certainly makes sense to evaluate shared cultural experiences and to ask what social arrangements should be developed or maintained to foster morally and aesthetically admirable forms of such experience.

A serious shortcoming in the theories of many democratic critics of traditional liberal theory is that with them, as with traditional liberal theory itself, the adequate evaluation of shared experience and of collective endeavors is not possible. Only if the shared experience of the collective endeavor were to contribute to the maximizing of individual self-development would it be, on these accounts, of value. But this seems misguided. Even if we hesitate to compare shared, collective progress with individual self-development or reject a comparison ascribing greater value to either, we should at least be able to ask of a social theory that it ascribe appropriate values to social relationships between persons in ways distinct from its evaluations of gains and losses to individuals in isolation from one another.

Some will suggest, of course, that neutral political institutions should permit but not promote such shared aesthetic experiences—that it is no proper function of government to take sides about what may be thought to be alternative conceptions of the good life.[24] But if this conception of government in fact leads to a privatization of activity, to individualistic persons pursuing private gains, while such shared concerns as schools and parks, transportation systems, protection of the environment, and public culture become increasingly impoverished, then institutions built on this conception of government must be evaluated on these grounds among others.

As we have seen, feminism is bringing about fundamental transformations in moral theory that will require transformations as well in social, political, economic, and legal theory. From a feminist point of view, radical changes are needed in, for instance, our standard conceptions of reason and emotion, of the public and the private, and of persons and their relationships. The implications for any theory of democracy of these changed conceptions are obviously enormous.

It may be that it is our historically located and changeable circumstances that have led women to interpret moral problems more in terms of social relationships between actual persons and less in terms of either abstract rules or individual interests. But it may also be that, on reflection, we will insist on seeing feminist concerns as the framework for moral theory within which other approaches must be fitted, among them the fair treatment of persons thought of as individuals in a political system. And then of course with a feminist approach to what morality requires, we may have views of what social arrangements should facilitate or foster that will be quite different from the views of any of the currently leading candidates from the liberal or Marxist traditions.

While we can acknowledge that the Marxist tradition enables us to see the realities of class oppression which the liberal tradition obscures, we can also recognize that the Marxist tradition may obscure as well as overlook the realities of gender oppression. And although the liberal tradition's respect for individual rights provides some moral guidelines we too will strive to preserve, we can recognize that without social ties of a deeper kind than offered by liberal theory, there may be no society within which to respect individuals.

Imagining a society without gender oppression involves imagining persons in inherently social relationships acting together to foster human development. This will mean dealing with such issues as protecting the environment, defusing intergroup violence, and caring enough about the children of future generations to summon the political will to do *now* what is essential. The "preservative love" that Sara Ruddick sees as guiding the activity of mothering may need to have analogues well beyond the family if we are to have a chance of preserving the life of humanity. Ruddick argues from the practices of mothering to political strategies for the peace movement. It is not only in the household and the marginal community that human relationships of trust and concern must be sought but at the global level.

Individualism and Communitarianism

Rousseau is often credited with the most astute recognition among all social philosophers of both the claims of the individual and the claims of the community.[25] No individual man, Rousseau thought, should ever be forced to submit to the will of another, and so no individual citizen should be asked to obey a government to whose decisions he does not consent. At the same time, the citizen should determine in accordance with what he takes to be the general will, the shared good of the whole community, and this he should try to determine by heeding his conscience, uninfluenced by the interests and pressures of his fellows.

From a feminist point of view, this image of the lonely citizen deciding in isolation, influenced as little as possible by the opinion of others, is highly suspect, and not only because Rousseau excluded women from the realm of citizenship. We should often want to decide with as much awareness as possible of others' views, not so that either we or they can use this knowledge to our own or their advantage, as so much of the social contract tradition would suppose we would, but so that we can all find cooperative solutions to mutual problems. We often seek to decide in a way more compatible with, rather than opposed to, the decisions of others. In this sense we seek to share decisions and consent, not to choose from the vantage point of a splendidly autonomous being.[26]

There is a long history of communitarian critiques of the isolated liberal individual. Communitarians have recognized the ways in which persons are constituted by their memberships in communities and the ways in which political life is built on traditions and practices as much as, or rather than, on rational agreements.[27] Feminists have compelling reasons to be skeptical of communitarian alternatives to individualism, since communitarians have so impoverished an account of how women are to break with the traditions that have, throughout history, so oppressed us. As Susan Okin demonstrates, such leading communitarians as Michael Sandel, Alasdair McIntyre, and Roberto Unger have virtually nothing to say about the traditional and continuing division of labor in the household that leaves women as a gender so disadvantaged. Marilyn Friedman points out that most nonfeminist defenders of a social conception of the self "provide no critical evaluation of the social roles" female selves in-habit; they leave as a mystery the process of subverting traditional roles in the ways that women so often need to do: "How can someone resist constituents of her very self? How can such independent attitudes be possible? Wouldn't they also be socially constituted?" Friedman's own suggestion for handling this conceptual problem is to acknowledge, as feminist views of the self can, that "selves are complex. Even though they are socially constituted, they can adopt points of view that are indepen-dent of this or that norm-governed relationship constituting their very identities."[28] A variety of relationships contribute to any one person's identity, and provide different and sometimes contradictory points of view. From them we learn techniques of critical reflection and develop capacities for resistance.[29]

In "Three Grades of Social Involvement," George Sher defends individ-ualism against what he takes to be three forms of communitarian attack on it. Nowhere does he consider the relational self as many feminists are trying to understand it. He simply asserts, at one point, that "a person's metaphysical (and moral) independence from his parents remains un-problematical."[30] From the point of view of the feminist relational self, this independence surely is problematical. For many years in a person's life, years in which childhood experiences shape the adult person she becomes, she exercises little independence. Even as an adult, it is part of what she is to be the child of given parents, with all the genetic and cultural history this involves, all the gender expectations or class advan-tage or racial disadvantage that attaches to it, and all the obligations and moral sentiments that the relationship brings with it.

While of course this is not *all* a person is, the unconscious ease with which many theorists seem to discount these constitutive aspects of the person illustrates the distorting abstraction on which individualism de-pends. On the other hand, a person is not only or primarily or necessarily to be identified with her community. Women especially, in recent de-cades, have loosened our ties with various of the communities with which we have found ourselves identified, and we have often formed new ties with other relational persons.

Consider a frequent declaration of personal independence: a young person rejects the religion of his parents, in which he was brought up. On the one hand, doing so indicates some inner core of individual choice; on the other, the young person can only exercise such choice in relation to a religion to which he has some connection through his parents, and only then if the years of mothering by which he has been shaped have equipped him with a sufficient degree of autonomy to make exercising choice possible.

Whether we focus on the capacity for independent choice that any person can aspire to develop or on the interpersonal ties within which the capacity must develop and remain embedded—at least at the level of personal history—will depend on the purposes of our inquiry. We should at any rate acknowledge that both individualism and communitarianism, especially as Sher characterizes them, are, for purposes of description, artificial abstractions from reality and, for purposes of evaluation, implausible recommendations. To suppose that selves-in-relation can be adequately discussed in terms of independent, isolated entities and their states, is misguided, but it is equally misguided to suppose that selves-in-relation are *only* what they are because of the communal, class, or historical contexts in which they are embedded, as Sher's characterization of the communitarian view would have them. Relational selves are relational, but they are also capable of radical change.

Parallel points can be made about evaluation. It can neither be satisfactory to value selves-in-relation in terms grounded only in values to independent, isolated individuals *nor* in terms of the values grounded only in the social wholes to which communitarians have attended—nations, ethnic groups, or local communities, and in terms of changes which occur at these levels. Selves-in-relation can make their own changes for better or for worse.

Sher's discussion of Michael Sandel's critique of individualism and Sandel's own discussion focus on persons and their *ends*. But the relational self of feminist theory is not only oriented toward purposive action. What we *are* is already a self related to other selves, regardless of our ends. For a relation between persons to make sense, we must be able to refer to the persons in the relation as well as to the relation. But we can reject the claims of individualism that the value of the relation must be reducible to values to the individuals in the relation; relations themselves can have value. We can also reject the claim that persons only have value insofar as they contribute to the value of communal relations. Both persons and relations can have value, as we can see in the concerns of feminist moral and social theory.

Various non-Western conceptions of the self see the self as more social and less individualistic than does the Western liberal tradition.[31] At the same time, the oppression of women is often greater in these societies than in Western ones. Part of the explanation may be that where female selves are incorporated into social roles reflective of male dominance in society, views that discern individual persons can represent progress; with such conceptions a woman can at least recognize her own reality as a person holding beliefs and experiencing dissatisfactions. This does not diminish the persuasiveness of feminist arguments that views which recognize persons as relational but that also offer scope for changing oppressive social roles represent still further progress. An adequate view of human beings involved in personal and political and social life will neither absorb us completely into traditional and communal groups nor leave us in the artificial isolation of liberal individualism. Democracy should be a way of life for persons understood as inherently relational *and* capable of transformation.

TEN

Noncontractual Society:
The Postpatriarchal Family as Model

I begin this final chapter with a bit more of the personal history touched on in chapter 1. When I returned to graduate school after a decade of work and life outside the academy, one of the first books I read carefully was the *Leviathan* by Thomas Hobbes. I was profoundly impressed by his description of the hypothetical "state of nature" with its "war of all against all" that could be alleviated only by rational agreement among men to "seek peace" and establish law. I can still quote longer passages from the *Leviathan* than from any other book, certainly including the Bible. It described the life I had experienced and was experiencing, professionally and personally, though the weapons that I felt were directed at me were psychological rather than made of metal. Not long afterwards I discovered game theory, and I felt as I imagined Hobbes to have felt when, in mid-life, he discovered geometry and, in Aubrey's account, fell in love with it.[1] I saw prisoner's dilemmas everywhere and marveled at how my experience of conflict could be so tellingly represented in such beautiful abstract formulations.

So it is not the case that I have never been dazzled by the attractions of rational choice theory or willing to work with its technical complexities. Doubts developed only slowly, as the conflict between rationality and morality itself came to seem to me intractable. In my article "Rationality and Reasonable Cooperation," published in 1977, I cautiously made a claim for the reasonable as distinct from the rational.[2] I still saw prisoner's dilemma situations as pervasive and the problems of rational choice theory as central to the human condition.

Perhaps David Gauthier's book *Morals by Agreement* represents the ultimate in the attempt to have rational choice theory provide a basis for decisions of any kind, including moral decisions. It and the approach it reflects have been widely influential; hence I will focus some attention on it. *Morals by Agreement* is an impressive attempt to deal with previous difficulties in such theories, but it raises even more fundamental questions than did they about whether we should try to deal with such a

192

wide range of issues within the framework and with the assumptions characteristic of rational choice theory. Such an earlier major work in the social contract tradition as John Rawls's *Theory of Justice* or such a widely read work in this tradition as Robert Nozick's *Anarchy, State, and Utopia* were more nearly political than full-fledged moral theories.[3] In offering his contribution to the tradition as a moral theory, Gauthier's work invites even more fundamental doubts about the entire approach. For while many may accept assumptions concerning non-tuistic[4] individuals rationally maximizing their interests as appropriate for political life, they may have doubts about the appropriateness of them for some other contexts. Doubting them somewhere, they may doubt them elsewhere.

By now, as many wounds have healed, I have come to see not only that not all of my life was or need be Hobbesian, but that perhaps little of life for most people is best prescribed for in terms drawn from the contractualist tradition. I try in this chapter to show why. If Gauthier's views on the moral agreements that may be possible among rational contractors turn out to be well-founded, they now seem to me to offer, at best, a solution to a problem that should not arise on a more satisfactory conception of mortality. For with an improved understanding of morality, the rational contracts of the marketplace would already be constrained by noncontractual social relations.

I am unpersuaded that Gauthier has solved the problems of rationality which I tried to grapple with years ago. I suspect that all the old questions about whether to trust or not in prisoner's dilemma situations could be revived in terms of whether or not to be "translucent."[5] And I suspect that problems analogous to those undermining rule utilitarianism would undermine as well Gauthier's claim that a choice is rational if it conforms to a *policy* that it would be rational to adopt. Why, we will have to ask, should we adopt a rational policy if, in a particular case, it would be irrational to do so?

But these questions are beside the point of this chapter. Even if Gauthier could solve such problems of rational choice my argument is that the solutions would only be good for very limited and constrained contexts, not for choice in general and not for deciding what we morally ought to do.

The Contractual Paradigm

Contemporary Western society is in the grip of contractual thinking. Realities are interpreted in contractual terms, and goals are formulated in terms of rational contracts. Leading current conceptions of rationality begin with assumptions that human beings are independent, self-interested, or mutually disinterested individuals; they then typically argue that it is often rational for human beings to enter into contractual relationships with each other.

On the side of description, assumptions characteristic of a contractual view of human relations underlie the dominant attempts to view social realities through the lenses of the social sciences.[6] They also underlie the principles upon which most persons in contemporary Western society claim their most powerful institutions are founded. We are told that modern democratic states rest on a social contract, that their economies should be thought of as a free market where producers and consumers, employers and employees make contractual agreements. And we should even, it is suggested, interpret our culture as a free market of ideas.[7]

On the side of prescription, leading theories of justice and equality, such as those of Rawls, Nozick, and Dworkin, suggest what social arrangements should be like to reflect more fully the requirements of contractual rationality.[8] And various philosophers claim that even morality itself is best understood in contractual terms.[9] The vast domain of rational choice theory, supposedly applicable to the whole range of human activity and experience, makes the same basic assumptions about individuals, contractual relations, and rationality as those in the social contract tradition.[10] And contractual solutions are increasingly suggested for problems that arise in areas not hitherto thought of in contractual terms, such as in dealing with unruly patients or in the context of bringing up children.

When examined, the assumptions and conceptions of contractual thinking seem highly questionable. As descriptions of reality they can be seriously misleading. Actual societies are the result of war, exploitation, racism, and patriarchy far more than the result of social contract. Economic and political realities are the outcome of economic strength triumphing over economic weakness more than of a free market. And rather than a free market of ideas, we have a culture in which the loudspeakers that are the commercial mass media drown out the soft voices of free expression. As expressions of normative concern, moreover, contractual theories hold out an impoverished view of human aspiration.

To see contractual relations between self-interested or mutually disinterested individuals as constituting a paradigm of human relations is to take a certain historically specific conception of "economic man" as representative of humanity. And it is, many feminists are beginning to agree, to overlook or to discount in very fundamental ways the experience of women.

An Alternative Perspective

In this chapter I look at society from a point of view wholly different from that of economic man. I take the point of view of women, especially of mothers, as the basis for trying to rethink society and its possible goals. Certainly there is no single point of view of women; their perspectives are potentially as diverse as those of men. But since the perspectives of women have all been largely discounted across the spectrum, I shall not try to deal here with diversity among such views. Instead I will give voice to one possible feminist outlook.

I will try to imagine what society would look like, for both descriptive and prescriptive purposes, if we replaced the paradigm of economic man with the paradigm of mother and child. I will try to explore how society and our goals for it might appear if, instead of thinking of human relations as contractual, we thought of them as *like* relations between mothers and children. What would social relations look like? What would society look like if we took the relation between mother and child as not just one relation among many, but as the *primary* social relation? And what sorts of aspirations might we have for such a society?[11]

On the face of it, it seems plausible to take the relation between mother and child as *the* primary social relation, since before there could have been any self-sufficient, independent men in a hypothetical state of nature, there would have to have been mothers and the children these men would have been. And the argument could be developed in terms of a conceptual as well as a causal primary. Before I begin this exploration, however, let me anticipate a likely reaction and say that I doubt that the view I am going to present is the one we should end up with. I doubt that we should take any one relation as paradigmatic for all the others. I have argued elsewhere for different moral approaches for different contexts, and have tried to map out which approaches are suitable for which contexts. I think we will continue to need to conceptualize different types of human relations differently, and to make different moral recommendations for such different domains as those of family living, cultural production, economic activity, and law, though I now think all should be embedded in the kind of understanding of persons and of moral considerations that feminist moral inquiry can provide.

There may then not be one type of human relation that is paradigmatic, but to think of relations between mothers and children *as* paradigmatic may be an important stage to go through in reconstructing a view of human relationships that can be adequate from a feminist point of view. Since the image of rational economic man in contractual relations is pervasive in contemporary society and expanding constantly to new regions around the globe, it may be a useful endeavor to try to see everything in this different way, as if the primary social relation is that between mother and child and as if all the others could and should be made over in the image of this one.

In any case, if we pay attention to this neglected relation between mother and child, perhaps we can put a stop to the imperialism of the model of economic man and assert with conviction that there are at least some domains where this model is definitely not appropriate. And we can show that morality must be as relevant to, and moral theory as appropriately based on, the context of mothering as on the context of contracting. To the extent that some of our relations should be seen as contractual, we should recognize how limited those relations are. And to the extent that some of morality should be understood in terms of what rational contractors would agree to, we should recognize that such a morality can only be suitable for a particular domain of human relations, not a model for morality in general.

Rational choice theorists point out that their theories are formulated for just those situations where individuals do seek to maximize their own interests and remain uninterested in each others' interests. Their theories, they say, are not intended to deal with family ties or with people in love. But the questions I raise here have to do with how we ought to treat, conceptually, a great variety of human relations. Of course we *can,* theoretically, treat them *as* contractual, but *should* we do so? Is it plausible to do so? And when we ask these questions we can see that of course it is not only in special cases that persons can be, and perhaps should be, and often are bound together in social ties of a noncontractual kind.

Defenders of rational choice theory point out that we can treat any entity *as* an individual. We can think of a family, a group, a nation as an individual and say that the contractualism of rational choice theory has to do with choices to be made in a context of other such individuals where mutually non-tuistic motives obtain. And we can admit that non-rational feelings, often strong, bind people together into such units. On this view, nothing I say in this chapter presents any problem for rational choice theory because the latter is talking about something different from what I am talking about. But this objection misses the point. I am not denying that as a logical possibility we can treat any entity *as* an individual. The issue is this: How *should* we treat, and think about, various social realities? Familiar traditions have treated flesh-and-blood human beings, each one taken alone, as individuals, and have interpreted the interactions between them as exchanges between *individuals*. I will try to suggest the artificiality of that treatment. It may capture some realities of men in the marketplace, but it misses the realities of mothering, where it is misleading to think of a mothering person and a child as two individuals linked by non-tuistic motives. These two human persons are such that the relation between them is partly constitutive of what they *are*. And if *they* should not be thought of as separate individuals acting on non-tuistic motives, perhaps much *more* of the social world should be seen in terms closer to these than to the terms of what the contract theorist is talking about.

In a book on the morality of groups, Larry May points out that we can of course admit that "social groups *can* be treated *as if* they were individual persons." But the question we may wish to address, he continues, is this: "Which way of conceptualizing social groups best fits the data of experience (from sociology, psychology, law, political science, etc.) in contemporary times?"[12] Similarly, we can acknowledge that of course we *can* treat social relations as if they were contracts between non-tuistic individual entities, from persons to corporations to states, and so on, but *should* we do so? What I am discussing in this chapter is what conception of social relations may best fit the data if we base it on the experience of women, and what conceptions are best for delineating what morality recommends. Rational choice theorists repeatedly point out that they are not assuming that human beings are in fact rational; they are prescribing for those who wish to be rational. Again, we can choose whether to think of ourselves as non-tuistic individual rational contractors or, for instance, as relational persons caring about other relational persons as well as about our own individual interests.

To see society in terms of family rather than marketplace relationships is not new. Feudal conceptions, for instance, drew analogies between monarchs and the heads of households. But these were views based on relations between patriarchal fathers and their wives and children, not on views of society seen in terms of mothering. To explore the latter is not to suggest a return to precontractual society, but to consider what further progress is needed.

Since it is the practice of mothering I shall be concerned with, rather than with women in the biological sense, I will use the phrase "mothering person" rather than "mother," in the same gender-neutral way that various writers now speak of "rational contractors." If men feel uncomfortable being referred to as, or even more so in being, mothering persons, this may possibly mirror the discomfort many mothers feel adapting to the norms and practices, and language, of "economic man."

I will look at the practice of mothering not as it has in fact existed in any society characterized by male dominance but in terms of what the characteristic features of this practice would be without male dominance. In method this may be comparable to what has been done in developing a concept of rational contracting. The concept developed while large segments of society were in fact still feudal, and actual human beings are certainly not in fact fully rational. These realities have not prevented the contractual relation from being taken as paradigmatic.

Furthermore, it may well be that the conception of the mother-child relation that I shall develop is somewhat historically specific. But perhaps no conception can avoid being that. My aim is only to have the conception I will try to develop capable of being considered an alternative to the conception of economic man in contractual relations, that is, of being no more historically limited, and contextually dependent, than that. To the extent that the mother/child relation will be an idealization, I hope it will not be more severely idealized than the relation between rational contractors that it is to replace; for the purposes of my exploration, it does not need to be less of an idealization.

Women and Family

The contractual model was hardly ever applied, as either description or ideal, to women or to relations within the family. The family was imagined to be "outside" the polis and "outside" the market in a "private" domain. This private domain was contrasted with the public domain, and with what, by the time of Hobbes and Locke, was thought of as the contractual domain of citizen and state and tradesman and market. Although women have always worked and although both women and children were later pressed into work in factories, they were still thought of as outside the domain in which the contractual models of "equal men" were developed. Women were not expected to demand equal rights either in the public domain or at home. Women were not expected to be economic men. And children were simply excluded from the realm of what was being interpreted in contractual terms as distinctively human.

The clearest example of the extraordinary bias to which such views can lead can be seen in the writings of Rousseau. Moral principles were to be applied to men and to women in ways thoroughly inconsistent with each other. Rousseau argued that in the polity no man should surrender his freedom. He thought that government could be based on a social contract in which citizens under law would be as free as in the state of nature because they would give the law to themselves. But, he argued, within the household the man must rule and the women must submit; women must be trained from childhood to serve and to submit to men.[13] Since the essence of being fully human was for Rousseau being free from submission to the will of another, women were to be denied the essential condition for being fully human. To grant women equality with men in the household (the only domain to be open to them) would bring about the dissolution of society.

The contrast, in this view, is total: complete freedom and equality in the exclusively male polity; absolute male authority and female submission in the household. Rousseau seems not to have considered the implications of such a view. If one really believes that two persons in a household, with ties of affection and time for discussion, can never reach decisions by consensus or by taking turns at deciding, but that one person must always possess full and permanent authority, what hope could there possibly be for the larger democratic, participatory, consensual political life Rousseau so eloquently advocated? On the other hand, if decisions in the political realm *can* be arrived at in such a way that the will of no man needs to be overpowered, as Rousseau thought, why cannot such concern for avoiding coercion be extended to relations between men and women in the family?

One way in which the dominant patterns of thought have managed to overlook such inconsistencies has been to see women as primarily mothers, and mothering as a primarily biological function. It has thus been thought that women's lives are taken up with activities which are not specifically human, in contrast with the rational contracting of distinctively human "economic man." The exclusion of women from the domain of voluntary contracting has been supposed to follow naturally and to require no justification.

The presupposition that women are more immersed in biological processes, more determined by instinctive and other "natural" forces than men, is still widely held. As we have seen, it is a misconception. A feminist perspective allows us to see how giving birth is a fully human project and mothering, with which women are so closely identified, a fully human activity when engaged in by human beings. If human mothering should be assimilated to the mothering of nonhuman animals, it would be as appropriate to think of governing the nation as like the governing of ant colonies, industrial production as like the building of beaver dams, exchange as like the relation of a large fish which protects and a small fish which grooms, and the conquest by force of arms that characterizes so much of human history as like the aggression of packs of animals.

Of course, women engage in many other sorts of human activity than that of bringing up children, and they can be as fully involved in pursuits other than motherhood as men are involved in pursuits other than fatherhood. The view that women are less human than men and that the experience of women is thus of less relevance for morality and social theory can not be defended. But even when we focus on the activity of motherhood itself, it cannot be maintained that this is a natural domain less relevant for our normative recommendations than some other domains imagined to be more distinctively human. Certainly, the activity of mothering includes many dull and repetitive tasks, as does farming, industrial production, banking, and work in a laboratory. But degree of dullness has nothing to do with degree of naturalness. Human mothering is as different from animal mothering as men are from animals. And of course this domain in which mothering persons and children interact is a very large domain of human activity and experience in which there are, obviously, human relations that are social relations.

On a variety of grounds there are good reasons to have mothering become an activity performed by men as well as by women. We may wish to continue to use the term 'mothering' to designate the activity, in recognition of the fact that it has been women, overwhelmingly, who have engaged in this activity.[14] Further, for the foreseeable future it is the point of view of women, including women engaged in mothering, which should be called on to provide a contrast with the point of view of men. A time may come when a phrase such as "the nurturing of children" would be preferable to "mothering." By then "parenting" might also be acceptable to those who at present find it misleading. But whatever we call it, and however many men are engaged in it, the practice of caring for children is one which will not be well discussed or understood or evaluated in the language or with the concepts of rationally contracting.

Clearly, the view that contractual relations are a model for human relations generally is especially unsuitable for considering the relations between mothering persons and children. It stretches credulity even further than most philosophers can tolerate it to imagine babies as little rational calculators contracting with their mothers for care, though Hobbes tried.[15] Of course the fundamental contracts have always been thought of as hypothetical rather than real. But one cannot imagine hypothetical babies contracting either. And mothering persons, in their care of children, demonstrate hardly any of the "trucking" or trading instinct claimed by Adam Smith to be the *most* characteristic aspect of human nature.[16] If the epitome of what it is to be human is thought to be a disposition to be a rational contractor, human persons creating other human persons through the processes of human mothering are overlooked. And human children developing human personhood are not recognized as engaged in a most obviously human activity.

David Hume, whom some admire for having moral views more compatible with "women's moral sense" than most philosophers, said that avarice is "a universal passion which operates at all times, in all places, and upon all persons."[17] Surely we can note that in the relation between mothering person and child, avarice is by no means always present. Yes, children may want more toys and mothers more compliance, but much of the time, in the relation between them, the avarice that fuels the model of "economic man" is not a salient feature.

An exchange in Charlotte Perkins Gilman's *Herland* illustrates the contrast between the motives ascribed to rational economic man building contractual society and the motives central to the practice of mothering. Herland is an imaginary society composed entirely of women. Because they reproduce by parthenogenesis, there are only mothers and daughters in the society. Everything is arranged to benefit the next generation. The society has existed peacefully for hundreds of years, with a high level of technological advancement but without any conception of a "survival of the fittest" ethic. Three young men from twentieth-century America, who manage to get to Herland, acknowledge that there are no wars, no kings, no priests, no aristocracies, that the women are all like sisters to each other and work together not by competing but by united action. But, the young men insist, things are much better at home, where competition prevails. One of them expounds on the advantages of competition, on how it develops fine qualities, saying that "without it there would be 'no stimulus to industry.'" Competition, he says, is necessary to provide an incentive to work; competition is "the motor power" of society.

The women of Herland are genuinely curious and good-naturedly skeptical, as they so often are in Gilman's novel. "Do you mean," they ask, "that no mother would work for her children without the stimulus of competition?" In Herland, the entire industrious society is strongly motivated to make the society better for the children: "The children in this country are the one center and focus of all our thoughts. Every step of our advance is always considered in its effects on them . . . You see, we are *Mothers.*"[18]

Of course, this is an idealized picture of mothering. But I am contrasting it with an idealized picture of rational contracting. Quite probably we would not want a society devoted entirely to mothering. But then would we want a society devoted entirely to better bargains? In developing these suggestions, it is instructive to see what is most seriously overlooked by a contractual view of society and to see how important what is overlooked really is.

Family and Society

Feminists have demanded that the principles of justice and freedom and equality on which it is claimed that democracy rests be extended to women and the family. They have demanded that women be treated as equals in the polity, in the workplace, and, finally, at home. They have demanded, in short, that in some respects full rights to enter freely the contractual relations of modern society be extended to take in the family.

But feminists are also considering whether the arguments should run the other way. Instead of importing into the household principles derived from the marketplace, perhaps we should export to the wider society the relations suitable for mothering persons and children. This approach suggests that just as relations between persons within the family should be based on concern and caring, rather than on contracts, so various relations in the wider society should be characterized by more care and concern. More openness and trust and human feeling than can even be aspired to in contractarian prescriptions should color political and social life. The household instead of the marketplace might then provide a model for society. Of course what we would mean by the household would not be the patriarchal household that was, before the rise of contractual thinking, also thought of as a model of society. No feminist would wish to go back to the political patriarchy replaced by social contract views, where political authority was seen as a version on a grander scale of patriarchal authority in the family. In arguing that the family might become a model for society, we would mean the relations between mothering persons and children without a patriarch, in societies free of the male dominance that has distorted these relations. We would take our conception of the *postpatriarchal* family as our possible model.

The family is a social institution of the utmost importance. It is a small society, a set of relations. The family has been, and still is, undergoing profound change at the present time, and the attendant upheavals in the personal lives of many persons hold out the promise of remarkable social change for the better.

The family is only beginning to receive the central attention from feminists that it deserves, partly because feminist theory is still in such exploratory stages, trying to understand all at once the multiplicity of forces—social, economic, political, legal, psychological, sexual, biological, and cultural—that affect women. Multiple causes shape the sex/gender structures within which human females and males develop feminine and masculine characteristics and come to occupy the roles that existing societies designate as female and male. We need to understand empirically how this happens. We also need normative theories of the family. Jane Flax, surveying various feminist writings on the family, says that to develop alternatives to the oppressive relations that now prevail, we need to think through

> what kinds of child care are best for parents and children; what family structures are best for persons at various stages of the life cycle . . . ; how the state and political processes should affect families; and how work and the organization of production should be transformed to support whatever family forms are preferred.[19]

It is an enormous task, but recent years have provided more new thought on these subjects than many previous decades.[20]

The major question remains: What are the possibilities of remaking society by remaking what have been thought of as personal relations? Societies are composed of persons in relation to one another. The *personal* relations among persons are the most affective and influential in many ways. But the extent to which they are central to wider social relations or could possibly provide a model for social and political relations of a kind that has been thought of as public—this remains an open question.

Western liberal democratic thought has been built on the concept of the individual seen as a theoretically isolable entity. This entity can assert interests, claim rights, and enter into contractual relations with other entities, but is not seen as related to others in inextricable or intrinsic ways. He is assumed to be motivated primarily by a desire to pursue his own interests, though he can recognize the need to agree to contractual restraints on the ways others may pursue their interests. To the extent that groups have been dealt with, they have largely been treated *as* individuals.

The difficulties of developing trust and cooperation and society itself on the sands of self-interested individuals pursuing their own gain are extreme.[21] Pure contractual society would be society perpetually in danger of breaking down. Perhaps what are needed for even adequate levels of social cohesion are persons bound together by relations of concern and caring and empathy and trust rather than merely by contracts it may be in their interest to disregard. Any enforcement mechanisms put in place to keep persons to their contracts will be as subject to disintegration as the contracts themselves; at some point contracts must be embedded in social relations that are noncontractual.

The relation between mothering person and child, hardly understandable in contractual terms, is a more fundamental human relation and may be a more promising one on which to build our recommendations for the future than is any relation between rational contractors. We should look to the relation between mothering person and child for suggestions of how better to describe such society as we now have. And we should look to it especially for a view of a future more fit for our children than a global battleground for rational, egoistic entities trying, somehow, to restrain their antagonisms by fragile contracts.

If we shift from the liberal contractual view of society to the Marxist one, we can note that the Marxist conception of relations between human beings is in various ways more satisfactory than the contractual one and more capable of accounting for social relations in general. However, the Marxist view of history as split into classes and driven by economic forces is hardly more capable of encompassing, and does not lend itself to reflecting, the experience of the relation between mothering person and child either. So I will continue to develop here the contrast between the relation between mothering person and child on the one hand and the contractual exchanges of economic man on the other.

The Mother/Child Relation

The relation between mothering person and child is not voluntary and therefore not contractual. The ties that bind mothering person and child are affectional and solicitous on the one hand, and emotional and dependent on the other. The degree to which bearing and caring for children has been voluntary for most mothers throughout most of history has been extremely limited; it is still quite limited for most mothering persons. The relation *should* be voluntary for the mothering person, but it cannot possibly be so for the young child, and it can only become, gradually, slightly more voluntary.

A woman may have decided voluntarily to have a child, but once that decision has been made, she will never again be unaffected by the fact that she has brought this particular child into existence. And even if the decision to have a child is voluntary, the decision to have this particular child, for either parent, cannot be. Technological developments can continue to reduce the uncertainties of childbirth, but unpredictable aspects are likely to remain great. Unlike the contract where buyer and seller can know what is being exchanged and which is void if the participants cannot know what they are agreeing to, a parent cannot know what a particular child will be like. And children are totally unable to choose their parents or for some years, any of their caretakers.

Recognizing how central to society the relation between mothering person and child is, yet how limited are the aspects of voluntariness in the relation may help us to gain a closer approximation to reality in our understanding of how little voluntariness exists in most human relations, especially at a global level. It will help us avoid the distortions arising from imagining the purely voluntary trades entered into by rational economic contractors to be characteristic of human relations in other domains.

Society may impose certain reciprocal obligations—obligations on parents to care for children when the children are young and on children to care for parents when the parents are old. But if there is any element of a bargain in the relation between mothering person and child, it is very different from the bargain supposedly characteristic of the marketplace. If a parent thinks, "I'll take care of you now so you'll take care of me when I'm old," that confidence must be based, unlike the contracts of political and economic bargains, on enormous trust and on a virtual absence of enforcement.[22] Few mothering persons have such an exchange in mind when they engage in the activities of mothering, and any such bargain would only be resorted to when the callousness or poverty of the society made the plight of the old person desperate. Survey after survey demonstrates that old persons hope not to have to be a burden on their children.[23] They prefer social arrangements that will allow them to refuse to cash in on any such bargain. So the intention and goal of mothering is to give of one's care without obtaining a return of a self-interested kind. The emotional satisfaction of a person engaged in mothering arises from the well-being and happiness of another human being and from the health of the relation between the two persons, not the gain that results from an egoistic bargain. The motive behind the activity of mothering is thus very different from that behind a market transaction.[24] And so is, perhaps even more clearly, the motive behind the child's project of growth and development.

205

Another aspect of the contrast between market relations and relations between mothering person and child lies in the extent to which any such relation is permanent and irreplaceable. The market makes of everything, even human labor and artistic expression and sexual desire, a commodity to be bought and sold, with one unit of economic value replaceable by any other of equivalent value. To the extent that political life reflects these aspects of the market, politicians are replaceable and political influence is bought and sold. Though rights may be thought of as outside the economic market, in contractual thinking they are seen as inside the wider market of the social contract, and they can be traded against each other. But the ties between parents and children are permanent ties, however strained or slack they become at times. And no person within a family should be a commodity to any other. Although various persons may participate in mothering a given child, and a given person may mother many children, still no child and no mothering person is to the other a merely replaceable commodity. More of our attitudes toward our society's cultural productions, for instance, might well be thought of in these terms rather than in the terms of the marketplace.

The relation between mothering person and child yields insight into our notions of equality. It shows us unmistakably that equality is not equivalent to having equal legal rights. All feminists are committed to equality and to equal rights in contexts where rights are appropriately at issue. But in many contexts, concerns other than rights are more salient and appropriate. And the equality at issue in the relation between mothering person and child is the equal consideration of persons, not a legal or contractual notion of equal rights.

Parents and children should not have equal rights in the sense that what they are entitled to decide or to do or to have should be the same. A family of several small children and an adult or two should not regularly make its decisions by majority vote.[25] But every member of a family is worthy of equal respect and consideration. Each person in a family is as important as a person as every other.

Sometimes the interests of children have been thought in some sense to count for more, justifying "sacrificing for the children." Certainly the interests of mothers have often counted for less than those of either fathers or children. Increasingly, we may come to think that the interests of all should count equally, but we should recognize that this claim is appropriately invoked only if the issue should be thought of as one of interest. Often it should not. Much of the time we can see that calculations of interest, and of equal interests, are as out of place as are determinations of equal rights. Both the rights and the interests of individuals seen as separate entities, and equality among them, should not exhaust our moral concerns. The flourishing of shared joy, of mutual affection, of bonds of trust and hope between mothering persons and children can illustrate this as clearly as anything can. Harmony, love, and cooperation cannot be broken down into individual benefits or burdens. They are goals we ought to share; they are relations *between* persons. And although the degree of their intensity may be different, many and various relations *between* persons are important also at the level of communities or societies. We can inquire whether the relations between the members of a society are trusting and mutually supportive or suspicious and hostile. To focus only on contractual relations and the gains and losses of individuals obscures these often more important relational aspects of societies.

In the relation between mothering person and child we obviously do not fulfill our obligations by merely leaving people alone. If one leaves an infant alone he will starve. If one leaves a two-year-old alone she will soon harm herself. The whole tradition that sees respecting others as constituted by noninterference is dramatically shown up as inadequate. It assumes that people can fend for themselves and provide through their own initiatives and efforts what they need. This Robinson Crusoe image of "economic man" is false for almost everyone, but it is totally false in the case of infants and children, and recognizing this can be salutary. It can lead us to see very vividly how unsatisfactory are those prevalent political views according to which we fulfill our obligations merely by refraining from interference and having laws and governments which only protect us from incursions by others. The arguments for government to provide positive enablements to those in need are at least as strong as those for government to protect us against interference. We ought to acknowledge that our fellow citizens and our fellow inhabitants of the globe have moral rights to the food, shelter, and medical care that are the necessary conditions of living and growing. When the resources exist for honoring such rights there are few excuses for not doing so, through governmental implementation where appropriate.[26] Human rights are not merely rights to be left to starve unattended. Seeing how unsatisfactory is the interpretation that sees rights in terms only of noninterference as an interpretation of the rights of children may help us to recognize a comparable truth about other rights. And the arguments—though in a different form—can be repeated for interests as distinct from rights.

The relation between mothering person and child gives us a view of privacy very different from the usual one. We come to see that to be in a position where others are *not* making demands on us is a rare luxury, not a normal state. To be a mothering person is to be subjected to the continual demands and needs of others. And to be a child is to be subjected to the continual demands and expectations of others. Both mothering persons and children need to extricate themselves from the thick and heavy social fabric in which we are entwined in order to enjoy any pockets of privacy at all.

Here the picture we form of our individuality and the concept we form of a self is entirely different from the one we get if we start with the self-sufficient individual of the "state of nature." If we begin with the picture of rational contractor entering into agreements with others, the natural condition is seen as one of individuality and privacy, and the problem is the building of society and government. From the point of view of the relation between mothering person and child, the problem is the reverse. The starting condition is an enveloping tie, and the problem is individuating oneself. The task is to carve out a gradually increasing measure of privacy in ways appropriate to a constantly shifting interdependency. For the child, the problem is to become gradually more independent. For the mothering person, the problem is to free oneself from an all-consuming involvement. For both, the progression is from society to greater individuality rather than from self-sufficient individuality to contractual ties.

Psychology and psychoanalysis have long been interested in the process by which children develop and individuate themselves. Especially relevant now are feminist explorations of the differential development of a sense of self in boys and in girls and of a possibly different moral sense. Philosophers are beginning to consider the normative issues involved. And social philosophers are beginning to consider what we should think about social relations if we take women as our starting point. That we need not start with the patriarchal family in forming our concepts of society has been recognized for several centuries, ever since Locke won out over Filmer. That it might be instructive to begin with the point of view of women, and within that with the relation between mothering person and child, to try to reconceptualize society and our goals for better societies are new ideas. A new concept of the "self" may be at the heart of such reconceptualizations. That new concept of "self" or "person" should have as much significance for our views of politics and society, and for our conceptualizations of the supposedly "impersonal" and "public" domain distinct from the supposedly "personal" and "private" sphere of the family, as have the concept of the self as rational calculator and the conceptualization of society as contractual. The same real persons can act in and inhabit both marketplace and household contexts. It is up to them to decide what sorts of institutions to encourage for the sake of what sorts of persons.

The relation between mothering person and child also yields a new view of power. We are accustomed to thinking of power as something that can be wielded by one person over another, a means by which one person can bend another to his will. An ideal has been to equalize power so that agreements can be forged and conflicts defused. But consider now the very different view of power in the relation between mothering person and child. The superior power of the mothering person is relatively useless for most of what she aims to achieve in bringing up the child. The mothering person seeks to *empower* the child to act responsibly; she neither wants to "wield" power nor to defend herself against the power "wielded" by the child. Though the mothering person is relatively powerful in the traditional sense, the relative powerlessness of the child is largely irrelevant to most of the project of growing up. When the child is physically weakest, as in infancy and illness, the child can "command" the greatest amount of attention and care from the mothering person because of the urgency of the child's needs.

The mothering person's stance is characteristically one of caring, of being vulnerable to the needs and pains of the child, and of fearing the loss of the child before the child is ready for independence. Certainly it is not characteristically a stance of domination. The child's project is one of developing, of gaining ever greater control over his or her own life, of relying on the mothering person rather than of submitting to superior strength. Of course the relation may in a degenerate form be one of domination and submission, but in a form in which the relation between mothering person and child is even adequately exemplified, the conceptions of power with which we are familiar, from Hobbes and Locke to Hegel and Marx, are of little use in understanding the aspects of power involved in the relation.[27] The power of a mothering person to empower others, to foster transformative growth, is a different sort of power from that of a stronger sword or a dominant will. And the power of a child to call forth tenderness and care is perhaps more different still.

Mothering and Social Theory

A final aspect of the relation between mothering person and child about which I would like to speculate is what a focus on this relation might imply for our views of normative social and political theory.

Hobbes thought we could build society on the equal vulnerability of every man to the sword of his fellows. Women have never fit into that picture. We are more vulnerable to the sword. And yet the sword is powerless to create new wielders of it. Only the power of mothers can in the long run triumph. The power of mothers is, however, continually being eclipsed by the power of children.

The vulnerability of men may bring them to seek peace and to covenant against violence. We can hope for progress in curbing the murderous conflicts, tempered by truces and treaties, to which this vulnerability has led, though our expectations under current conditions must realistically be very modest.

But let us speculate about a different vulnerability and a different development. Mothering persons are certainly vulnerable to the demands and needs of children. We do not know whether this vulnerability is innate. Some claim that women lack a mothering instinct. Others claim that the experiences of carrying a child, of laboring and suffering to give birth, and of suckling inevitably cause mothers to be especially sensitive to the cries and needs of a child. Others claim that fathers, placed in the position of being the only persons capable of responding to the needs of a child, develop similar responsiveness. Whatever the truth, no one can become a mothering person without becoming sensitive to the needs of relatively helpless or less powerful others. And to become thus sensitive is to become vulnerable. If the vulnerability is chosen, so much the better. Mothering persons become in this way vulnerable to the claims of morality and to its social and political implications.

It is not, however, the morality of following abstract, universal rules so much as the morality of being responsive to the needs of actual, particular others in relations with us. The traditional view, reasserted by countless philosophers and others, that women are less likely than men to be guided by the highest forms of morality, would only be plausible if morality were no more than the abstract and rational rules of pure and perfect principle.[28] For traditional morality, increasingly recognizable as developed from a male point of view, there seems to be either the pure principle of the rational lawgiver or the self-interest of the individual contractor—the unreal universality of *all* or the real *self* of individual interest.

Both views lose sight of acting *for* particular others in actual contexts. Mothering persons cannot lose sight of the particularity of the child being mothered nor of the actuality of the circumstances in which the activity is taking place. Mothering persons may tend to resist harming or sacrificing those particular others for the sake of abstract principles or total faith; on the other hand, it is for the sake of *others* or for the sake of relationships between persons, rather than to further their own interests, that such resistance is presented by mothering persons. Morality, for mothering persons, must guide us in our relations with actual, particular children, enabling them to develop their own lives and commitments. For mothering persons, morality can never seem adequate if it offers no more than ideal rules for hypothetical situations: morality must connect with the actual context of real, particular others in need. At the same time, morality, for mothering persons, cannot possibly be a mere bargain between rational contractors. That morality in this context could not be based directly on self-interest or mutual lack of interest is obvious; that a contractual escape is unavailable or inappropriate is clear enough. And all of these points can have as strong implications for social and political morality and for questions of how institutions ought to be structured and social and political goals pursued as have the traditional moralities of egos in conflict and universal rules.

The morality that could offer guidance for those engaged in mothering might be a superior morality to those available at present. It would be a morality based on caring and concern for actual human others, and it would have to recognize the limitations of both egoism and perfect justice. If we turn to the social and political theories that would be compatible with such a view of morality, we see that they would have to be very different not only from the patriarchal models of precontractual conceptions but also from the contractual models that so dominate current thinking. Contractual relations would not be ruled out, but they would cease to seem paradigmatic of human relations, and the regions within which they could be thought to be justified would be greatly reduced.

The Child's Perspective

What about the point of view of the child? A most salient characteristic of the relation between mothering person and child is the child's relative powerlessness. The child cannot possibly rely on the Hobbesian safeguard of the equal vulnerability of the caretaker. Not even when the caretaker is asleep is she vulnerable to the sword of the small child, and it will be years, if ever, before the child can match the caretaker in even physical strength, let alone social and economic and psychological power. Whatever claims the child makes against a mothering person must be based on something other than superior strength, and the child should come to trust the restraint of one who could—but does not wish to—cause the child harm.

The child in relation to the mothering person is permanently in the best possible position from which to recognize that right is *not* equivalent to might, that power, including the power to teach and enforce a given morality, is not equivalent to morality itself. Becoming a person is not so much learning a morality that is being taught as it is developing the ability to decide for oneself what morality requires of one. Children characteristically go beyond the mothering persons in their lives to become autonomous beings. They do not typically respond to the mothering persons they leave behind with proposals for better bargains for themselves now that they have the power to enforce their terms. The relation between mothering person and child is such that disparity of power is a given. Though the positions may reverse themselves, unequal power is ever-present. But it is often also irrelevant to what matters in the relation.

When young men are invited to enter the public realm of contractual relations, they are encouraged to forget their past lack of power and to assume a position of equality or superiority. But we should probably none of us ever forget what it is like to be a child and to lack power. Taking the relation between child and mothering person as the primary social relation might encourage us to remember the point of view of those who cannot rely on the power of arms to uphold their moral claims. It might remind us of the distinction between the morality that, as mature autonomous persons, we come to construct for ourselves, and the moral injunctions which those with superior force can hold us to.

Models of Society

In an earlier paper, "Marx, Sex, and the Transformation of Society," I looked at the relation between man and woman, if transformed by love into a relation of mutual concern and respect, as a possible model for transformed relations in the wider society.[29] It now seems to me that this possibility is more remote and uncertain, and less illuminating as a model, than the relation between mothering person and child.

There are good reasons to believe that a society resting on no more than bargains between self-interested or mutually uninterested individuals will not be able to withstand the forces of egoism and dissolution pulling such societies apart. Although there may be some limited domains in which rational contracts are the appropriate form of social relations, as a foundation for the fundamental ties which ought to bind human beings together they are clearly inadequate. Perhaps we can learn from a nonpatriarchal household better than from further searching in the marketplace what the sources might be for justifiable trust, cooperation, and caring.

On the first occasion when I spoke about considering the relation between mothering person and child as the primary social relation, a young man in the audience asked who the mothers are and who the children are in society, by which he meant society outside the family. It was meant as a hostile question, but it is actually a very good one. The difficulty so many persons have in imagining an answer may indicate how distorted are the traditional contractual conceptions. Such persons can imagine a society on the model of economic man, a society built on a contract between rationally self-interested persons, because these are the theories they have been brought up with. They cannot imagine society resembling in any way a group of persons bound together by ongoing relations of caring and trust between persons in positions such as those of mothers and children where, as adults, we would sometimes be one and sometimes the other. The fear that so many adults feel of being treated like children may indicate a great deal about the deficiencies of actual parental practices and about the lack of respect and consideration accorded children much of the time. It does not indicate that all such conceptions are inappropriate.

Suppose now we ask, In the relation between mothering person and child, who are the rational contractors? Where is the rational self-interest? The model of economic man makes no sense in this context. Anyone in the social contract tradition who has noticed the relation of mothering person and child has supposed it to belong to some domain outside the realm of the free market and outside the public realm of politics and law. Such theorists have supposed the context of mothering to be of much less significance for human history and of much less relevance for moral theory than the realms of trade and government, or they have imagined mothers and children as somehow outside human society altogether in a region labeled "nature." But mothering and the development of children are at the heart of human society.

If the dynamic relation between mothering person and child is taken as the primary social relation, then it is the model of "economic man" that can be seen to be deficient as a model for society and morality, and unsuitable for all but a special context. A domain such as law, if built on no more than contractual foundations, can then be recognized as one limited domain among others; law protects some moral rights when people are too immoral or weak to respect them without the force of law. But it is hardly a majestic edifice that can serve as a model for morality. Neither can the domain of politics, if built on no more than self-interest or mutual lack of interest, and assuming and reflecting conflict of interest among all, provide us with a model with which to understand and improve morality and culture and society. Neither, even more clearly, can the market itself.

When we explore the implications of these speculations we may come to realize that instead of seeing the family as an anomalous island in a sea of rational contracts making up economic and political and social life, perhaps it is instead economic man who belongs on a relatively small island surrounded by social ties of a less hostile, cold, and precarious kind.

From a feminist perspective, existing society needs different descriptions from those it has received in the dominant traditions. Even more clearly, the society that should be reshaped by feminist moral inquiry and culture should be different from any we know, and from most so far envisioned. When we try to imagine the restructuring of society that feminism invites, we can see that every domain of society needs transformation, from the military, law, politics, and economic activity, to cultural production, education, the health and welfare systems, and the family. And then we can see that not only would every domain need to be transformed, but so also would the relationships between them. Some which have been central and dominant might become peripheral and less important. Others which have been peripheral would become the very center of our attention and the dominant concern of society. Instead of a society determined by violent conflict modified by the authority and restraints of law and preoccupied with economic gain, we might have a society which saw as its *most* important task the flourishing of children and the creation of human relationships worthy of the aspirations of the children who will become women as well as men.

Epilogue:

The Feminist Future

Lamentations about the decline of the social order, or Western Civilization, or the United States, abound. We are told repeatedly that stability is crumbling, that the center cannot hold, that the sources of authority have been undermined. In the despairing words of a recent essay, "Many regard our epoch as a post age. Postindustrial, postcapitalist, postliberal, posttheological, posthumanist—these posts join in the description of our condition as postmodern. In the postmodern era, God is dead; art is exhausted; philosophy is finished; literature is merely preserved."[1] If the discussion is more specifically about the United States, the decline is asserted, or feared, or predicted; if it is challenged, it is recognized nonetheless as a grave danger.

Although there are indeed extremely serious problems plaguing the United States, and Western civilization, and the world, it is often unclear how much such lamentations reflect genuine concern about the difficulties of confronting such problems, and how much they reflect nostalgia for unchallenged dominance by established male elites.[2]

Andreas Huyssen's description of turn-of-the-century associations between fear of the masses and fear of the feminine lends support to this conjecture. Over and over, the masses were identified with women, true culture with men:

> The notion . . . gained ground during the nineteenth century that mass culture is somehow associated with woman while real, authentic culture remains the prerogative of men . . . When the 19th and early 20th centuries conjured up the threat of the masses 'rattling at the gate,' to quote Hall . . . the masses knocking at the gate were also women . . . It is indeed striking to observe how the political, psychological, and aesthetic discourse around the turn of the century consistently and obsessively genders mass culture and the masses as feminine, while high culture, whether traditional or modern, clearly remains the privileged realm of male activities.[3]

215

The Decline of the Past

Perhaps many of the changes we are seeing in contemporary society and culture reflect the decline of male dominance. It is probably true that the conceptual order of the barracks community is threatened, that the stability of masculine supremacy is being undermined, and that the traditional hierarchy of gender is in danger. Male dominance is surely being challenged. Few feminists will lament the decline of the old order of gender or pay heed to the attempts of some defenders of that order to blame feminism for the problems of the contemporary world. Feminists are indeed in the process of reshaping human relationships and rebuilding human lives; women are indeed changing our relationships with men, with children, with each other, and with the world. All the structures of thought that permeate human life and all the social arrangements that uphold male dominance are being reevaluated. But this is a promising renewal, an occasion for hope. If we are entering a postpatriarchal era, an era in which male domination will be overturned, that will be reason for rejoicing.

In reviewing four books on the decline of the United States, Paul Kennedy, himself the author of a book on the rise and fall of national power, made no mention of the women's movement or even of the civil rights movement.[4] This lack of attention is characteristic of many discussions of the lamented decline facing the United States and the West, unless these movements are themselves taken as signs of the decline. Putting aside the conservative nostalgia of the latter views, let's consider the attempts to evaluate the rise or fall of societies without considering the situation of women and minorities in them. From a feminist point of view, this neglect is even more culpable than evaluating the standing of societies without considering the place in them, say, of the idea of democracy and how movements for democracy where it does not yet exist are likely to affect the strength of such a society and whether it should be thought of as "ascendant" or "in decline." Clearly, global standing should involve normative evaluation as well as estimates of power divorced from moral condition.

To replace the order of male domination with gender equality would be even more fundamental than replacing the order of feudalism with democratic institutions. There can be little doubt that movement toward the latter has had profound effects on a society's place in the world; movement toward the former is no doubt doing so now.

The question of whom a nation is "stronger" for is of course relevant.

And the ways societies allow for and handle social change are important in affecting their health. We need to ask, too, whether societies with high levels of gender and racial domination should retain their traditional strength, or whether a decrease represents, on the contrary, global progress. A feminist point of view enables us to deal with all these issues quite differently from the way they are typically treated.[5] Rather than fin-de-siècle despair, we can look forward to a less brutal world. We do not seek the return of past glories longed for by conservatives; they never were glories for us. We may not share the fear of many liberals that change is getting out of hand; for us, it is often too slow. Many entrenched concentrations of power such as the corporate and governmental structures that sustain male dominance and the cultural and educational institutions that reflect and support these structures show too few signs of change. The prospect of their yielding to feminist criticism and maternal sanity can be welcomed by everyone.

The changes which feminism and the women's movement have brought about in recent years and throughout the world have been revolutionary.[6] But they have involved on the part of women little vengeance and virtually no violence. They have built on the experience of women, on the practices and traditions of women reflectively analyzed, and on the thought and imagination of feminism experimentally put into practice. These changes have the potential to transform culture and thus society and to create a future that will be better for all children.

The threat of violence against women seeking change is real and alarming, but violence against women has been there all along. Means are being developed to combat it more effectively than in the past and to keep it from being concealed. Revolutions, it is true, cannot occur without pain, and women, as well as men, have suffered it. But by now very many women can attest to the changes having been well worth the pain. And many men are coming to appreciate rather than to resist the experience of mutuality with women and the joys of building such better relationships with their children as can only be achieved through involvement in their daily care. Many men want to share in developing the feminist future; those who do not may well be left behind.

The Future of Feminist Moral Inquiry

If we begin with the recommendations about feminist morality discussed in chapters 2, 3, and 4, and include the rethinking of culture and society and politics discussed in subsequent chapters, what might their implications be for the future?

I argued in my book *Rights and Goods* that we need different moral approaches for different domains of society, and those arguments seem still valid. The type of moral approach suitable for respecting rights in a legal context is not the best type for choosing various governmental policies. And the type of moral approach suitable for decisions in an economic marketplace is not the type best suited to decisions among family members and friends. I advocated a division of moral labor in which we would accept different moral considerations as salient for different domains of human activity, and I tried to delineate the approaches suitable for various domains.

However, such a view still leaves us with the difficulty of integrating the various approaches recommended and deciding which approach to follow for a specific problem when the approaches seem to conflict. It can be a serious difficulty, and we can hope that perhaps a feminist approach to morality can provide the framework or the more comprehensive moral theory within which the more specialized approaches can be fitted. But can feminist moral theory serve in this way to unify other approaches? Can it incorporate, for instance, a Kantian approach for law, a utilitarian approach for public policy, an approach permitting a considerable degree of self-interested choice in the marketplace, and so forth? Can a feminist morality provide the sorts of recommendations suitable for those domains in which women have not been the primary moral agents, or will it be limited to such domains as the family, early education, and caring for the sick and elderly? Can feminist moral theory be the sort of theory that can, where nonfeminist theory cannot, appropriately provide recommendations for all domains and all contexts?

At the very least, feminist moral approaches will elevate to moral significance those contexts and problems neglected by nonfeminist moral theory, requiring that *any* moral theory claiming to be applicable to all moral problems be scrutinized for its suitability for handling problems within the family, and in the context of giving care. Many traditional moral theories will fail this test. But feminist moral approaches will be more ambitious: they will ask for a reconsideration of all those other domains, such as of law and state and market, where moral principles recommended by nonfeminist moral theories have been thought applicable. They will ask how these domains might have to be reconstructed and transformed in the light of feminist approaches to morality. Since the latter are characteristically respectful of context, they may well allow what appear to be various traditional moral principles to be salient in various particular domains, if they can be embedded in a wider approach compatible with feminist concerns. But feminist approaches are not likely to lose sight of the way these principles should be limited to particular domains rather than generalized to all moral problems. To argue, for instance, that utilitarian recommendations to maximize the preference satisfaction of individuals can be suitable for certain governmental policy choices is not at all to subscribe to a utilitarian moral theory for all moral problems. But a feminist approach to morality might agree that after its requirements and most urgent goals had been met—for the flourishing of children, say—then perhaps utilitarian principles would be the appropriate ones to employ in a limited region of human activity. This would, however, be because utilitarian principles in this domain could be justified in terms of feminist moral inquiry, not because, as utilitarianism has characteristically claimed, the right course of action is always just what will maximize the satisfaction of individuals.

Since feminist approaches to morality are suspicious of rather than eager to offer highly abstract theories and simple principles, they are more likely to emphasize methods of moral inquiry and processes of moral improvement than to propound finished, comprehensive theories. But feminist approaches to morality will seek, I believe, to develop patterns of moral concern and expression suitable for any and all contexts. Then, within these patterns, more limited recommendations may be acceptable for particular domains.

For instance, a feminist approach might hold that within a pattern of morality recognizing a more satisfactory, relational concept of persons, it is acceptable to treat persons, in some contexts and some of the time, as if the artificially abstract individualistic terms of the Kantian and utilitarian traditions were satisfactory for that domain. As long as we do not lose sight of the way we are abstracting from reality, and as long as we keep our understanding of the limited aspects of this way of thinking, we may find the use of individualistic liberal conceptions to be a helpful device.

Similar arguments could be made about various nonfeminist moral principles. Such abstract principles as those of freedom and equality may well be acceptable for various domains if embedded in patterns of morality arrived at through the course of feminist moral inquiry. But what the latter can be expected to provide is an understanding of which principles are suitable for which contexts, and why traditional nonfeminist moral principles that have been claimed to be universally valid are often not suitable for many contexts when the experience of women is accorded its proper due.

Let us now try to develop further what some feminist recommendations for the future might include.

Conceptualizing Feminist Society

First, how should we conceptualize feminist society? The major prefeminist conceptions include three alternative views.

(1) Law is supreme. Whatever the law does not forbid, it permits; thus law covers everything. The state has a monopoly on the legitimate use of violence to uphold law. The state enforces law and thus has ultimate authority in the society. Economic activity and cultural production and education are permitted to develop under law as participants in them choose; they are not directly controlled by the state but may be regulated by it. Government is legitimate only if it rests on the consent of the governed (who are formally or effectively male heads of household); when it does, it is supreme. This is a picture of society offered by, among others, the liberal tradition of political thought.

(2) The economic base determines everything else in society. A capitalist economic system will have a capitalist state, law that upholds capitalist economic relations, and a government that reflects the economic interests of the dominant class. Cultural production and educational institutions will be structured to reinforce the economic system. Society is built on an economic foundation and the means and relations of production in this foundation bring about the characteristics of other segments of society. This is the model of society provided, roughly, by Marxist analyses.

(3) The segments of society are overlapping but relatively independent; none determines or is supreme over all others. The political system can be distinguished from the economic system, but neither determines the other; other segments of society such as the cultural or the educational are also distinguishable and relatively independent. Society is seen as pluralistic with multiple sources of influence. Interests conflict; none overpower with regularity. A number of recent empirical theories in sociology and political science present this depiction of society.

None of these familiar descriptions of society includes recognition of the centrality of the gender structure of society. A feminist description of past and current social reality will assure that gender will be attended to as a central factor organizing society in fundamental and pervasive ways, and feminist evaluations of society will include assessments of the aspects of gender in them. Feminist recommendations for the future may show why the influence of gender should be greatly reduced as we strive for a society that is genuinely democratic. Or we may recommend that the values incorporated in the gender structure be transformed so that feminist concerns have priority.

To say that feminist concerns should have priority is not to advocate female dominance or a replacement of men by women in the gender structure of existing societies. Among feminist values is a rejection of domination itself. As we have seen repeatedly, most feminists do not aim to integrate women on equal terms into the structures of male-dominated society; we seek to change these structures into ones hospitable to and reflective of feminist values. Among the implications of a feminist aim to overcome domination are, in my view, as I have argued in this book, a commitment to the liberation of culture and to the development of social arrangements that will shape the future of society through cultural imagination and free discussion rather than through organized violence and economic power.

Of the three conceptions referred to, the first—a pyramidal one—is incompatible with a feminist view of how society ought to be organized. It unduly elevates, for law, a supremacy brought about by force, and it unduly privileges the power of the state to determine the shape of society. It ignores the coercion produced by economic power, and it overlooks the unsuitability of law and legalistic approaches for dealing with a wide range of human problems. As description, it seems to miss many other important sources of influence in society, such as social movements and cultural innovation, as well as family relationships and racial or ethnic or other group ties.

The view that an economic foundation determines all the layers of society built upon it also seems inadequate from a feminist point of view. It is descriptively insufficient and normatively pallid. Surely there are political forces other than economic effects. And the women's movement itself has shown the influence of changed consciousness on social change. Although the surge of women into the labor force has undoubtedly been a strong influence on that consciousness and on the women's movement, at least some of the shift of women from the household to the workplace has been brought about by consciously chosen values rather than by economic causes. And Marxism cannot explain such aspects of the women's movement as the resistance to the sexual objectification of women and the determination to oppose rape, sexual harassment, and domestic violence. Moreover, the society for which feminists strive will be one going far beyond the ending of economic class privilege.

The third view—that of society as composed of partially overlapping but relatively independent domains or segments—is more compatible

221

with feminist views of society than the others. It is unsatisfactory all the same: not only has it ignored the structure of gender domination that affects all these segments, as have the other models, but it may obscure even more than the others do the way domination has operated throughout society.

Let us imagine a feminist alternative to these views. To understand society as it exists at present, a feminist view would first of all recognize the centrality and pervasiveness of the gender structure of society. It would see the way male dominance operates throughout society. Now let us suppose male dominance were to be overcome. What would all the different segments of society be like, and what would the relations between them be like? How they fit together would in all likelihood be transformed as would each domain. Is there any point in trying to imagine all this?

Much philosophical and theoretical effort has been devoted to prescribing ideal liberal alternatives to existing society. But the elaborate delineation of ideal societies of perfect justice, an enterprise which has dominated mainstream political philosophy for some time, has seemed to many critics to be of limited usefulness. Annette Baier has expressed this position:

> Descriptions of ideal societies imply nothing about how to act in this society. Even if one derives the vague injunction to act so as to change the actual society in the direction of the ideal one, one is still left with all the hard questions concerning how one is to do it . . . Is one to sacrifice only oneself for one's cause, or drag others with one? Is one to lie, cheat, and kill so that there can be a society without liars, cheats, or killers? Knowing what sort of society a utilitarian or a contractarian would deem satisfactory tells us nothing about our or their duty now, in this society.[7]

Many feminists have shared these reservations about ideal theory along with our objections to the various ideals promoted.[8] It may thus be appropriate that I am devoting only a very few pages of this book to questions of what an ideal feminist society might be like. From the point of view of many of the draining political struggles which need to be fought in society as it is, such a utopian sketch might appear distracting. Countless women struggle to survive, and to allow children to survive, in economic conditions that became even more grim in the Reagan-Bush era than they were before the women's movement. When women need desperately to have actual conditions improve, ideal conditions may seem irrelevantly remote.[9] Still, to the extent that a tentative depiction of goals to be sought is useful to guide cultural and political effort and to lend it encouragement, its absence may be missed. Images of possible feminist society should be part of the cultural stage.

Looking Ahead

Suppose we change the gender domination the previously outlined conceptualizations of society obscure. We might then be left with some segments of society relatively intact and distinguishable from other segments—a democratic political system, say, with true equality for women at all levels. But if all such segments are infused with feminist values, and if all are embedded in a society hospitable to feminism, then the relative positions of the segments might change in fundamental ways, as well as many of their internal characteristics.

A feminist society would be fundamentally different from a society composed of individuals each pursuing his own interest, especially his own economic interest, and evaluating public institutions by how well they facilitate or contribute to his own advancement—the traditional model of liberal and pluralistic society. It would be different as well from Marxist conceptions of society with their neglect of the issues of women and the family, and different as well from conservative communitarian views with their upholding of patriarchy.

Feminist society might be seen as having various relatively independent and distinct segments, with some not traditionally thought of as especially central and influential now being so, and with all such segments embedded in a wider network of social relations characterized by social caring and trust. Certainly the levels of caring and trust appropriate for the relations of all members of society with all others will be different from the levels appropriate for the members of a family with one another. But social relations in what can be thought of as society as a whole will not be characterized by indifference to the well-being of others, or an absence of trust, as they are in many nonfeminist conceptions. What kinds and amounts of caring and trust might characterize the relations of the most general kind in society should be decided on the basis of experience and practice with institutions that have overcome male dominance.

From the point of view of the self-interested head of household, the individual's interest in his own family may be at odds with the wider political and public interest. And aspects of mothering in patriarchal society have contributed to parochialism and racism. But from a satisfactorily worked-out feminist and moral point of view, the picture of the particularistic family in conflict with the good of society is distorted. The postpatriarchal family can express universal emotions and can be guided by universally shared concerns. A content and healthy child eager to learn and to love elicits general approval. A child whose distress can be prevented or alleviated should elicit universal efforts to deal with the distress and prevent its recurrence. Any feminist society can be expected to cherish new persons, seeing in the face and body of a child both the specialness of a unique person and the universal features of a child's wonder and curiosity and hope. It should seek to build institutions and practices and a world worthy of that hope, and needed for each child to flourish.

Although feminist society would be likely to have democratic political processes, an independent judicial system to handle the recalcitrant, and markets to organize some economic activity, these and other institutions would be evaluated in terms of how well they worked to achieve feminist goals. And other segments of society might be recognized as far more central in doing so. Cultural expression would continually evaluate imaginative alternatives for consideration. It would provide entertainment not primarily to serve commercial interests or to relieve for a few hours the distress of persons caught in demeaning and exploitative jobs or with no jobs at all, but to enrich the lives of respected members of cultural and social communities.

The major implications of a feminist ethic on such areas of human activity traditionally noticed as having specifically moral significance—the state, the law, and the market—might be to limit drastically their influence rather than to change completely the principles by which they are guided. Consider the principles of democracy on which there is such widespread agreement around the globe. A feminist ethic would almost surely agree that government should be founded on the consent of the governed, though it might require the consent to be interpreted in actual rather than hypothetical terms.[10] But as soon as we moved to questions of what government should do, we would hear questions about the reach of law and of bureaucratic authority, as well as questions about adequate social support for the kinds of social activity a feminist ethic would recognize ought to be undertaken. And a feminist approach would differ significantly from a nonfeminist one. If nongovernmental efforts do not succeed in meeting needs, government should be called on to do so itself. Everyone should have, by right, access to the means to live and to develop. On the other hand, government might often do better to empower families—in various and expanded senses—to provide for their members rather than to multiply its own bureaucratic layers.

With respect to many social programs, the United States is especially backward compared with those industrialized countries which have a background of strong social democratic influence. A comparison of provisions for maternal health care, child care, parental leave, and early education makes this clear.[11] Certainly a feminist view of how society ought to be restructured may have a harder time realizing its goals in a society as ideologically overcommitted to capitalism as is the United States. But in other ways, such as awareness of sexual victimization, feminist transformations may have gone further in the United States than elsewhere. In any case, all societies will need fundamental change along feminist lines. And the changes to improve the future of children should be motivated not by the desire to win the competition, which may now be the economic competition with Japan and Germany rather than the military competition with the Soviet Union but by the understanding that all children deserve the care that will enable them to flourish.

A society organized along feminist lines might put the proper care and suitable development of all children at the very center of its concerns. Instead of allowing, as so often at present, family policies and arrangements for child care and for the education and health of children to be marginal concerns, vastly less important than military strength and corporate profits, a feminist society might understand the future of children to be its highest priority. As the children grew up with the levels of concern and attention needed for all to flourish and with feminist values guiding their development, the needs for the traditional functions of state power might greatly diminish; fewer children would grow up to be lawbreakers or irresponsible agents in need of ever more detailed legislative restraints.

Among the most important transformations needed in the ways human beings organize their lives are changes in prevailing relationships between "man" and "nature." Feminists have shown the connections between the attitudes that nature is to be conquered and dominated and the association of nature with the feminine. Prior to the sixteenth century, there had been a reluctance to violate an earth seen as a generative and nurturing mother. But by the seventeenth century, sexual metaphors burgeoned: the earth was seen as a female to be dominated, a woman who should be mastered.[12] Many feminists believe that there remain connections between men's domination of women and their exploitation and destruction of the environment, and that achieving respect for nature will require achieving respect for women.[13] Feminist concerns for the well-being of future children include awareness of the urgent need for harmonious relationships between human beings and the global environment.

Of course feminist moralities and the arrangements they will recommend will not of themselves provide solutions to all problems, but they may make remarkable contributions compared to previous moralities and arrangements.

From Family to Society

Long before we reach anything resembling feminist society we can indicate the directions, from where we are, that a feminist ethic would suggest we move in. We need to consider how we should connect a feminist morality most appropriate for moral problems that arise within a family, or among persons with close ties to one another, with what we think of as the moral foundations of the state, law, politics, and interactions among strangers. A feminist ethic will not be blind to the need for procedural principles to settle disputes among strangers or to the appeal of principles of justice and equality as prima facie starting points for reaching agreements among conflicting positions. And a feminist ethic will of course be concerned with increasing the general happiness. But a feminist ethic will never forget that such principles and starting points and concerns should not be more than a part, perhaps a rather small part, of morality. A feminist ethic will not try to generalize these principles and approaches to all other domains.

Generalizing from the "public" domain of law and politics to the whole of morality has been the dominant tendency of philosophical ethics in the modern era. In Bernard Williams's view, the development of the rationalistic moralities exemplified by Kantian and utilitarian moral theories was not based on people's own experience but on certain "social features of the modern world, which impose on personal deliberation and on the idea of practical reason itself a model drawn from a particular understanding of public rationality." This ideal of rationality has been made to look as if it has been independently arrived at and then applied to the public world; instead, Williams argues, this way of thinking needed by modern political life has been imposed on personal life and imagined to be satisfactory for all of ethics.[14]

Peter Railton's interpretation of the rise of morality based on what an abstract, rational individual might agree to, or on the moral law such individuals might give to themselves, is similar:

> Expanding social and political units brought within single regimes
> or polities substantially heterogeneous populations. After the Euro-

pean wars of religion, for example, the emerging national societies had to contend in their public discourse with considerable diversity in the population's background beliefs, values, and norms. If mutually beneficial co-operation—including the cessation of hostilities—was to be secured, the most effective terms in which that benefit could find expression might be rather abstract and general, or be addressed to individuals seen in an abstract and general way . . . The abstract individual of modern normative theory is in a number of ways modeled upon the abstract citizen of the modern nation-state, where the possibility of securing mutual restraint and civil peace by drawing on richly articulated community values and norms, or upon shared understandings of the place and purpose of individuals . . . has receded.[15]

The ways in which utilitarian and rational choice theories reflect a generalization to the moral level of assumptions and motivations thought suitable for the marketplace can also be discerned. The moral agent must consider the interests of others as well as of himself, but the starting assumptions of discrete individuals with their conflicting interests are carried over from the economic realm to the realm of moral theory.

Any feminist ethic will be likely to resist such expansions as these of moral concepts and approaches developed for law and politics and the marketplace. And it will call for significant rethinking of them for the legal and political and economic domains themselves.

It is certainly true, as Marilyn Friedman and Susan Okin argue, that justice is relevant to arrangements within the family. The fact that so often "men do not serve women as women serve men" is a violation of distributive justice; wife battering and child abuse are occasions for corrective justice.[16] But we can at the same time recognize that justice in the family sets little more than the moral minimums to be observed. Bringing this about is no easy matter; still, most of what families should provide is in a range over and above these moral minimums. Building relations of trust and consideration far exceeds what justice can assure. When we consider the activity of mothering we see how many of its values are "beyond justice." The activity is not a one-way giving that can be divided up equally between women and men, though many of the minimal tasks involved can and should be. As Nel Noddings writes, "Infants contribute to the mother-child relationships by responding in characteristic (and idiosyncratic) ways to their mothers." Their smiles and attention contribute to the relation and show how mutuality or reciprocity can characterize relations even when one member is weaker than another. In Noddings's view, "much of the energy required to maintain caring relations comes from the cared for."[17]

Certainly the activity of mothering can be exploitative if women are confined to it or expected to perform it at the expense of pursuing other activities. But the activity itself is potentially among the most humanly promising, as it allows future persons to flourish and satisfying human relationships to grow. Friedman emphasizes that relationships can be exploitative and harmful as well as enriching, and she suggests that our aim should be "to advance 'beyond caring,' that is, beyond *mere* caring dissociated from a concern for justice."[18] We can agree that caring relationships need a floor of justice if they lack it. But what those who seek to develop an ethic of care often suggest is that we should progress beyond mere justice, which has been so dominant a focus of so much traditional moral theory.[19] And we need to do this not only within the family, where care has prevailed and justice has not, but in the society as well.

Of course there will remain occasions for the application of law and occasions for bureaucratic decision making. But these occasions might be greatly reduced in a feminist society in comparison with their current sway. Feminists are reconceptualizing the roles and meanings of friendship and community and political life. Kathleen Jones, for example, suggests how a transformed conception of "citizenship" will be needed for a "woman-friendly polity." She notes that "in place of the more distant and alienated interactions of citizens of bureaucratic systems," various feminists have proposed more intimate forms of interaction and "have based models of political life on idealized models of the family and on friendship groups. In this analysis affective ties replace functional ones as the cement of the social order, the creative development of personality substitutes for the pursuit of instrumental goals, and a shared sense of community takes the place of the competitive norms of capitalist culture. Similarly, trust supplants suspicion as the motivating political impulse."[20] To an appreciable extent, the citizen becomes sister or friend.

How do we connect feminist moral approaches with the principles of the market and with the contractual transactions between strangers that comprise such an overwhelming part of economic activity in industrialized societies? Again, a feminist ethic may agree that market principles are suitable for *some* transactions, but it is highly unlikely to be willing to generalize these principles to many other domains than the economic, or even to agree that they are suitable for all or most economic activity.[21] Many enterprises would gain if they resembled families more and groups of hostile strangers less. Many economic transactions are not between strangers but between fellow inhabitants of a neighborhood or fellow participants in an endeavor; and all persons have reason to share a concern with what their economic activity is doing to the environment and with how to harmonize it with the future needs of their communities and the world. That having ties and concerns such as these leads persons to depart from rather than to conform to the "laws of the market" is often a morally superior rather than inferior situation—as a feminist ethic would readily recognize.

The Cultural Shaping of Feminist Society

To a large extent we cannot discern the feminist future because we are entering unexplored territory, and we need and want to be open to what our new experiences suggest. Our practices are experiments in living differently, in experiencing our sexuality in new ways, in trying to order our societies in ways they have heretofore not been ordered, in thinking anew about almost everything, in expressing culturally and celebrating some changes, and calling for others. Our theories analyze and evaluate these practices and recommend others.

There are many reasons to think the feminist future needs to be and can be expected to be developed gradually, on the basis of lived experience, with openness to new possibilities, and a deep sense of responsibility for living children, future generations, and global well-being. After all, mothers have been bringing up children well enough while the structures of thought and of art, the clashes of armies and struggles of classes, paid hardly any attention. A feminist future in which feminist moral inquiry and culture reshape the organization of society will require fundamental reorderings and rethinkings of existing practices and theories. The changes will be enormous, but there are many reasons to think both women and men will swim in them rather than drown.

Feminist transformations of culture and society are unlike any previous transformations. Probably we should not try to map out the future of feminist culture and society any more than we should map out the future of a child. We can specify certain essential conditions that ought to be assured for the child to be well and capable and headed in some admirable directions. We can hope to have helped the child develop, and, with love in our hearts, we can hope to be able to watch the child live. But the future will be for the child to make, and the same can be said of the feminist future.

Notes

Chapter 1

1. Flora Davis, author of *Moving the Mountain: The Women's Movement in America since 1960* (New York: Simon and Schuster, 1991), interviewed by Jacqueline Shaheen, "The Women's Movement, Then and Now," *New York Times*, New Jersey edition, 8 March 1992, 3.

2. Although I think of them as part of the more comprehensive women's movement, I here speak of "women's movements" in the plural, since those of black women or lesbians or Latinas, for instance, have often been based on different patterns of organization and expression.

3. Conversation with Sara Ruddick has been helpful in developing my views here.

4. For a brief account, see F. Davis, *Moving the Mountain*, chaps. 10 and 19.

5. See Gail Warshofsky Lapidus, *Women in Soviet Society: Equality, Development, and Social Change* (Berkeley: University of California Press, 1978). See also Rochelle Ruthchild, review of *Soviet Women: Walking the Tightrope*, by Francine duPlessix Gray, *Women's Review of Books* 8 (December 1990): 25–26; and Slavenka Drakulic, *How We Survived Communism and Even Laughed* (New York: Norton, 1992).

6. Arthur C. Danto, *Connections to the World* (New York: Harper and Row, 1989), 274.

7. Sheila Rowbothan, "The Trouble with 'Patriarchy,'" *New Statesman* 21 (8 December 1979): 970; and Carole Pateman, *The Sexual Contract* (Stanford, Calif.: Stanford University Press, 1988), 20.

8. Alison M. Jaggar, *Feminist Politics and Human Nature* (Totowa, N.J.: Rowman and Allanheld, 1983).

9. Ann Ferguson, *Blood at the Root: Motherhood, Sexuality and Male Domination* (London: Pandora, 1989). Ferguson explains the difference between (2) and (3), which are often confused.

10. A. Ferguson, *Blood at the Root*, 102; Carol Brown, "Mothers, Fathers, and Children: From Private to Public Patriarchy," in *Women and Revolution*, ed. Lydia Sargent (Boston: South End Press, 1981). See also Carole Pateman, "The Patriarchal Welfare State," in *The Disorder of Women: Democracy, Feminism and Political Theory* (Stanford, Calif.: Stanford University Press. 1989).

11. Mary Field Belenky et al., eds., *Women's Ways of Knowing: The Development of Self, Voice, and Mind* (New York: Basic Books, 1986).

12. I avoid the term 'standpoint' here because I think it unnecessary for my purposes to become engaged in the debate within feminism concerning standpoint theory. See Nancy C. M. Hartsock, *Money, Sex, and Power: Toward a Feminist Historical Materialism* (New York: Longman, 1983); and Alison Wylie, "The Philosophy of Ambivalence: Sandra

Harding on *The Science Question in Feminism*," in *Science, Morality and Feminist Theory*, ed. Marsha Hanen and Kai Nielsen (Calgary: University of Calgary Press, 1987).

13. Catherine A. MacKinnon, *Toward a Feminist Theory of the State* (Cambridge: Harvard University Press, 1989), 83, 98, 121.

14. On conceptualizing culture, I have found helpful Margaret S. Archer, *Culture and Agency: The Place of Culture in Social Theory* (Cambridge, Eng.: Cambridge University Press, 1988); Clifford Geertz, *The Interpretation of Cultures* (New York: Basic Books, 1973); and E. Valentine Daniel; *Fluid Signs: Being a Person the Tamil Way* (Berkeley: University of California Press, 1984).

15. C. Geertz, *Interpretation of Cultures*, 89.

16. Richard Johnson, "What Is Cultural Studies Anyway?" *Social Text: Theory/Culture/ Ideology* 16 (Winter 1986–87): 43.

17. See Sandra Harding, "Why Has the Sex/Gender System Become Visible Only Now?" in *Discovering Reality: Feminist Perspectives on Epistemology, Metaphysics, Methodology, and Philosophy of Science*, ed. Sandra Harding and Merrill B. Hintikka (Dordrecht, Holland: Reidel, 1983).

18. Frederic Jameson, "Postmodernism, or the Cultural Logic of Late Capitalism," *New Left Review* 146 (July-August 1984): 53–93; and Dana Polan, "Brief Encounters: Mass Culture and the Evacuation of Sense," in *Studies in Entertainment: Critical Approaches to Mass Culture*, ed. Tania Modleski (Bloomington: Indiana University Press, 1986), 181.

19. Patricia Mellencamp, "Video Politics: Guerrilla TV, Ant Farm, Eternal Frame," *Discourse: Journal for Theoretical Studies in Media and Culture* 10 (Spring-Summer 1988): 94.

20. See Jane Flax, "Gender as a Social Problem: In and for Feminist Theory," *Amerikastudien/American Studies* 31: 193–213; Nancy Fraser, "Michel Foucault: A 'Young Conservative'?" *Ethics* 96 (October 1985): 165–84; and Nancy Fraser and Linda J. Nicholson, "Social Criticism without Philosophy: An Encounter between Feminism and Postmodernism," in *Feminism/Postmodernism*, ed. Linda J. Nicholson (New York: Routledge, 1990).

21. For a discussion of the differences between postmodernism and poststructuralism, see Andreas Huyssen, *After the Great Divide: Modernism, Mass Culture, Postmodernism* (Bloomington: Indiana University Press, 1986), chap. 10.

22. Catharine R. Stimpson, *Where The Meanings Are: Feminism and Cultural Spaces* (New York: Routledge, 1990), 191.

23. Linda Alcoff, "Cultural Feminism versus Post-Structuralism: The Identity Crisis in Feminist Theory," *Signs: Journal of Women in Culture and Society*, 13 (Spring 1988): 419.

24. For various reasons why a stand against essentialism should not become a strict methodological requirement for feminist inquiry, see Elizabeth Rapaport, "Generalizing Gender: Reason and Essence in the Legal Thought of Catharine MacKinnon," in *A Mind of One's Own: Feminist Essays on Reason and Objectivity*, ed. Louise Antony and Charlotte Witt (Boulder, Colo: Westview Press, 1992); and Jane Roland Martin, "Methodological Essentialism and Other Dangerous Traps," Paper presented to Society for Women in Philosophy, New York City, December 1991.

25. Alison M. Jaggar, "Feminist Ethics: Projects, Problems, Prospects," in *Feminist Ethics*, ed. Claudia Card (Lawrence: University Press of Kansas, 1991), 95.

26. Lynda Lange, "On (Re)Claiming Feminism: Postmodern Doubts and Political Amnesia" Paper presented at the annual meeting of the American Philosophical Association, Central Division, Chicago, April 1991.

27. Susan Bordo, "Feminism, Postmodernism, and Gender-Scepticism," in *Feminism/ Postmodernism*, ed. L. Nicholson, 143, 145.

28. Mary E. Hawkesworth, "Knowers, Knowing, Known: Feminist Theory and Claims of Truth," *Signs* 14 (Spring 1989): 557.

29. L. Lange, "On (Re)Claiming Feminism."

30. Susan Hekman, "Reconstituting the Subject: Feminism, Modernism, and Postmodernism," *Hypatia: A Journal of Feminist Philosophy* 6 (Summer 1991): 44–63. Among those expressing the doubts referred to is Nancy C. M. Hartsock, "Rethinking Modernism: Minority vs. Majority Theories," *Cultural Critique* 7 (1987): 187–202.

31. S. Hekman, "Reconstituting the Subject," 59.

32. Nancy C. M. Hartsock, "Postmodernism and Political Change: Issues for Feminist Theory," *Cultural Critique* 14 (Winter 1989–90): 23, 32.

33. Nancy C. M. Hartsock, "Foucault on Power: A Theory for Women?" in *Feminism/ Postmodernism*, ed. L. Nicholson, 160.

34. Ailbhe Smyth, "A (Political) Postcard from a Peripheral Pre-Postmodern State (of Mind) or How Alliteration and Parentheses Can Knock You Down Dead in Women's Studies," *Women's Studies International Forum* 15 (May-June 1992): 331–37.

35. See A. Huyssen, *After the Great Divide*, viii–x.

36. For extended argument, see Virginia Held, *Rights and Goods: Justifying Social Action* (New York: Free Press, 1984).

37. See Elizabeth V. Spelman, *Inessential Woman: Problems of Exclusion in Feminist Thought* (Boston: Beacon Press, 1988).

38. For discussion of related arguments, see Sandra Harding, *The Science Question in Feminism* (Ithaca, N.Y.: Cornell University Press, 1986).

39. See Cherrie Moraga and Gloria Anzaldua, eds., *This Bridge Called My Back: Writings by Radical Women of Color* (New York: Kitchen Table Press, 1981), and *All the Women Are White, All the Blacks Are Men, But Some of Us Are Brave*, ed. Gloria T. Hull, Patricia Bell Scott, and Barbara Smith (New York: Feminist Press, 1982). See also bell hooks, *Feminist Theory: from Margin to Center* (Boston: South End Press, 1984); and Patricia Hill Collins, *Black Feminist Thought: Knowledge, Consciousness, and the Politics of Empowerment* (Boston: Unwin Hyman, 1990).

On how debates within feminism can contribute to the energy and strength of feminism rather than be divisive and disempowering, see *Conflicts in Feminism*, ed. Marianne Hirsch and Evelyn Fox Keller (New York: Routledge, 1990).

40. Emily Martin, *The Woman in the Body: A Cultural Analysis of Reproduction* (Boston: Beacon Press, 1987), 4.

41. See Dorothy Dinnerstein, *The Mermaid and the Minotaur: Sexual Arrangements and Human Malaise* (New York: Harper and Row, 1977).

42. See Linda Alcoff, "The Problem of Speaking for Others," *Cultural Critique* 20 (Winter 1991–92): 5–32.

43. Annette C. Baier, "Whom Can Women Trust?" in *Feminist Ethics*, ed. C. Card.

Chapter 2

1. See Virginia Held, "The Political 'Testing' of Moral Theories," *Midwest Studies in Philosophy*, 7 (Spring 1982): 343–63; and *Rights and Goods*, chaps. 4 and 15.

2. Richard De George, "Ethics and Coherence," *Proceedings and Addresses of The American Philosophical Association* 64 (November 1990), 39–52.

3. C. Stimpson, *Where the Meanings Are*, 181.

4. C. MacKinnon, *Toward a Feminist Theory of the State*, 116.

5. Mary Stevenson (Personal correspondence, 8 December 1991) describes several incidents where agents are "taken by surprise" by such experience.

6. John Rawls, *A Theory of Justice* (Cambridge: Harvard University Press, 1971).

7. See Norman Daniels, "Wide Reflective Equilibrium and Theory Acceptance in Ethics," *Journal of Philosophy* 76 (May 1979): 256–82; and Richard Brandt, "The Science of Man and Wide Reflective Equilibrium," *Ethics* 100 (January 1990): 259–78.

8. J. Rawls, *Theory of Justice*, 47.

9. See Nel Noddings, *Caring: A Feminine Approach to Ethics and Moral Education* (Berkeley: University of California Press, 1984); Carol Gilligan, *In a Different Voice: Psychological Theory and Women's Development* (Cambridge: Harvard University Press, 1982); Eva Feder Kittay and Diana T. Meyers, eds., *Women and Moral Theory* (Totowa, N.J.: Rowman and Littlefield, 1987); C. Card, ed. *Feminist Ethics;* and Margaret Urban Walker, "Moral Understandings: Alternative 'Epistemology' for a Feminist Ethics," *Hypatia* 4 (Summer 1989): 15–28.

10. See Amélie Oksenberg Rorty, ed., *Explaining Emotions* (Berkeley: University of California Press, 1980). See also Anthony Kenny, *Action, Emotion and the Will* (London: Routledge, 1963); and Irving Thalberg, *Perception, Emotion and Action* (Oxford: Blackwell, 1977).

11. Sara Ruddick, *Maternal Thinking: Toward a Politics of Peace* (Boston: Beacon Press, 1989), 70.

12. G. W. F. Hegel, *The Phenomenology of Mind,* pt. 6, A, b, trans. J. Baillie (New York: Harper, 1967), 496.

13. Charles Fried, *An Anatomy of Values* (Cambridge: Harvard University Press, 1970).

14. Bernard Williams, *Moral Luck: Philosophical Papers 1973–1980* (Cambridge, Eng.: Cambridge University Press, 1981), 18.

15. See Marilyn Friedman, "The Social Self and the Partiality Debates," in *Feminist Ethics,* ed. C. Card. See also Lawrence A. Blum, "Gilligan and Kohlberg: Implications for Moral Theory," *Ethics* 98 (April 1988): 474–91.

16. See G. W. H. Hegel, *Philosophy of Right,* trans. T. Knox (Oxford: Clarendon Press, 1952).

17. Thomas Nagel, *The View from Nowhere* (New York: Oxford University Press, 1986).

18. Alison M. Jaggar, "Taking Consent Seriously: Feminist Ethics and Actual Moral Dialogue," in *The Applied Ethics Reader,* ed. Earl Winkler and Jerrold Coombs (Oxford: Blackwell, 1993).

19. An exception may be N. Noddings, *Caring.*

20. See Susan Sherwin, "Feminist and Medical Ethics: Two Different Approaches to Contextual Ethics," *Hypatia* 4 (Summer 1989): 57–72.

21. See Kathryn Pauly Morgan, "Strangers in a Strange Land: Feminists Visit Relativists," in *Perspectives on Relativism,* ed. D. Odegaard and C. Stewart (Toronto: Agathon Press, 1990).

22. Stephen Darwall, "Autonomous Internalism and the Justification of Morals," *Noûs* 24 (April 1990): 265. See also S. Darwall, *Impartial Reason* (Ithaca, N.Y.: Cornell University Press, 1983).

23. Annette C. Baier, "Trust and Anti-Trust," *Ethics* 96 (January 1986): 231–60.

24. For discussion of both the limitations of abstract legal categories and the utility for

African Americans of the concept of rights, see Patricia J. Williams, *The Alchemy of Race and Rights* (Cambridge: Harvard University Press, 1991), esp. chap. 8.

25. Annette C. Baier, "The Need for More than Justice," in *Science, Morality and Feminist Theory*, ed. M. Hanen and K. Nielsen, 53.

26. J. Rawls, *Theory of Justice,*. 5.

27. Alan Gewirth, *Reason and Morality* (Chicago: University of Chicago Press, 1978), 10.

28. Iris Marion Young, "Impartiality and the Civic Public," in *Feminism as Critique: On the Politics of Gender*, ed. Seyla Benhabib and Drucilla Cornell (Minneapolis: University of Minnesota Press, 1987), 69. See also Mari J. Matsuda, "Affirmative Action and Legal Knowledge: Planting Seeds in Plowed-Up Ground," *Harvard Women's Law Journal* 11 (Spring 1988): 1–17.

29. Maria C. Lugones and Elizabeth V. Spelman, "Have We Got a Theory for You! Feminist Theory, Cultural Imperialism and the Demand for 'The Woman's Voice,'" *Women's Studies International Forum* (Hypatia) 6, no. 6 (1983): 581. See also Uma Narayan, "Working across Difference: Some Considerations on Emotions and Political Practice," *Hypatia* 3 (Summer 1988): 31–47.

30. G. Hull et al., *All the Women Are White.*

31. S. Darwall, "Autonomous Internalism," 266.

Chapter 3

1. See, e.g., Cheshire Calhoun, "Justice, Care, Gender Bias," *Journal of Philosophy* 85 (September 1988): 451–63.

2. Lorraine Code, "Second Persons," in *Science, Morality and Feminist Theory*, ed. M. Hanen and K. Nielsen, 360.

3. See, e.g., Sue Rosenberg Zalk and Janice Gordon-Kelter, eds., *Revolutions in Knowledge: Feminism in the Social Sciences* (Boulder, Colo.: Westview Press, 1992).

4. Genevieve Lloyd, *The Man of Reason: "Male" and "Female" in Western Philosophy* (Minneapolis: University of Minnesota Press, 1984), 104. For detailed argument that the association between reason and maleness is fundamental and lasting rather than incidental and expendable, see Phyllis Rooney, "Gendered Reason: Sex Metaphor and Conceptions of Reason," *Hypatia* 6 (Summer 1991): 77–103.

5. G. Lloyd, *Man of Reason*, 2.

6. G. Lloyd, *Man of Reason*, 3, 4. For a feminist view of how reason and emotion in the search for knowledge might be reevaluated, see Alison M. Jaggar, "Love and Knowledge: Emotion in Feminist Epistemology," *Inquiry* 32 (June 1989): 151–76.

7. David Heyd, *Supererogation: Its Status in Ethical Theory* (New York: Cambridge University Press, 1982), 134.

8. J. O. Urmson, "Saints and Heroes," in *Essays in Moral Philosophy*, ed. A. I. Melden (Seattle: University of Washington Press, 1958), 202. I am indebted to Marcia Baron for pointing out this example and the preceding one in her "Kantian Ethics and Supererogation," *Journal of Philosophy* 84 (May 1987): 237–62.

9. Alan Ryan, "Distrusting Economics," *New York Review of Books*, 18 May 1989, 25–27. For a different treatment, see Jane Mansbridge, ed., *Beyond Self-Interest* (Chicago: University of Chicago Press, 1990).

10. Pioneering works are Joyce Trebilcot, ed., *Mothering: Essays in Feminist Theory* (Totowa, N.J.: Rowman and Allanheld, 1984); and S. Ruddick, *Maternal Thinking.*

11. Christine Di Stefano, *Configurations of Masculinity: A Feminist Perspective on Modern Political Theory* (Ithaca, N.Y.: Cornell University Press, 1991), 81–83.

12. Thomas Hobbes, *The Citizen: Philosophical Rudiments Concerning Government and Society*, ed. B. Gert (Garden City, N.Y.: Doubleday, 1972), 205.

13. C. Di Stefano, *Configurations of Masculinity*, 84.

14. C. Di Stefano, *Configurations of Masculinity*, 92, 104.

15. For examples of relevant passages, see Mary Mahowald, ed., *Philosophy of Woman: Classical to Current Concepts* (Indianapolis: Hackett, 1978); and Linda Bell, ed., *Visions of Women* (Clifton, N.J.: Humana Press, 1985). For discussion, see Susan Moller Okin, *Women in Western Political Thought* (Princeton: Princeton University Press, 1979); and Lorenne Clark and Lynda Lange, eds., *The Sexism of Social and Political Theory: Women and Reproduction from Plato to Nietzsche* (Toronto: University of Toronto Press, 1979).

16. A. Baier, "Trust and Anti-Trust," 247–48.

17. K. Morgan, "Strangers in a Strange Land."

18. Kathryn Pauly Morgan, "Women and Moral Madness," in *Science, Morality and Feminist Theory*, ed. M. Hanen and K. Nielsen, 223.

19. Alison M. Jaggar, "Feminist Ethics: Some Issues for the Nineties," *Journal of Social Philosophy* 20 (Spring-Fall 1989): 91. See also Alison M. Jaggar, "Feminist Ethics," in *Feminist Ethics*, ed. C. Card.

20. One well-argued statement of this position is Barbara Houston, "Rescuing Womanly Virtues: Some Dangers of Moral Reclamation," in *Science, Morality and Feminist Theory*, ed. M. Hanen and K. Nielsen.

21. See E. Spelman, *Inessential Woman*. See also Sarah Lucia Hoagland, *Lesbian Ethics: Toward New Value* (Palo Alto, Calif.: Institute of Lesbian Studies, 1989); and Katie Geneva Cannon, *Black Womanist Ethics* (Atlanta, Ga.: Scholars Press, 1988).

22. M. Walker, "Moral Understandings," 19, 20. See also I. Young, "Impartiality and the Civic Public."

23. See C. Gilligan, *In a Different Voice*; and E. Kittay and D. Meyers, eds., *Women and Moral Theory*. See also Joan C. Tronto, "Beyond Gender Difference to a Theory of Care," *Signs* 12 (Summer 1987): 644–63.

24. A. Baier, "The Need for More than Justice," 55.

25. K. Morgan, "Strangers in a Strange Land," 2.

26. See A. Baier, "Trust and Anti-Trust"; and Laurence Thomas, "Trust, Affirmation, and Moral Character: A Critique of Kantian Morality," in *Identity, Character, and Morality: Essays in Moral Psychology*, ed. Owen Flanagan and Amélie Oksenberg Rorty (Cambridge: MIT Press, 1990).

27. S. Sherwin, "Feminist and Medical Ethics."

28. See John Rawls, "Justice as Fairness: Political not Metaphysical," *Philosophy and Public Affairs* 14 (Summer 1985): 251–75; idem, "The Priority of Right and Ideas of the Good," *Philosophy and Public Affairs* 17 (Fall 1988): 251–76; idem, "The Idea of Overlapping Consensus," *Oxford Journal of Legal Studies* 7 (Spring 1987): 1–25; Ronald Dworkin, "Liberalism," in *Public and Private Morality*, ed. Stuart Hampshire (Cambridge, Eng.: Cambridge University Press, 1978). See also Charles Larmore, *Patterns of Moral Complexity* (Cambridge, Eng.: Cambridge University Press, 1987).

29. A. Baier, "The Need for More than Justice," 53–54.

30. See Linda Nicholson, *Gender and History: The Limits of Social Theory in the Age of the Family* (New York: Columbia University Press, 1986); and Jean Bethke Elshtain, *Public*

Man, Private Woman (Princeton: Princeton University Press, 1981). See also C. Pateman, *The Sexual Contract.*

31. See S. Okin, *Women in Western Political Thought;* and A. Jaggar, *Feminist Politics.*

32. Simone de Beauvoir, *The Second Sex,* trans. H. Parshley (New York: Bantam, 1953).

33. See Sherry B. Ortner, "Is Female to Male as Nature Is to Culture?" in *Woman, Culture, and Society,* ed. Michelle Z. Rosaldo and Louise Lamphere (Stanford, Calif.: Stanford University Press, 1974).

34. See Marilyn Friedman, "Feminism and Modern Friendship: Dislocating the Community," *Ethics* 99 (January 1989): 275–90; and L. Code, "Second Persons."

35. See Seyla Benhabib, "The Generalized and the Concrete Other. The Kohlberg-Gilligan Controversy and Moral Theory," in *Women and Moral Theory,* ed. E. Kittay and D. Meyers; Caroline Whitbeck, "Feminist Ontology: A Different Reality," in *Beyond Domination: New Perspectives on Women and Philosophy,* ed. Carol C. Gould (Totowa, N.J.: Rowman and Allanheld, 1983); Janice Raymond, *A Passion for Friends: Toward a Philosophy of Female Affection* (Boston: Beacon Press, 1986); and Marilyn Friedman, "Individuality without Individualism: Review of Janice Raymond's *A Passion for Friends,*" *Hypatia* 3 (Summer 1988): 131–37.

36. See. T. Nagel, *View from Nowhere.* For a feminist critique, see S. Bordo, "Feminism, Postmodernism, and Gender-Scepticism."

37. See Naomi Scheman, "Individualism and the Objects of Psychology," in *Discovering Reality,* ed. S. Harding and M. Hintikka.

38. On Marxist theory, see L. Sargent, ed., *Women and Revolution;* A. Jaggar, *Feminist Politics;* and A. Ferguson, *Blood at the Root.* On communitarian theory, see M. Friedman, "Feminism and Modern Friendship" and "The Social Self and the Partiality Debates," in *Feminist Ethics,* ed. C. Card.

39. B. Williams, *Moral Luck;* S. Hampshire, ed., *Public and Private Morality;* Alasdair MacIntyre, *After Virtue: A Study in Moral Theory* (Notre Dame, Ind.: University of Notre Dame Press, 1981). For discussion, see Susan Moller Okin, *Justice, Gender, and the Family* (New York: Basic Books, 1989).

40. On the Stone Center concept of the self, see especially Jean Baker Miller, "The Development of Women's Sense of Self," Wellesley, Mass.: Stone Center Working Paper No. 12 (1984); Janet Surrey, "The 'Self-in-Relation': A Theory of Women's Development," Working Paper No. 13 (1985); and Judith Jordan, "The Meaning of Mutuality," Working Paper No. 23 (1986). For a feminist but critical view of this work, see Marcia Westkott, "Female Relationality and the Idealized Self," *American Journal of Psychoanalysis* 49 (September 1989): 239–50.

41. Jean Baker Miller, *Toward a New Psychology of Women* (Boston: Beacon Press, 1976); Nancy Chodorow, *The Reproduction of Mothering: Psychoanalysis and the Sociology of Gender* (Berkeley: University of California Press, 1978).

42. C. Gilligan, *In a Different Voice.*

43. J. Jordan, "The Meaning of Mutuality," 2.

44. Jennifer Nedelsky, "Law, Boundaries, and the Bounded Self," *Representations* 30 (Spring 1990): 169, 181. See also Martha Minow, *Making All the Difference: Inclusion, Exclusion, and American Law* (Ithaca, N.Y.: Cornell University Press, 1990).

45. Jennifer Nedelsky, "Reconceiving Autonomy: Sources, Thoughts and Possibilities," *Yale Journal of Law and Feminism* 1 (Spring 1989): 9. See also Diana T. Meyers, *Self, Society, and Personal Choice* (New York: Columbia University Press, 1989). For a discussion of

why feminist criticisms of the ideal of autonomy need not weaken arguments for women's reproductive rights, see Sally Markowitz, "Abortion and Feminism," *Social Theory and Practice* 16 (Spring 1990): 1–17.

46. J. Nedelsky, "Reconceiving Autonomy," 11.

47. J. Nedelsky, *"Reconceiving Autonomy,"* 12. *See also Mari J. Matsuda, "Liberal Jurisprudence and Abstracted Visions of Human Nature,"* New Mexico Law Review 16 (Fall 1986): 613–30.

48. See M. Belenky et al., *Women's Ways of Knowing.*

49. A. Jaggar, "Feminist Ethics," 11.

Chapter 4

1. See George Sher, "Other Voices, Other Rooms? Women's Psychology and Moral Theory," in *Women and Moral Theory,* ed. E. Kittay and D. Meyers.

2. See Carolyn G. Heilbrun, "Feminist Criticism in Departments of Literature," *Academe* 69 (September–October 1983).

3. See R. M. Hare, *Freedom and Reason* (New York: Oxford University Press, 1965), 88–89; and J. Rawls, *Theory of Justice,* 121.

4. C. Gilligan, *In a Different Voice;* and N. Noddings, *Caring.* A useful discussion of the philosophical significance of Gilligan's work is Owen Flanagan and Kathryn Jackson, "Justice, Care, and Gender: The Kohlberg-Gilligan Debate Revisited," *Ethics* 97 (April 1987): 622–37.

5. Lawrence Kohlberg, *The Philosophy of Moral Development* (San Francisco: Harper and Row, 1981); and L. Kohlberg and R. Kramer, "Continuities and Discontinuities in Child and Adult Moral Development," *Human Development* 12, no. 2 (1969): 93–120. Kohlberg, studying the moral development of boys, posited six stages of moral development. In his later work he introduced an additional stage: $4\frac{1}{2}$.

6. See Lawrence J. Walker, "Sex Differences in the Development of Moral Reasoning: A Critical Review," *Child Development* 55 (June 1984): 677–91.

7. See N. Chodorow, *The Reproduction of Mothering.*

8. See Constance Boucher Holstein, "Irreversible, Stepwise Sequence in the Development of Moral Judgment: A Longitudinal Study of Males and Females," *Child Development* 47 (March 1976): 51–61.

9. Carol Gilligan, "Moral Orientation and Moral Development," in *Women and Moral Theory,* ed. E. Kittay and D. Meyers, 25.

10. See Norma Haan, "Hypothetical and Actual Moral Reasoning in a Situation of Civil Disobedience," *Journal of Personality and Social Psychology* 32 (August 1975): 255–70.

11. For suggestions on how Gilligan's stages, like Kohlberg's, might be thought to be historically and culturally based, rather than more universally, see Linda Nicholson, "Women, Morality, and History," *Social Research* 50 (Autumn 1983): 514–36. Claudia Card observes: "Different kinds of relationships have been differently distributed among women and men in patriarchal society: a larger share of the responsibilities of certain personal and informal relationships to women, a larger share of the responsibilities of formal and impersonal relationships defined by social institutions to men. It is plausible that a result has been the creation of a significant difference in ethical orientation." Claudia Card, "Gender and Moral Luck," in *Identity, Character, and Morality,* ed. O. Flanagan and A. Rorty, 200.

12. Sara Ruddick, "Maternal Thinking," *Feminist Studies* 6 (Summer 1980): 342–67; reprinted in *Mothering: Essays in Feminist Theory,* ed. J. Trebilcot, 214, 218.

13. See Genevieve Lloyd, "Reason, Gender, and Morality in the History of Philosophy," *Social Research* 50 (Autumn 1983): 490–513.

14. See N. Hartsock, *Money, Sex, and Power,* chaps. 10 and 11.

15. See Debra Nails, "Social-Scientific Sexism: Gilligan's Mismeasure of Man," *Social Research* 50 (Autumn 1983), 643–64.

16. See C. Pateman, *The Sexual Contract.*

17. See David Gauthier, *Morals by Agreement* (Oxford: Clarendon Press, 1986).

18. N. Hartsock, *Money, Sex, and Power,* 39.

19. See M. Friedman, "Feminism and Modern Friendship."

20. Lawrence A. Blum, *Friendship, Altruism and Morality* (London: Routledge, 1980), 1.

21. Owen J. Flanagan, Jr., and Jonathan E. Adler, "Impartiality and Particularity," *Social Research* 50 (Autumn 1983): 576–96.

22. See N. Noddings, *Caring.*

23. N. Noddings, *Caring,* 91–92, 94.

24. For arguments that there is no objective truth in ethics, see Gilbert Harman, *The Nature of Morality* (New York: Oxford University Press, 1977); and J. L. Mackie, *Inventing Right and Wrong* (New York: Penguin, 1977). For arguments that ethics is indeed capable of knowledge of moral "facts," see Geoffrey Sayre-McCord, ed., *Essays on Moral Realism* (Ithaca, N.Y.: Cornell University Press, 1988).

25. Michael Slote, "Morality and Self-Other Asymmetry," *Journal of Philosophy* 81 (April 1984): 180.

26. See especially A. MacIntyre, *After Virtue.*

27. See S. Okin, *Justice, Gender, and the Family.*

28. Eva Kittay, "Womb Envy: An Explanatory Concept," in *Mothering: Essays in Feminist Theory,* ed. J. Trebilcot.

29. See Margaret A. Simons, "Motherhood, Feminism and Identity," *Women's Studies International Forum (Hypatia)* 7, no. 5 (1984): 349–59.

30. N. Noddings, *Caring,* 31, 43, 49.

31. S. Ruddick, *Maternal Thinking,* 68.

32. See C. Gilligan, *In a Different Voice,* 104; and N. Noddings, *Caring,* 43.

33. That some women enthusiastically send their sons off to war may be indicative of a greater than usual acceptance of male myths rather than evidence against this claim, since the enthusiasm seems most common in societies where women have the least influence in the formation of prevailing religious and other beliefs.

34. A. Baier, "The Need for More than Justice," 50.

35. Niccolo Machiavelli, *The Prince,* trans. G. Bull (New York: Penguin, 1961), chap. 18, 101. See also S. Hampshire, ed., *Public and Private Morality;* and Virginia Held, "On Ronald Dworkin's Liberalism and Conservatism," in *Two Centuries of Philosophy in America,* ed. Peter Caws (London: Blackwell, 1980).

36. S. Ruddick, "Maternal Thinking," was first published in 1980.

37. Dr. Antonia Novello, Surgeon General, warned that "the home is actually a more dangerous place for American women than the city streets" because domestic violence is the single largest cause of injury to women in the U.S. *New York Times,* 17 October 1991.

38. A. Jaggar, *Feminist Politics.*

Chapter 5

1. See Richard Wollheim, *On Art and the Mind* (Cambridge: Harvard University Press, 1974); and John Dewey, *Art As Experience* (New York: Putnam, 1934).

2. See Virginia Held, "Corporations, Persons, and Responsibility," in *Shame, Responsibility, and the Corporation,* ed. Hugh Mercer Curtler (New York: Haven, 1987); Peter A. French, *Collective and Corporate Responsibility* (New York: Columbia University Press, 1984); Larry May, *The Morality of Groups* (Notre Dame, Ind.: University of Notre Dame Press, 1987); Larry May and Stacey Hoffman, eds., *Collective Responsibility* (Savage, Md.: Rowman and Littlefield, 1991); and Gregory Mellema, *Individuals, Groups, and Shared Moral Responsibility* (New York: Peter Lang, 1988).

3. On the topic of imagination, see Hide Ishiguro, "Imagination," in *British Analytic Philosophy,* ed. Bernard Williams and A. Montefiore (New York: Humanities Press, 1966); and Richard Wollheim, *The Thread of Life* (Cambridge: Harvard University Press, 1984).

4. For some parallel developments in aesthetics, see Carolyn Korsmeyer, "Pleasure: Reflections on Aesthetics and Feminism," *Journal of Aesthetics and Art Criticism,* in press.

5. Michel Foucault, *The History of Sexuality: An Introduction,* vol. 1 (New York: Vintage, 1990), 27.

6. For a related discussion, see Amélie Oksenberg Rorty, "Imagination and Power," in *Mind in Action: Essays in the Philosophy of Mind* (Boston: Beacon Press, 1988).

7. For further discussion, see Virginia Held, "Culture or Commerce: On the Liberation of Expression," *Philosophic Exchange* 19 and 20 (1988–89): 73–87, and "Philosophy and the Media," *Journal of Social Philosophy* 20 (1989): 116–24.

8. John Stuart Mill, *On Liberty,* ed. Elizabeth Rapaport (Indianapolis, Ind.: Hackett, 1978); see Frederick Schauer, *Free Speech: A Philosophical Inquiry* (Cambridge, Eng.: Cambridge University Press, 1982).

9. For a brief account, see David Held, *Introduction to Critical Theory: Horkheimer to Habermas* (Berkeley: University of California Press, 1980).

10. See James Curran, Michael Gurevitch, and Janet Wollacott, eds., *Mass Communication and Society* (Beverly Hills, Calif.: Sage, 1977); Michael Gurevitch, Tony Bennett, James Curran, and Janet Wollacott, eds., *Culture, Society, and the Media* (New York: Methuen, 1982); and the journal *Media, Culture, and Society.*

11. Meaghan Morris, "Banality in Cultural Studies," *Discourse* 10 (Spring-Summer 1988): 19. The phrase "cultural dopes" is from Stuart Hall, and the quotation that follows is from Mica Nova.

12. Susan Faludi documents the complicity of the media in promoting the backlash that grew in strength during the 1980s in the United States against feminism and the modest gains made by women. Publications from right to left blamed the women's movement, rather than its opponents, for the stresses and woes women were experiencing; films and television programs spread the message that women should "recant their independent ways." Susan Faludi, *Backlash: The Undeclared War against American Women* (New York: Crown, 1991), xi.

13. Donald Lazere, ed., *American Media and Mass Culture: Left Perspectives* (Berkeley: University of California Press, 1987), 9; Kate Moody, *Growing Up On Television: The TV Effect* (New York: New York Times Book, 1980).

14. Jeff Silverman writes, "Advertisers want a peaceful marketplace . . . When adver-

tisers object to the content of a show, which, by contract, they prescreen, they have the right, also by contract, to withdraw their support." Advertisers withdraw support "if they sense that a particular show, or episode, is too controversial to be associated with their products." In the same article, producer Barney Rosenzweig is quoted as saying, "It's censorship based on economics"; and Steven Bochco, producer of "Hill Street Blues" and "L.A. Law" is quoted as saying, "We're sensing a much stronger resistance to ideas than in the last half dozen years. And I would say it's getting worse." The worsening of the problem, which has been there all along, is attributed to lean economic times. Jeff Silverman, "TV's Creators Face a New Caution," *New York Times,* 8 December 1991, B1.

15. Almost $129 billion was spent in 1990. See Stuart Elliott, "A forecast for '91 Spending Is Revised." *New York Times,* 12 December 1991, D1.

16. "Ad Clutter: Even in Restrooms Now," *New York Times,* 18 February 1988, D1.

17. Herbert J. Gans, *Popular Culture and High Culture* (New York: Basic Books, 1974), viii.

18. See Neil Postman, *Amusing Ourselves to Death: Public Discourse in the Age of Show Business* (New York: Penguin, 1985).

19. See E. Ann Kaplan, *Rocking around the Clock: Music Television, Postmodernism, and Consumer Culture* (New York: Methuen, 1987); and S. Faludi, *Backlash.* See also Judith Williamson, "Woman Is an Island: Femininity and Colonization," and Patricia Mellencamp, "Situation Comedy, Feminism, and Freud: Discourses of Gracie and Lucy," both in *Studies in Entertainment,* ed. T. Modleski.

20. See, e.g., Judith Mayne, "L.A. Law and Prime-Time Feminism," *Discourse* 10 (Spring-Summer 1988): 30–47.

21. Bill Carter, "HBO Turns 'Baby-Sitters Club' into a Series of Specials," *New York Times,* 10 September 1991, C11. Carter writes: "It is a pattern that has become familiar to educators, feminists and parents of girls: Children's shows on network television always steer clear of properties they believe will be of special interest to girls."

22. *National Assessment of Educational Progress.* Report of U.S. Department of Education, 27 September 1990.

23. See, e.g., Raymond Williams, *Problems in Materialism and Culture* (London: Verso, 1980).

24. See Michael Parenti, *Inventing Reality: The Politics of the Mass Media* (New York: St. Martin's Press, 1986); and Michael Morgan, "Television and Democracy," in *Cultural Politics in Contemporary America,* ed. Ian Angus and Sut Jhally (New York: Routledge, 1989). See also Daniel Hallin, "Sound Bite News: Television Coverage of Elections 1968–1988," Woodrow Wilson International Center for Scholars, 1991.

25. Mark Crispin Miller, *Boxed In: The Culture of TV* (Evanston, Ill.: Northwestern University Press, 1988), 7, 8, 14, 17.

26. Angela Y. Davis, *Women, Culture, and Politics* (New York: Vintage, 1990), 201.

27. The networks' share of the prime-time audience fell steadily from 93% in 1976–77 to 62% in 1990–91; a slight reversal of the trend was recorded by 1991–92. "The Media Business," *New York Times,* 13 April 1992, D7. See Jon Margolis, "Are Americans Moving Away from Popular Culture?" *Chicago Tribune,* 24 November 1991.

28. On the increasing commercialization of the film industry, see Tom O'Brien, *The Screening of America: Movies and Values from "Rocky" to "Rain Man"* (New York: Ungar, 1990); and Mark Crispin Miller, ed., *Seeing through Movies* (New York: Pantheon, 1990).

29. For discussion of the role of culture in social change, see M. Archer, *Culture and Agency.*

30. See F. Davis, *Moving the Mountain;* Jo Freeman, *The Politics of Women's Liberation* (New York: Longman, 1975); and Elly Bulkin, Minnie Bruce Pratt, and Barbara Smith, *Yours in Struggle: Three Perspectives on Anti-Semitism and Racism* (Brooklyn, N.Y.: Long Haul Press, 1984).

31. On how popular music can be effective in mobilizing large numbers of people for politically progressive ends, see Reebee Garofalo, ed., *Rockin' the Boat: Mass Music and Mass Movements* (Boston: South End Press, 1992), especially Peter Wicke, "The Times They Are A-Changin': Rock Music and Political Change in East Germany" and Anna Szemere, "The Politics of Marginality: A Rock Musical Subculture in Socialist Hungary in the Early 1980's."

32. Linda Gordon, "What's New in Women's History?" in *Feminist Studies, Critical Studies,* ed. Teresa de Lauretis (Bloomington: Indiana University Press, 1986), 21.

33. See Gerda Lerner, *The Majority Finds Its Past: Placing Women in History* (New York: Oxford University Press, 1979); and S. Zalk and J. Gordon-Kelter, eds., *Revolutions in Knowledge.*

34. See Catharine R. Stimpson, "Multiculturalism: A Big Word at the Presses," *New York Times Book Review,* 22 September 1991. See also Chandra Talpade Mohanty, "On Race and Voice: Challenges for Liberal Education in the 1990's," *Cultural Critique* 14 (Winter 1989–90): 179–208; Joan Scott, "The New University: Beyond Political Correctness," *Boston Review,* March 1992, and "Readers Forum," same journal (May-August 1992): 30–34; Marilyn Frye, "Getting It Right," and Alice Kessler-Harris, "The View from Women's Studies," both in *Signs* 17 (Summer 1992): 781–805.

35. See Michael Parenti, *Power and the Powerless* (New York: St. Martin's Press, 1978), chap. 11.

36. See Alasdair MacIntyre, "Moral Arguments and Social Contexts," *Journal of Philosophy* 80 (October 1983): 590; and, in the same issue, Virginia Held, "The Independence of Intellectuals," 572–82.

37. On enabling access to expression and funding noncommercial culture, see Virginia Held, "Access, Enablement, and the First Amendment," in *Philosophical Foundations of the Constitution,* ed. Diana T. Meyers and Kenneth Kipnis (Boulder, Colo.: Westview, 1988).

38. On the exploitation of children by commercial television, see Stephen Kline, "Limits to the Imagination: Marketing and Children's Culture," in *Cultural Politics,* ed. I. Angus and S. Jhally; and Tom Engelhardt, "Children's Television: The Shortcake Strategy," in *Watching Television,* ed. Todd Gitlin (New York: Pantheon, 1986).

39. J. Mill, *On Liberty;* and Alexander Nehamas, "Plato and the Mass Media," *Monist* 71 (April 1988): 214–34.

40. See *A Public Trust: Report of the Carnegie Commission on the Future of Public Broadcasting* (New York: Bantam, 1979).

41. See V. Held, *Rights and Goods.*

Chapter 6

1. Mary O'Brien's observation is apt: "Birth was not, and will not become, a worthy subject for male philosophy. It is neglected so that man may make himself . . . Feminist philosophy will be a philosophy of birth and regeneration." Mary O'Brien, *The Politics of Reproduction* (London: Routledge, 1983), 156, 200.

2. See Carolyn Merchant, *The Death of Nature: Women, Ecology, and the Scientific Revolu-*

tion (New York: Harper and Row, 1982); and Susan Griffin, *Woman and Nature: The Roaring Inside Her* (New York: Harper and Row, 1978).

3. For a historical account of attitudes toward death and of cultural practices surrounding dying, see Philippe Ariès, *The Hour of Our Death*, trans. H. Weaver (New York: Knopf, 1981). For a helpful discussion of views of death in the works of Goethe, Conrad, Melville, and Camus, see Konstantin Kolenda, "Facing Death: Four Literary Accounts," *Philosophic Exchange* SUNY Brockport, nos. 14–15 (1984–85).

4. Ernest Becker writes: "We admire most the courage to face death; we give such valor our highest and most constant adoration; it moves us deeply in our hearts because we have doubts about how brave we would be . . . And so the hero has been the center of human honor and acclaim since probably the beginning of specifically human evolution." Ernest Becker, *The Denial of Death* (New York: Free Press, 1973), 11–12.

5. Adrienne Rich, *Of Woman Born: Motherhood as Experience and Institution* (New York: Bantam, 1977), 149.

6. Writing of frequently encountered practices, the authors of a text on human ecology cite a study which finds that "the average poor mother in Colombia . . . goes through a progression of attempts to limit the number of her children. She starts with ineffective native forms of contraception and moves on to quack abortion, infanticide, frigidity, and all too often suicide." Paul R. Ehrlich and Anne H. Ehrlich, *Population, Resources, Environment: Issues in Human Ecology*, 2d ed. (San Francisco: W. H. Freeman, 1972), 278.

7. Personal conversation.

8. The traditional conceptions of Hobbes, Locke, and others are mirrored in contemporary contractual and rational choice theories. For discussion of how Hobbes's conceptualizations reflect a specifically masculine point of view and a denial of mothers and mothering, see C. Di Stefano, *Configurations of Masculinity*.

9. In male-dominated society, when reasons to give birth have been noticed, they have usually been men's reasons more than women's: the birth rate should be increased to provide new recruits for war, and so forth. But even bad reasons to give birth are distinctively human.

10. Thomas Nagel notes the very different attitudes we have toward our nonexistence prior to our births, which causes us little concern, and our nonexistence after our deaths, about which many people feel great anxiety. This illustrates in a very familiar way the disanalogy between our views of our own births and deaths. Thomas Nagel, *Mortal Questions* (London: Cambridge University Press, 1979), 8.

11. Eva Kittay, conversation with author, 20 January 1988.

12. T. Nagel, *The View from Nowhere*, 113–14.

13. Iris Marion Young, "Pregnant Embodiment: Subjectivity and Alienation," *Journal of Medicine and Philosophy* 9 (February 1984): 45.

14. Emily Martin shows how the framework of discussion of modern childbirth has been constructed by the medical profession and how the imagery of birth might be recreated from the points of view of women. See E. Martin, *The Woman in the Body*.

15. See Tillie Olsen, *Silences* (New York: Delacorte, 1979).

16. Since images of birth from the point of view of those giving birth are almost nonexistent, the ones presented in *The Birth Project* are startlingly novel. *The Birth Project* is a series of needlepoint and embroidery works designed and created under the direction of the artist Judy Chicago; it was shown at the R. H. Love Gallery in Chicago in 1986, and elsewhere.

17. A. Rich, *Of Woman Born,* 12.

18. See Mary Daly, *Gyn/Ecology: The Metaethics of Radical Feminism* (Boston: Beacon Press, 1978). Daly, focusing especially on religious myths, believes that men as a gender display the disease of necrophilia: they desire women to be "victimized into a state of living death," (59). But see Nancy C. M. Hartsock, "Prologue to a Feminist Critique of War and Politics," in Judith Stiehm, ed., *Women's Views of the Political World of Men* (Dobbs Ferry, N.Y.: Transnational Publishers, 1984); and "Masculinity, Heroism, and the Making of War," in Adrienne Harris and Ynestra King, eds., *Rocking the Ship of State: Toward a Feminist Peace Politics* (Boulder, Colo.: Westview, 1989).

19. In a 380-page book on "reproductive rituals" in some 200 societies, the anthropologists Karen Ericksen Paige and Jeffrey M. Paige discuss no celebrations of actual birth. What are meant by "reproductive rituals" in the vast amount of theorizing and discussion they examine, and in their own theory to account for the rituals, are male genital mutilation, menarcheal ceremonies, menstrual segregation practices, *couvade,* and restrictions on pregnant women. See K. E. Paige and J. M. Paige, *The Politics of Reproductive Ritual.* (Berkeley: University of California Press, 1981.) See also E. Kittay, "Womb Envy," 109–15.

20. Conversation with E. Kittay, January 20, 1988.

21. For a useful collection of what male philosophers over the centuries have said about women, see M. Mahowald, ed., *Philosophy of Woman;* also L. Bell, ed., *Visions of Women.* For discussion of such views see S. Okin, *Women in Western Political Thought;* and G. Lloyd, *The Man of Reason.*

22. See Christine Pierce, "Natural Law Language and Women," in *Woman in Sexist Society: Studies in Power and Powerlessness,* ed. Vivian Gornick and Barbara K. Moran (New York: Basic Books, 1971).

23. Shulamith Firestone, *The Dialectic of Sex: The Case for Feminist Revolution* (New York: Morrow, 1970).

24. For a useful account of how a recognition of women's difference from men in the area of reproduction could and should be rendered socially "costless," see Christine A. Littleton, "Reconstructing Sexual Equality," *California Law Review* 75 (1987): 201–59.

25. Brigitte Jordan, *Birth in Four Cultures: A Cross-cultural Investigation of Childbirth in Yucatan, Holland, Sweden and the United States* (Montreal: Eden Press, 1980).

26. See A. Rich, *Of Woman Born,* chap. 6; Barbara Ehrenreich and Deirdre English, *Witches, Midwives and Nurses: A History of Women Healers* (New York: Feminist Press, 1973) and *For Her Own Good: 150 Years of Experts' Advice to Women* (New York: Doubleday, 1978).

27. Barbara Katz Rothman describes the commodification of motherhood under capitalism and the devaluation of mothers under patriarchy; she considers how the medical aspects of motherhood could be reconstructed by feminism. See *Recreating Motherhood: Ideology and Technology in Patriarchal Society* (New York: Norton, 1989).

28. See Judith Walzer Leavitt, *Brought to Bed: Childbearing in America 1750 to 1950* (New York: Oxford University Press, 1986).

29. Alison M. Jaggar, "Human Biology in Feminist Theory: Sexual Equality Reconsidered," in *Beyond Domination,* ed. C. Gould, 37–38.

30. S. de Beauvoir, *The Second Sex,* 239; Sherry B. Ortner, "Is Female to Male as Nature Is To Culture?" in *Woman, Culture, and Society,* ed. M. Rosaldo and L. Lamphere, 74–75. Though Ortner has modified her views, this essay and its formulations continue to be very influential.

31. See Hannah Arendt, *The Human Condition* (Chicago: University of Chicago Press, 1958). Arendt did not consider herself a feminist and cannot plausibly be classified as one, but from personal conversations I can record that she was beginning, late in her life, to acknowledge the validity of some feminist views.

32. S. de Beauvoir, *The Second Sex*, 58–59. For Beauvoir, "the support of life became for man an activity and a project through the invention of the tool; but in maternity woman remained closely bound to her body, like an animal. It is because humanity calls itself in question in the matter of living—that is to say, values the reasons for living above mere life—that, confronting woman, man assumes mastery." For an excellent critical discussion of Beauvoir on procreation, see Alison M. Jaggar and William L. McBride, " 'Reproduction' as Male Ideology," in *Women's Studies International Forum. Hypatia* 8, no. 3 (1985): 185–96.

33. S. de Beauvoir, 58. For an argument that links male valuing of destruction and death over life and birth to male envy of women's procreative capacities, see E. Kittay, "Womb Envy," 120.

34. S. Ortner, "Is Female to Male," 76.

35. S. Ortner, "Is Female to Male," 87.

36. E. g., Aristotle, Kant, Hegel, Lévi-Strauss, Arendt.

37. S. Ortner, "Is Female to Male," 79.

38. See A. Jaggar and W. McBride, " 'Reproduction.' "

39. A. Jaggar, *Feminist Politics,* 76, 68.

40. In his introduction to *The Origin of the Family,* Engels wrote: "The determining factor in history is, in the final instance, the production and reproduction of immediate life. This, again, is of a twofold character; on the one side the production of the means of existence, of food, clothing and shelter and the tools necessary for that production; on the other side, the production of human beings themselves, the propagation of the species." Frederick Engels, *The Origin of the Family, Private Property and the State,* ed. Eleanor Leacock (New York: International Publishers, 1972), 71.

41. See Mariarosa Dalla Costa and Selma James, *The Power of Women and the Subversion of Community* (Bristol, Eng.: Falling Wall Press, 1973); and L. Sargent, ed., *Women and Revolution.*

42. Ann Ferguson and Nancy Folbre, "The Unhappy Marriage of Patriarchy and Capitalism," in *Women and Revolution,* ed. L. Sargent, 317, 319.

43. A. Jaggar and W. McBride, " 'Reproduction,' " 194–95.

44. See M. O'Brien, *Politics of Reproduction.* See also Mary O'Brien, "Reproducing Marxist Man," in *The Sexism of Social and Political Theory,* ed. L. Clark and L. Lange, 104.

45. O'Brien, *Politics of Reproduction,* 22–53.

46. O'Brien, *Politics of Reproduction,* 14. See also Reyes Lazaro, "Feminism and Motherhood: O'Brien vs. Beauvoir," *Hypatia* 1 (Fall 1986): 87–102.

47. "Reproductive process," O'Brien writes, "is not only the material base of the historical forms of the social relations of reproduction, but . . . is also a dialectical process, which changes historically." The first significant change in the process occurred as a change in male reproductive consciousness, with the discovery of physiological paternity. "The second and much more recent change in reproductive praxis is brought about by . . . contraceptive technology." *Politics of Reproduction,* 21.

48. See Gena Corea, *The Mother Machine: Reproductive Technologies from Artificial Insemination to Artificial Wombs* (New York: Harper and Row, 1985). See also Anne Donchin,

"The Future of Mothering: Reproductive Technology and Feminist Theory," *Hypatia* 1 (Fall 1986): 121–37.

49. N. Hartsock, *Money, Sex, and Power,* 197. For other examples see Eva Feder Kittay, "Woman as Metaphor," *Hypatia* 3 (Summer 1988): 63–86. For an interpretation of Cartesian thought as an expression of the "*re*-birthing and re-imaging of knowledge and the world as masculine" (441), see Susan Bordo, "The Cartesian Masculinization of Thought," *Signs* 11 (Spring 1986): 439–56. Bordo suggests that "the possibility of objectivity . . . is conceived by Descartes as a kind of *re*-birth, on one's own terms, this time" (448).

50. I am grateful to Cass Sunstein for this terse example.

51. See A. Rich, *Of Woman Born,* 80–97 for discussion.

52. M. O'Brien, *Politics of Reproduction,* 147.

53. A Rich, *Of Woman Born,* 81, 86.

54. The best example may still be Charlotte Perkins Gilman's *Herland* (New York: Pantheon, 1979). Also suggestive is Marge Piercy's *Woman on the Edge of Time* (New York: Fawcett, 1976).

55. See, e.g., Iris Marion Young, "Humanism, Gynocentrism and Feminist Politics," *Women's Studies International Forum (Hypatia)* 8, no. 3 (1985): 173–83.

Chapter 7

1. See Jeffrey A. Gray, "Sex Differences in Emotional Behavior in Mammals Including Man: Endocrine Bases." *Acta Psychologica* 35 (1971): 29–46; Ronald P. Rohner, "Sex Differences in Aggression," *Ethos* 4 (1976): 57–72; Eleanor Emmons Macoby and Carol Nagy Jacklin, *The Psychology of Sex Differences* (Stanford, Calif.: Stanford University Press, 1974).

2. See the typology of "determinants" of human behavior in Melford E. Spiro, *Gender and Culture: Kibbutz Women Revisited* (New York: Schocken Books, 1980).

3. C. MacKinnon, *Toward a Feminist Theory,* 137, 145, 113, 179.

4. Ironically, MacKinnon's views include some claims parallel to those in the discredited views of such conservatives as George Gilder, who argue that unless women are subordinate, men become impotent. In *Sexual Suicide* (New York: Quadrangle, 1973), Gilder maintains that this justifies female subordination.

5. One such critic is Camille Paglia, in *Sexual Personae: Art and Decadence from Nefertiti to Emily Dickinson* (New Haven, Conn.: Yale University Press, 1990).

6. Recent figures indicate that over a third of women are victims of some form of sexual abuse in childhood. See Diana Russell, *The Secret Trauma: Incestuous Abuse of Women and Girls* (New York: Basic Books, 1986).

7. Estimates are that almost half of women are victims of attempted rape or rape at least once in our lives. See Diana Russell and Nancy Howell, "The Prevalence of Rape in the United States Revisited," *Signs* 8 (Summer 1983): 668–95. Studies of male college students who were asked if they would use force and/or rape if they knew they would not get caught disclosed that 60 percent of those surveyed admitted some likelihood that they would. Barbara Roberts, "The Death of Machothink: Feminist Research and the Transformation of Peace Studies," *Women's Studies International Forum* 7, no. 4 (1984): 195–200.

8. The effects of viewing violence have been studied and are not benign. Normal men become more willing to act aggressively toward women after viewing sexual material that

contains aggression against women. See E. Donnerstein, "Pornography: Its Effects on Violence Against Women," in *Pornography and Sexual Aggression,* ed. N. Malamuth and E. Donnerstein (Orlando, Fla.: Academic Press, 1984); and E. Donnerstein and L. Berkowitz, "Victim Reactions in Aggressive Erotic Films as a Factor in Violence against Women," *Journal of Personality and Social Psychology* 41 (1981): 710–24.

9. C. MacKinnon, *Toward a Feminist Theory,* 139.

10. For an exploration into the psychology and sexual fantasies of a warrior caste, see Klaus Theweleit, *Women, Floods, Bodies, History,* vol. 1 of *Male Fantasies,* trans. S. Conway (Minneapolis: University of Minnesota Press, 1987). Barbara Ehrenreich concludes in a foreword that the Freikorpsmen whose fantasies were studied hated women, especially women's sexuality and women's bodies, and she speculates that these men may have devoted their lives to producing death as a way to escape women. Their dread of women arose, she suggests "in the pre-Oedipal struggle of the fledgling self" (p. xiii) and may have been not so different in these men from the dread in "normal" men of engulfment and annihilation in the holes and swamps of women's bodies.

11. It is now thought that there may have been relatively peaceful, gynecocentric, and often goddess-worshipping societies in the late Paleolithic and early Neolithic eras. See Rohrlich, "Prehistoric Puzzles," *Women's Review of Books* 7 (June 1990): 14–16. See also Riane Eisler, *The Chalice and the Blade* (San Francisco: Harper, 1987).

12. Heidi Hartmann, "The Unhappy Marriage of Marxism and Feminism: Towards a More Progressive Union," in *Women and Revolution,* ed. L. Sargent, 15.

13. See Barrie Thorne, "Feminist Rethinking of the Family: An Overview," in *Rethinking the Family: Some Feminist Questions,* ed. Barrie Thorne (New York: Longman, 1982).

14. Judith Stiehm, "The Man Question," in *Women's Views,* 221–22.

15. N. Hartsock, "The Barracks Community," in *Women and Men's Wars,* ed. Judith Stiehm (New York: Pergamon, 1983), 283–84.

16. N. Hartsock, "The Barracks Community," 286.

17. See Barbara Roberts, "No Safe Place: The War against Women," *Our Generation* 15 (1983): 7–26; and "Death of Machothink," 196.

18. Jane Held, "The British Peace Movement: A Critical Examination of Attitudes to Male Violence within the British Peace Movement as Expressed with Regard to the 'Molesworth Rapes.'" *Women's Studies International Forum* 11, n. 3 (1988): 211–21.

19. Birgit Brock-Utne, "The Peace Concepts through Three United Nations Women Decade Conferences." Oslo: International Peace Research Institute, PRIO Working Paper (January 1986).

20. Betty Reardon, *Sexism and the War System* (New York: Teachers College Press, 1985).

21. B. Roberts, "No Safe Place," and "Death of Machothink." 197. See also Cynthia Enloe, *Does Khaki Become You? The Militarization of Women's Lives* (Boston: South End Press, 1983).

22. B. Roberts, "Death of Machothink," 198.

23. Helen Caldicott, *Missile Envy: The Arms Race and Nuclear War,* rev. ed. (New York: Bantam, 1986).

24. Carol Cohn, "Sex and Death in the Rational World of Defense Intellectuals," *Signs* 12 (Summer 1987): 687–718.

25. Paul Fussell, *The Great War and Modern Memory* (London: Oxford University Press, 1975), 270.

26. Claire M. Tylee, "'Maleness Run Riot'—The Great War and Women's Resistance to Militarism," *Women's Studies International Forum* 11, no. 3 (1988): 204. Most of Tylee's article is a refutation of Sandra Gilbert's article (*Signs* 1983), claiming that the war gave women a sense of power and that women supported the war. Tylee attributes this impression to government propaganda, which tried to make men and women believe that women supported the war and sacrificed men gladly, but she rejects this view.

27. Tania Modleski, "A Father Is Being Beaten: Male Feminism and the War Film," *Discourse* 10 (Spring-Summer 1988): 62–77.

28. The language is Polish. I owe this point to Jozef Goldblat.

29. C. Enloe, *Does Khaki Become You?* 13, 14.

30. N. Hartsock, "Masculinity, Heroism," 134, 135.

31. James Redfield, *The Tragedy of Hector* (Chicago: University of Chicago Press, 1975), 101.

32. N. Hartsock, "Masculinity, Heroism," 141.

33. N. Hartsock, "Masculinity, Heroism," 141.

34. James Redfield, *Nature and Culture in the Iliad* (Chicago: University of Chicago Press, 1975), xiii.

35. Ernest Becker, *The Denial of Death* (New York: Free Press, 1973), 1, 2.

36. C. Cohn, "Sex and Death."

37. N. Hartsock, "Masculinity, Heroism," 147.

38. Nancy Huston, "Tales of War and Tears of Women," in *Women and Men's Wars,* ed. J. Stiehm.

39. S. Ruddick, *Maternal Thinking,* 24.

40. S. Ruddick, *Maternal Thinking,* 17.

41. S. Ruddick, *Maternal Thinking,* 148.

42. See Amy Swerdlow, "Pure Milk, Not Poison: Women Strike for Peace and the Test Ban Treaty of 1963," in *Rocking the Ship of State,* ed. A. Harris and Y. King.

43. Judith Stiehm, "The Protected, the Protector, the Defender," in *Women and Men's Wars,* 37.

44. See Birgit Brock-Utne, *Educating for Peace: A Feminist Perspective* (New York: Pergamon, 1985).

45. Barbara Deming, *We Are All Part of One Another: A Barbara Deming Reader,* ed. Jane Meyerding (Philadelphia: New Society Educational Foundation, 1984), 177–78.

46. B. Deming, *We Are All Part of One Another,* 179, 180.

47. Ann Snitow, "A Gender Diary," in *Rocking the Ship of State,* ed. A. Harris and Y. King, 50–52.

48. S. Ruddick, *Maternal Thinking,* 156, 157.

49. Barbara Omolade, "We Speak for the Planet," in *Rocking the Ship of State,* ed. A. Harris and Y. King, 181.

50. For further discussion, see Virginia Held, "Terrorism, Rights, and Political Goals," in *Violence, Terrorism, and Justice,* ed. R. G. Frey and Christopher W. Morris (Cambridge, Eng.: Cambridge University Press, 1991).

51. To avoid overpopulation, responsible limiting of childbearing is needed; global experience shows that among the most important factors conducive to a lowering of birth rates are raising the social status of women, and increasing opportunities for women to

be employed outside the home. See P. Ehrlich and A. Ehrlich, *Population, Resources, Environment*. According to Stephen Sinding, director of population sciences at the Rockefeller Foundation, "among the general factors affecting childbearing, like infant mortality, nutritional levels and social security, the education and status of women is the most important." (*New York Times,* 31 May 1992, A12). The World Bank, in its annual world development report issued in May 1992, stated that better education for women was crucial in reducing the number of children born into poverty.

52. Ynestra King, Afterword, *Rocking the Ship of State,* ed. A. Harris and Y. King, 281–82.

Chapter 8

1. For an account of the treatment of women in the history of political thought, and of how its assumptions persist, see S. Okin, *Women in Western Political Thought;* L. Clark and L. Lange, eds., *The Sexism of Social and Political Theory;* Carole Pateman and Elizabeth Gross, eds., *Feminist Challenges: Social and Political Theory* (Sydney, Australia: Allen and Unwin, 1986); J. Elshtain, *Public Man, Private Woman;* and Mary Lyndon Shanley and Carole Pateman, eds., *Feminist Interpretations and Political Theory* (University Park, Pa.: Pennsylvania State University Press, 1991). For detailed discussion of theoretical issues concerning women's lack of legal equality in the nineteenth century, see Mary Lyndon Shanley, *Feminism, Marriage, and the Law in Victorian England: 1850–1895* (Princeton: Princeton University Press, 1989).

2. Realizations occurring in the women's movement as a whole were sometimes anticipated in, and sometimes reflected by, academic work on women's issues and feminist theory. I will not try here to sort out the connections or directions of these influences.

3. My own participation in these debates occurred in papers presented in the early 1970s, for instance on the equal obligations of mothers and fathers.

4. See Zillah Eisenstein, *The Radical Future of Liberal Feminism* (New York: Longman, 1981). For an account of how even the relatively simple goal of passing an Equal Rights Amendment to the Constitution was blocked, see Jane Mansbridge, *Why We Lost the ERA* (Chicago: University of Chicago Press, 1986).

5. S. Okin, *Women in Western Political Thought,* 282.

6. C. Pateman, *Disorder of Women,* 183–85.

7. For further discussion, see V. Held, *Rights and Goods,* chap. 8; see also Carol C. Gould, "Private Rights and Public Virtues: Women, the Family, and Democracy," in *Beyond Domination;* and Carol C. Gould, *Rethinking Democracy: Freedom and Social Cooperation in Politics, Economy and Society* (Cambridge, Eng.: Cambridge University Press, 1988).

8. For further argument see Nancy Fraser, "Women, Welfare, and the Politics of Need Interpretation," *Hypatia* 2 (Winter 1987): 102–22.

9. See S. Harding, "The Sex/Gender System."

10. A. Jaggar, *Feminist Politics,* 308–16.

11. See Larry Blum, Marcia Homiak, Judy Housman, and Naomi Scheman, "Altruism and Women's Oppression," in *Women and Philosophy: Toward a Theory of Liberation,* ed. Carol C. Gould and Marx W. Wartofsky (New York: Putnam, 1976); and B. C. Postow, "Economic Dependence and Self-Respect," *Philosophical Forum* 10 (Winter-Summer 1978–79): 181–205.

12. C. Littleton, "Reconstructing Sexual Equality," 228; see also M. Minow, *Making All the Difference.*

13. C. Littleton, "Reconstructing Sexual Equality," 206.

14. See Catharine A. MacKinnon, *Feminism Unmodified: Discourses on Life and Law* (Cambridge: Harvard University Press, 1987).

15. Iris Marion Young, "The Ideal of Community and the Politics of Difference," *Social Theory and Practice* 12 (Spring 1986): 1–26.

16. See Cynthia Fuchs Epstein, *Deceptive Distinctions: Sex, Gender, and the Social Order* (New Haven: Yale University Press, 1988).

17. See B. Ehrenreich and D. English, *For Her Own Good.*

18. Daniel N. Maltz and Ruth A. Borker, "A Cultural Approach to Male-Female Miscommunication," in *Language and Social Identity*, ed. John J. Gumperz (Cambridge: Cambridge University Press, 1982), 196–216. See also Carol Gilligan, Nona P. Lyons, and Trudy J. Hanmer, eds., *Making Connections: The Relational Worlds of Adolescent Girls at Emma Willard School* (Cambridge: Harvard University Press, 1990).

19. Deborah Tannen, *You Just Don't Understand: Women and Men in Conversation* (New York: Ballantine Books, 1991).

20. See Nancy C. M. Hartsock, "The Feminist Standpoint: Developing the Ground for a Specifically Feminist Historical Materialism," in *Discovering Reality*, ed. S. Harding and M. Hintikka.

21. C. Gilligan, *In a Different Voice,* 134.

22. S. Ruddick, "Remarks on the Sexual Politics of Reason," in *Women and Moral Theory,* ed. E. Kittay and D. Meyers.

23. For a relevant discussion see N. Scheman, "Individualism."

24. C. Gilligan, "Moral Orientation and Moral Development," 24.

25. E. Kittay and D. Meyers, eds., *Women and Moral Theory,* 10.

26. Thomas Hobbes, *Leviathan,* ed. C. B. Macpherson (Baltimore, Md.: Penguin Books, 1971).

Chapter 9

1. For discussion of this combination, see Frank Cunningham, *Democratic Theory and Socialism* (Cambridge, Eng.: Cambridge University Press, 1987).

2. Other works which can be considered in this category are Michael Harrington, *Socialism* (New York: Bantam, 1973); Joshua Cohen and Joel Rogers, *On Democracy: Toward a Transformation of American Society* (New York: Penguin Books, 1983).

3. See C. B. Macpherson, *The Political Theory of Possessive Individualism* (New York: Oxford University Press, 1972).

4. Anne Phillips, *Engendering Democracy.* (University Park, Pa.: Penn State University Press, 1991), 6.

5. C. B. Macpherson, *Democratic Theory: Essays in Retrieval* (Oxford: Clarendon Press, 1973) 51, 54. I omit any special attention to Macpherson's exclusive use of masculine pronouns—standard at the time—in passages such as this. In his later work he modified the practice to some extent.

6. C. Macpherson, *Democratic Theory,* 54–55. See also N. Hartsock, *Money, Sex, and Power.* For discussion of the concept of self-development, see C. Gould, *Rethinking Democracy.*

7. See Gerald MacCallum, "Negative and Positive Freedom," *Philosophical Review* 76 (July 1967): 312–34.

8. C. Macpherson, *Democratic Theory,* 60.

9. The phrase is Husseen Abdilahi Bulhan's; he uses it in *Franz Fanon and the Psychology of Oppression* to characterize slaves and oppressed persons of color. Citing the work of Orlando Patterson and Chester Pierce, he means by it a status in which, in the words of Bartky's summary, "one's person lacks integrity, worth and autonomy . . . one is subject to violations of space, time, energy, mobility, bonding and identity." In Sandra Lee Bartky, *Femininity and Domination: Studies in the Phenomenology of Oppression* (New York: Routledge, 1990), 133, n. 6; 85, 86.

10. S. Bartky, *Femininity and Domination*, 87, 85, 97.

11. See Roberta M. Hall and Bernice R. Sandler, "The Classroom Climate: A Chilly One for Women?" Washington, D.C.: Project on the Status and Education of Women, Association of American Colleges, 1982.

12. A. Ferguson and N. Folbre, "The Unhappy Marriage," in *Women and Revolution*, 317, 319. See also Ann Ferguson, "On Conceiving Motherhood and Sexuality," in *Mothering: Essays in Feminist Theory*, ed. J. Trebilcot; and A. Ferguson, *Blood at the Root*.

13. C. Macpherson, *Democratic Theory*, 42.

14. C. Macpherson, *Democratic Theory*, 14.

15. C. Macpherson, *Democratic Theory*, 76, 74.

16. C. Macpherson, *Democratic Theory*, 133.

17. Brian Barry, *The Liberal Theory of Justice* (London: Oxford University Press, 1973), 166.

18. Rawls's assumption about the persons for whom his theory of justice was developed is that they do not take an interest in one another's interests (J. Rawls, *Theory of Justice*, 13). David Gauthier's formulation of a similar notion of mutual unconcern follows Wicksteed's requirement of "non-tuism," and is somewhat less restrictive. It requires that persons "be conceived as not taking an interest in the interests of those with whom they exchange," though their preferences may involve some third person not party to the interaction in question (D. Gauthier, *Morals by Agreement*, 87).

19. See C. B. Macpherson, "Pluralism, Individualism, and Participation," in *The Rise and Fall of Economic Justice, and Other Papers* (New York: Oxford University Press, 1985).

20. Jane Mansbridge examines two types of democracy: "adversary democracy," where interests conflict, and "unitary democracy," where interests are shared. She provides an enlightening critique of the way prevailing democratic theory regularly assumes that interests conflict. Feminist views of democracy would surely give more emphasis to the kind of participatory democracies Mansbridge studied, where the ultimate concern was what was thought of as solidarity, community, fraternity, or sisterhood. "It was from this concern," Mansbridge writes, "that their commitment to equality, face-to-face assembly, and consensus primarily derived." Jane Mansbridge, *Beyond Adversary Democracy* (Chicago: University of Chicago Press, 1983), viii.

21. C. Macpherson, *Democratic Theory*, 50.

22. C. B. Macpherson, "Problems of Human Rights in the Late Twentieth Century," in *Rise and Fall*, 23.

23. C. B. Macpherson, *Life and Times of Liberal Democracy* (New York: Oxford University Press, 1977), 19–20, 100, 114.

24. On the conception of government as neutral arbiter, see chap. 3, n. 28 for references.

25. Jean-Jacques Rousseau, *The Social Contract*, ed. Charles Frankel (New York: Hafner, 1947); for discussion, see Robert Paul Wolff, *In Defense of Anarchism* (New York: Harper,

1970); and Marshall Berman, *The Politics of Authenticity; Radical Individualism and the Emergence of Modern Society* (New York: Atheneum, 1970).

26. Some feminists are reviving and reinterpreting the Aristotelian conception of "civic friendship," recognizing its relevance while discarding its dependence on the perspective of privileged men. See J. Mansbridge, *Beyond Adversary Democracy,* chap. 2; and Sibyl Schwarzenbach, "A Political Reading of the Reproductive Soul in Aristotle," *History of Philosophy Quarterly* 9 (July 1992): 243–64.

27. See A. MacIntyre, *After Virtue;* and Michael J. Sandel, *Liberalism and the Limits of Justice* (Cambridge, Eng.: Cambridge University Press, 1982).

28. M. Friedman, "The Social Self," 170–171, 173.

29. See D. Meyers, *Self, Society, and Personal Choice.*

30. George Sher, "Three Grades of Social Involvement," *Philosophy and Public Affairs* 18 (Spring 1989): 140.

31. See Ifeanyi Menkiti, "Person and Community in African Traditional Thought," in *African Philosophy: An Introduction,* 3d ed., ed. Richard A. Wright (New York: University Press of America, 1984); and Sandra Harding, "The Curious Coincidence of Feminine and African Moralities: Challenges for Feminist Theory," in *Women and Moral Theory,* ed. E. Kittay and D. Meyers.

Chapter 10

1. A. D. Lindsey, in his introduction to the Everyman edition of the *Leviathan* (New York: Dutton, 1947), the one I read as a student, quotes Aubrey thus: "He was forty years old before he looked on geometry which happened accidentally; being in a gentleman's library Euclid's *Elements* lay open, and it was the 47th Proposition, Lib. I. So he reads the proposition. 'By God,' says he, 'this is impossible.' So he reads the demonstration of it, which referred him back to another which he also read, *et sic deinceps,* that at last he was demonstratively convinced of that truth. This made him in love with geometry" (viii).

2. Virginia Held, "Rationality and Reasonable Cooperation," *Social Research* 44 (Winter 1977): 708–44.

3. J. Rawls, *Theory of Justice;* Rawls has subsequently made explicit that his theory of justice is political only. Robert Nozick, *Anarchy, State, and Utopia* (New York: Basic Books, 1974).

4. See chap. 9, n. 18.

5. In trying to decide whether others can be trusted to cooperate, rather than expected to cheat, in mutually beneficial interactions, we need not assume, in David Gauthier's view, that persons are fully transparent and incapable of deception. He does, however, assume that persons can be translucent "so that their dispositions to co-operate or not may be ascertained by others, not with certainty, but as more than mere guesswork." *Morals by Agreement,* 174.

6. As Carole Pateman writes, "One of the most striking features of the past two decades is the extent to which the assumptions of liberal individualism have permeated the whole of social life." All those fields influenced by rational choice theory—and that includes most of the social sciences—thus "hark back to classical liberal contract doctrines, and claims that social order is founded on the interactions of self-interested, utility-maximizing individuals, protecting and enlarging their property in the capitalist market." *The Problem of Political Obligation: A Critique of Liberal Theory* (Berkeley: University of California Press, 1985) 182–83.

7. On the social contract, see T. Hobbes, *Leviathan;* John Locke, *Two Treatises of Government,* ed. Peter Laslett (New York: Mentor, 1965); J. -J. Rousseau, *The Social Contract; The Declaration of Independence;* and of course a literature too vast to mention. As Pateman writes of this tradition, "a corollary of the liberal view . . . is that social contract theory is central to liberalism. Paradigmatically, contract is the act through which two free and equal individuals create social bonds, or a collection of such individuals creates the state." *Problems of Political Obligation,* 180. On economic life as a free market, see Adam Smith, *The Wealth of Nations,* ed. M. Lerner (New York: Random House, 1937) and virtually the whole of classical and neoclassical economics. The phrase "free market of ideas" has been entrenched in judicial and social discussion since Oliver Wendell Holmes used it in *Abrams v. United States,* 250 U.S. 616 (1919).

8. J. Rawls, *Theory of Justice;* R. Nozick, *Anarchy, State;* and Ronald Dworkin, *Taking Rights Seriously* (Cambridge: Harvard University Press, 1977).

9. David A. J. Richards, *A Theory of Reasons for Action* (New York: Oxford University Press, 1971); and D. Gauthier, *Morals by Agreement.*

10. For a sample, see the symposium "Explanation and Justification in Social Theory," in *Ethics* 97 (October 1986).

11. The paradigm of economic man has long been criticized from Marxist and various other points of view, but because these leave out the perspectives of mothers as fully as do those they criticize, I omit such views in pursuing the alternative I develop here.

12. L. May, *The Morality of Groups,* 3.

13. J. -J. Rousseau, *The Social Contract; Emile,* trans. B. Foxley (New York: Dutton, 1911).

14. See Susan Peterson, "Against 'Parenting,'" in *Mothering: Essays in Feminist Theory,* ed. J. Trebilcot.

15. In the *Leviathan* Hobbes imagines that in exchange for nourishment, children tacitly agree to obey their mothers. Pt. II, chap. 20.

16. A. Smith, *Wealth of Nations,* I, chap. 2.

17. Annette Baier, "Hume: The Women's Moral Theorist?" in *Women and Moral Theory,* ed. E. Kittay and D. Meyers; David Hume, *Essays Moral, Political, and Literary,* vol. 1, ed. T. H. Green and T. H. Gross (London: Longmans, 1898), 176.

18. C. Gilman, *Herland,* 60, 66.

19. Jane Flax, "The Family in Contemporary Feminist Thought: A Critical Review," in *The Family in Political Thought,* ed. Jean Bethke Elshtain (Amherst: University of Massachusetts Press, 1982), 252.

20. The collection of readings in Barrie Thorne, ed., *Rethinking the Family* (New York: Longman, 1982) is a useful source. See also *Mothering,* ed. J. Trebilcot, and such feminist utopian novels as M. Piercy, *Woman on the Edge of Time.*

21. See V. Held, *Rights and Goods,* chap. 5.

22. In some societies, social pressures to conform with the norms of reciprocal care— of children by parents and later of parents by children—can be very great. But these societies are usually at a stage of development antecedent to that of contractual society.

23. The gerontologist Elaine Brody says about old people that "what we hear over and over again—and I'm talking gross numbers of 80 to 90 percent in survey after survey— is 'I don't want to be a burden on my children.'" Interview by Lindsay Van Gelder, *Ms. Magazine* 14 (January 1986): 48.

24. In an illuminating account of mothering arrangements among black women, Patricia

Hill Collins writes that "othermothers—women who assist blood mothers by sharing mothering responsibilities—traditionally have been central to the institution of Black motherhood . . . Organized, resilient, women-centered networks of bloodmothers and othermothers are key in understanding this centrality. Grandmothers, sisters, aunts, or cousins act as othermothers by taking on child-care responsibilities for one another's children." The networks often include "fictive kin," beyond biologically related persons. P. Collins, *Black Feminist Thought,* 119–120. Obviously such networks cannot be understood in terms of contractual relationships.

25. For a different view, see Howard Cohen, *Equal Rights for Children* (Totowa, N.J.: Littlefield Adams, 1980); for discussion, see Laura M. Purdy, *In Their Best Interest? The Case against Equal Rights for Children* (Ithaca, N.Y.: Cornell University Press, 1992).

26. See Robert E. Goodin, *Protecting the Vulnerable: A Reanalysis of Our Social Responsibilities* (Chicago: University of Chicago Press, 1985).

27. For related discussions, see N. Hartsock, *Money, Sex, and Power;* and S. Ruddick, *Maternal Thinking.*

28. For examples of the view that women are more deficient than men in understanding morality and acting morally, see selections in M. Mahowald, ed., *Philosophy of Woman;* L. Kohlberg, *Philosophy of Moral Development;* and L. Kohlberg and R. Kramer, "Continuities and Discontinuities."

29. Virginia Held, "Marx, Sex, and the Transformation of Society," *The Philosophical Forum* 5 (Fall-Winter 1973–74): 168–84.

Epilogue

1. Mark C. Taylor, "Descartes, Nietzsche, and the Search for the Unsayable," *New York Times Book Review,* 1 February 1987.

2. For a related view, see Rosi Braidotti, "The Subject in Feminism," *Hypatia* 6 (Summer 1991): 155–72.

3. A. Huyssen, *After the Great Divide,* 47.

4. Paul Kennedy, "Fin-de-Siècle America," *New York Review of Books,* 28 June 1990, 31–40.

5. For consideration of this question in interpreting history, see Joan Kelly, "Did Women Have a Renaissance?" in *Becoming Visible: Women in European History,* ed. Renate Bridenthal and Claudia Koonz (New York: Houghton Mifflin, 1977); and G. Lerner, *The Majority Finds Its Past.*

6. See Vivian Gornick, "Who Says We Haven't Made a Revolution?" *New York Times Magazine,* 15 April 1990, 24.

7. Annette C. Baier, *Postures of the Mind: Essays on Mind and Morals* (Minneapolis: University of Minnesota Press, 1985), 210–11.

8. Starting with *The Public Interest and Individual Interests* (New York: Basic Books, 1970) most of my work has considered what we ought to do from where we are here and now, rather than what ideal principles of perfect justice or equality would hold.

9. For a portrayal of how far women still have to go to attain even minimal levels of respect and equality, see Marilyn French, *The War against Women* (New York: Simon and Schuster, 1992).

10. A. Jaggar, "Taking Consent Seriously."

11. See *Beyond Rhetoric: A New American Agenda for Children and Families.* Final Report of the National Commission on Children (Washington, D.C.: U.S. Government Printing

Office, 1991); *Who Cares for America's Children?* Report of the National Academy of Sciences (National Academy Press, 1990); Fred M. Hechinger, "Why France Outstrips the United States in Nurturing Its Children," *New York Times,* 1 August 1990; and report by Robert Pear on the Report of the White House Task Force on Infant Mortality, *New York Times,* 6 August 1990, A1, B9.

12. See C. Merchant, *Death of Nature,* 170–89.

13. See Karen Warren, "Feminism and Ecology: Making Connections," *Environmental Ethics* 9 (1987): 3–20.

14. Bernard Williams, *Ethics and the Limits of Philosophy* (Cambridge: Harvard University Press, 1985), 18.

15. Peter Railton, "Moral Theory as a Moral Practice," *Noûs* 25 (April 1991): 188.

16. Marilyn Friedman, "Beyond Caring: The De-Moralization of Gender," in *Science, Morality and Feminist Theory,* ed. M. Hanen and K. Nielsen, 101, quoting Marilyn Frye; see also S. Okin, *Justice, Gender, and the Family.*

17. Nel Noddings, "A Response," *Hypatia* 5 (Spring 1990): 123.

18. M. Friedman, "Beyond Caring," 105.

19. A good example of such an argument is A. Baier's "The Need for More Than Justice."

20. Kathleen B. Jones, "Citizenship in a Woman-Friendly Polity," *Signs* 15 (Summer 1990): 807.

21. See Elizabeth S. Anderson, "Is Women's Labor a Commodity?" *Philosophy and Public Affairs* 19 (Winter 1990): 71–92.

Selected Bibliography

Alcoff, Linda. "Cultural Feminism versus Post-Structuralism: The Identity Crisis in Feminist Theory." *Signs: Journal of Women in Culture and Society* 13 (Spring 1988): 405–36.
———. "The Problem of Speaking for Others." *Cultural Critique* 20 (Winter 1991–92): 5–32.
Anderson, Elizabeth S. "Is Women's Labor a Commodity?" *Philosophy and Public Affairs* 19 (Winter 1990): 71–92.
Angus, Ian, and Sut Jhally, eds. *Cultural Politics in Contemporary America.* New York: Routledge, 1989.
Antony, Louise, and Charlotte Witt, eds. *A Mind of One's Own: Feminist Essays on Reason and Objectivity.* Boulder, Colo.: Westview Press, 1992.
Archer, Margaret S. *Culture and Agency: The Place of Culture in Social Theory.* Cambridge, Eng.: Cambridge University Press, 1988.
Arendt, Hannah. *The Human Condition.* Chicago: University of Chicago Press, 1958.
Ariès, Philippe. *The Hour of Our Death,* trans. H. Weaver. New York: Knopf, 1981.
Baier, Annette C. *Postures of the Mind: Essays on Mind and Morals.* Minneapolis: University of Minnesota Press, 1985.
———. "Trust and Anti-Trust." *Ethics* 96 (January 1986): 231–60.
———. "Hume: The Women's Moral Theorist?" In *Women and Moral Theory,* ed. Eva Feder Kittay and Diana T. Meyers. Totowa, N.J.: Rowman and Allanheld, 1987.
———. "The Need for More than Justice." In *Science, Morality and Feminist Theory,* ed. Marsha Hanen and Kai Nielsen. Calgary: University of Calgary Press, 1987.
———. "Whom Can Women Trust?" In *Feminist Ethics,* ed. Claudia Card. Lawrence: University Press of Kansas, 1991.
Baron, Marcia. "Kantian Ethics and Supererogation." *Journal of Philosophy* 84 (May 1987): 237–62.
Barry, Brian. *The Liberal Theory of Justice.* London: Oxford University Press, 1973.
Bartky, Sandra Lee. *Femininity and Domination: Studies in the Phenomenology of Oppression.* New York: Routledge, 1990.
Beauvoir, Simone de. *The Second Sex,* trans. H. Parshley. New York: Bantam, 1953.
Becker, Ernest. *The Denial of Death.* New York: Free Press, 1973.
Belenky, Mary, Blythe Clinchy, Nancy Goldberger, and Jill Tarule. *Women's Ways of Knowing: The Development of Self, Voice, and Mind.* New York: Basic Books, 1986.
Bell, Linda, ed. *Visions of Women.* Clifton, N.J.: Humana, 1985.
Benhabib, Seyla. "The Generalized and the Concrete Other: The Kohlberg-Gilligan Controversy and Moral Theory." In *Women and Moral Theory,* ed. Eva Feder Kittay and Diana T. Meyers. Totowa, N.J.: Rowman and Littlefield, 1987.

Benhabib, Seyla, and Drucilla Cornell, eds. *Feminism as Critique: On the Politics of Gender.* Minneapolis: University of Minnesota Press, 1987.

Berger, Fred R., ed. *Freedom of Expression.* Belmont, Calif.: Wadsworth, 1980.

Blum, Lawrence A. *Friendship, Altruism and Morality.* London: Routledge, 1980.

————. "Gilligan and Kohlberg: Implications for Moral Theory." *Ethics* 98 (April 1988): 474–91.

Blum, Larry, Marcia Homiak, Judy Housman, and Naomi Scheman. "Altruism and Women's Oppression." In *Women and Philosophy: Toward a Theory of Liberation,* ed. Carol C. Gould and Marx W. Wartofsky. New York: Putnam, 1976.

Bordo, Susan. "The Cartesian Masculinization of Thought." *Signs* 11 (Spring 1986): 439–56.

————. "Feminism, Postmodernism, and Gender-Scepticism." In *Feminism/Postmodernism,* ed. Linda J. Nicholson. New York: Routledge, 1990.

Braidotti, Rosi. "The Subject in Feminism." *Hypatia: A Journal of Feminist Philosophy* 6 (Summer 1991): 155–72.

Bridenthal, Renate, and Claudia Koonz, eds. *Becoming Visible: Women in European History.* New York: Houghton Mifflin, 1977.

Brock-Utne, Birgit. *Educating for Peace: A Feminist Perspective.* New York: Pergamon Press, 1985.

————. "The Peace Concepts through Three United Nations Women Decade Conferences." Oslo: International Peace Research Institute: PRIO Working Paper (January 1986).

Brown, Carol. "Mothers, Fathers, and Children: From Private to Public Patriarchy." In *Women and Revolution,* ed. Lydia Sargent. Boston: South End Press, 1981.

Bulkin, Elly, Minnie Bruce Pratt, and Barbara Smith. *Yours in Struggle: Three Perspectives on Anti-Semitism and Racism.* Brooklyn, N.Y.: Long Haul Press, 1984.

Caldicott, Helen. *Missile Envy: The Arms Race and Nuclear War.* Revised edition. New York: Bantam, 1986.

Calhoun, Cheshire. "Justice, Care, Gender Bias." *Journal of Philosophy* 85 (September 1988): 451–63.

Cannon, Katie Geneva. *Black Womanist Ethics.* Atlanta, Ga.: Scholars Press, 1988.

Card, Claudia. "Gender and Moral Luck." In *Identity, Character, and Morality: Essays in Moral Psychology,* ed. Owen Flanagan and Amélie Oksenberg Rorty. Cambridge: MIT Press, 1990.

————, ed. *Feminist Ethics.* Lawrence: University Press of Kansas, 1991.

Carnegie Commission on the Future of Public Broadcasting. *A Public Trust.* New York: Bantam, 1979.

Chodorow, Nancy. *The Reproduction of Mothering: Psychoanalysis and the Sociology of Gender.* Berkeley: University of California Press, 1978.

Clark, Lorenne, and Lynda Lange, eds. *The Sexism of Social and Political Theory: Women and Reproduction from Plato to Nietzsche.* Toronto: University of Toronto Press, 1979.

Code, Lorraine. "Second Persons." In *Science, Morality and Feminist Theory,* ed. Marsha Hanen and Kai Nielsen. Calgary: University of Calgary Press, 1987.

Cohen, Howard. *Equal Rights for Children.* Totowa, N.J.: Littlefield, Adams, 1980.

Cohen, Joshua, and Joel Rogers. *On Democracy: Toward a Transformation of American Society.* New York: Penguin Books, 1983.

Cohn, Carol. "Sex and Death in the Rational World of Defense Intellectuals." *Signs* 12 (Summer 1987): 687–718.

Collins, Patricia Hill. *Black Feminist Thought: Knowledge, Consciousness, and the Politics of Empowerment.* Boston: Unwin Hyman, 1990.

Corea, Gena. *The Mother Machine: Reproductive Technologies from Artificial Insemination to Artificial Wombs.* New York: Harper and Row, 1985.

Cunningham, Frank. *Democratic Theory and Socialism.* Cambridge, Eng.: Cambridge University Press, 1987.

Curran, James, Michael Gurevitch, and Janet Wollacott, eds. *Mass Communication and Society.* Beverly Hills, Calif.: Sage, 1977.

Dalla Costa, Mariarosa, and Selma James. *The Power of Women and the Subversion of Community.* Bristol, Eng.: Falling Wall Press, 1973.

Daly, Mary. *Gyn/Ecology: The Metaethics of Radical Feminism.* Boston: Beacon Press, 1978.

Daniel, E. Valentine. *Fluid Signs: Being a Person the Tamil Way.* Berkeley: University of California Press, 1984.

Daniels, Norman. "Wide Reflective Equilibrium and Theory Acceptance in Ethics." *Journal of Philosophy* 76 (May 1979): 256–82.

Danto, Arthur C. *Connections to the World.* New York: Harper and Row, 1989.

Darwall, Stephen L. *Impartial Reason.* Ithaca, N.Y.: Cornell University Press, 1983.

———. "Autonomous Internalism and the Justification of Morals." *Noûs* 24 (April 1990): 257–67.

Davis, Angela Y. *Women, Culture, and Politics.* New York: Vintage, 1990.

Davis, Flora. *Moving the Mountain: The Women's Movement in America since 1960.* New York: Simon and Schuster, 1991.

De George, Richard. "Ethics and Coherence." *Proceedings and Addresses of The American Philosophical Association* 64 (November 1990): 39–52.

de Lauretis, Teresa, ed. *Feminist Studies, Critical Studies.* Bloomington: Indiana University Press, 1986.

Deming, Barbara. *We Are All Part of One Another: A Barbara Deming Reader,* ed. Jane Meyerding. Philadelphia: New Society Educational Foundation, 1984.

Dinnerstein, Dorothy. *The Mermaid and the Minotaur: Sexual Arrangements and Human Malaise.* New York: Harper and Row, 1977.

Di Stefano, Christine. *Configurations of Masculinity: A Feminist Perspective on Modern Political Theory.* Ithaca, N.Y.: Cornell University Press, 1991.

Donchin, Anne. "The Future of Mothering: Reproductive Technology and Feminist Theory." *Hypatia* 1 (Fall 1986): 121–37.

Dworkin, Ronald. *Taking Rights Seriously.* Cambridge: Harvard University Press, 1977.

Ehrenriech, Barbara, And Deirdre English. *Witches, Midwives, and Nurses: A History of Women Healers.* New York: Feminist Press, 1973.

———. *For Her Own Good: 150 Years of Experts' Advice to Women.* Garden City, N.Y.: Doubleday/Anchor, 1979.

Eisenstein, Zillah. *The Radical Future of Liberal Feminism.* New York: Longman, 1981.

Eisler, Riane. *The Chalice and the Blade.* San Francisco: Harper and Row, 1987.

Elshtain, Jean Bethke. *Public Man, Private Woman.* Princeton: Princeton University Press, 1981.

———, ed. *The Family in Political Thought.* Amherst: University of Massachusetts Press, 1982.

Engels, Frederick. *The Origin of the Family: Private Property and the State,* ed. Eleanor Leacock. New York: International Publishers, 1972. Originally published 1884.

Enloe, Cynthia. *Does Khaki Become You? The Militarization of Women's Lives.* Boston: South End Press, 1983.

Epstein, Cynthia Fuchs. *Deceptive Distinctions: Sex, Gender, and the Social Order.* New Haven: Yale University Press, 1988.

Faludi, Susan. *Backlash: The Undeclared War Against American Women.* New York: Crown, 1991.

Ferguson, Ann. "On Conceiving Motherhood and Sexuality." In *Mothering: Essays in Feminist Theory,* ed. Joyce Trebilcot. Totowa, N.J.: Rowman and Allanheld, 1984.

———. *Blood at the Root: Motherhood, Sexuality and Male Domination.* London: Pandora, 1989.

Ferguson, Ann, and Nancy Folbre. "The Unhappy Marriage of Patriarchy and Capitalism." In *Women and Revolution,* ed. Lydia Sargent. Boston: South End Press, 1981.

Firestone, Shulamith. *The Dialectic of Sex: The Case for Feminist Revolution.* New York: Morrow, 1970.

Flanagan, Owen J., and Jonathan E. Adler. "Impartiality and Particularity." *Social Research* 50 (Autumn 1983): 576–96.

Flanagan, Owen, and Kathryn Jackson. "Justice, Care, and Gender: The Kohlberg-Gilligan Debate Revisited." *Ethics* 97 (April 1987): 622–37.

Flax, Jane. "The Family in Contemporary Feminist Thought: A Critical Review." In *The Family in Political Thought,* ed. Jean Bethke Elshtain. Amherst: University of Massachusetts Press, 1982.

———. "Gender as a Social Problem: In and for Feminist Theory." *Amerikastudien/American Studies* 31 (1986): 193–213.

Foucault, Michel. *The History of Sexuality: An Introduction.* Vol. 1. New York: Vintage, 1990; Gallimard, 1976.

Fraser, Nancy. "Women, Welfare and the Politics of Need Interpretation." *Hypatia* 2 (Winter 1987): 103–22.

———. "Michel Foucault: A 'Young Conservative'?" *Ethics* 96 (October 1985): 165–84.

Fraser, Nancy, and Linda Nicholson. "Social Criticism without Philosophy: An Encounter between Feminism and Postmodernism." In *Feminism/Postmodernism,* ed. Linda J. Nicholson. New York: Routledge, 1990.

Freeman, Jo. *The Politics of Women's Liberation.* New York: Longman, 1975.

French, Marilyn. *The War against Women.* New York: Simon and Schuster, 1992.

French, Peter A. *Collective and Corporate Responsibility.* New York: Columbia University Press, 1984.

Friedman, Marilyn. "Beyond Caring: The De-Moralization of Gender." In *Science, Morality and Feminist Theory,* ed. Marsha Hanen and Kai Nielsen. Calgary: University of Calgary Press, 1987.

———. "Individuality without Individualism: Review of Janice Raymond's *A Passion for Friends.*" *Hypatia* 3 (Summer 1988): 131–37.

———. "Feminism and Modern Friendship: Dislocating the Community." *Ethics* 99 (January 1989): 275–90.

———. "The Social Self and the Partiality Debates." In *Feminist Ethics,* ed. Claudia Card. Lawrence: University Press of Kansas, 1991.

Frye, Marilyn. "Getting It Right." *Signs* 17 (Summer 1992): 781–805.

Garofalo, Reebee, ed. *Rockin' the Boat: Mass Music and Mass Movements.* Boston: South End Press, 1992.

Gauthier, David. *Morals by Agreement.* Oxford: Clarendon Press, 1986.

Geertz, Clifford. *The Interpretation of Cultures.* New York: Basic Books, 1973.

Gewirth, Alan. *Reason and Morality.* Chicago: University of Chicago Press, 1978.

Gilligan, Carol. *In A Different Voice: Psychological Theory and Women's Development.* Cambridge: Harvard University Press, 1982.

———. "Moral Orientation and Moral Development." In *Women and Moral Theory,* ed. Eva Feder Kittay and Diana T. Meyers. Totowa, N.J.: Rowman and Littlefield, 1987.

Gilligan, Carol, Nona P. Lyons, and Trudy J. Hanmer, eds. *Making Connections: The Relational Worlds of Adolescent Girls at Emma Willard School.* Cambridge: Harvard University Press, 1990.

Gilman, Charlotte Perkins. *Herland.* New York: Pantheon, 1979. Written in 1915.

Gitlin, Todd, ed. *Watching Television.* New York: Pantheon, 1986.

Goodin, Robert E. *Protecting the Vulnerable: A Reanalysis of Our Social Responsibilities.* Chicago: University of Chicago Press, 1985.

Gordon, Linda. "What's New in Women's History?" In *Feminist Studies, Critical Studies,* ed. Teresa de Lauretis. Bloomington: Indiana University Press, 1986.

Gornick, Vivian. "Who Says We Haven't Made a Revolution?" *New York Times Magazine,* 15 April 1990.

Gornick, Vivian, and Barbara K. Moran, eds. *Woman in Sexist Society: Studies in Power and Powerlessness.* New York: Basic Books, 1971.

Gould, Carol C., ed. *Beyond Domination: New Perspectives on Women and Philosophy.* Totowa, N.J.: Rowman and Allanheld, 1984.

———. *Rethinking Democracy: Freedom and Social Cooperation in Politics, Economy and Society.* Cambridge, Eng.: Cambridge University Press, 1988.

Gould, Carol C., and Marx W. Wartofsky, eds. *Women and Philosophy.* New York: Putnam, 1976.

Griffin, Susan. *Woman and Nature: The Roaring Inside Her.* New York: Harper and Row, 1978.

Gurevitch, Michael, Tony Bennett, James Curran, and Janet Wollacott, eds. *Culture, Society and the Media.* New York: Methuen, 1982.

Haan, Norma. "Hypothetical and Actual Moral Reasoning in a Situation of Civil Disobedience." *Journal of Personality and Social Psychology* 32 (August 1975): 255–70.

Hall, Roberta M., and Bernice M. Sandler. *The Classroom Climate: A Chilly One for Women?* Washington D.C.: Project on the Status and Education of Women, Association of American Colleges, 1982.

Hall, Stuart. "Notes on Deconstructing 'the Popular.'" In *People's History and Socialist Theory,* ed. Raphael Samuel. London: Routledge, 1981.

Hampshire, Stuart, ed. *Public and Private Morality.* Cambridge, Eng.: Cambridge University Press, 1978.

Hanen, Marsha, and Kai Nielsen, eds. *Science, Morality and Feminist Theory.* Calgary: University of Calgary Press, 1987.

Harding, Sandra. "Why Has the Sex/Gender System Become Visible Only Now?" In *Discovering Reality,* ed. Sandra Harding and Merrill B. Hintikka. Dordrecht, Holland: Reidel, 1983.

———. *The Science Question in Feminism.* Ithaca, N.Y.: Cornell University Press, 1986.

————. "The Curious Coincidence of Feminine and African Moralities: Challenges for Feminist Theory." In *Women and Moral Theory,* ed. Eva Feder Kittay and Diana T. Meyers. Totowa, N.J.: Rowman and Littlefield, 1987.

Harding, Sandra, and Merrill B. Hintikka, eds. *Discovering Reality: Feminist Perspectives on Epistemology, Metaphysics, Methodology and Philosophy of Science.* Dordrecht, Holland: Reidel, 1983.

Hare, R. M. *Freedom and Reason.* New York: Oxford University Press, 1965.

Harman, Gilbert. *The Nature of Morality.* New York: Oxford University Press, 1977.

Harrington, Michael. *Socialism.* New York: Bantam, 1973.

Harris, Adrienne, and Ynestra King, eds. *Rocking the Ship of State: Towards a Feminist Peace Politics,* Boulder, Colo.: Westview, 1989.

Hartmann, Heidi. "The Unhappy Marriage of Marxism and Feminism: Towards a More Progressive Union." In *Women and Revolution,* ed. Lydia Sargent. Boston: South End Press, 1981.

Hartsock, Nancy C. M. *Money, Sex, and Power: Toward a Feminist Historical Materialism.* New York: Longman, 1983.

————. "The Barracks Community in Western Political Thought." In *Women and Men's Wars,* ed. Judith Stiehm. New York: Pergamon, 1983.

————. "The Feminist Standpoint: Developing the Ground for a Specifically Feminist Historical Materialism." In *Discovering Reality.* ed. Sandra Harding and Merrill B. Hintikka. Dordrecht, Holland: Reidel, 1983.

————. "Masculinity, Heroism and the Making of War." In *Rocking the Ship of State,* ed. Adrienne Harris and Ynestra King. Boulder, Colo.: Westview, 1989.

————. "Postmodernism and Political Change: Issues for Feminist Theory." *Cultural Critique* 14 (Winter 1989–90): 15–33.

————. "Foucault on Power: A Theory for Women?" In *Feminism/Postmodernism,* ed. Linda J. Nicholson. New York: Routledge, 1990.

Hawkesworth, Mary E. "Knowers, Knowing, Known: Feminist Theory and Claims of Truth." *Signs* 14 (Spring 1989): 553–57.

Hegel, G. W. F. *The Phenomenology of Mind,* trans. J. B. Baillie. New York: Harper, 1967. Originally published 1807.

————. *Philosophy of Right,* trans. T. M. Knox. Oxford: Clarendon Press, 1952. Originally published 1821.

Hekman, Susan. "Reconstituting the Subject: Feminism, Modernism, and Postmodernism." *Hypatia* 6 (Summer 1991): 44–63.

Held, David. *Introduction to Critical Theory: Horkheimer to Habermas.* Berkeley: University of California Press, 1980.

Held, Jane. "The British Peace Movement: A Critical Examination of Attitudes to Male Violence within the British Peace Movement as Expressed with Regard to the 'Molesworth Rapes.'" *Women's Studies International Forum* 11 (1988): 211–21.

Held, Virginia. "Reasonable Progress and Self-Respect." *Monist* 57 (January 1973): 12–27.

————. "Marx, Sex, and the Transformation of Society." *Philosophical Forum* 5 (Fall-Winter 1973–74): 168–84.

————. "Rationality and Reasonable Cooperation." *Social Research* 44 (Winter 1977): 708–44.

————. "The Obligations of Mothers and Fathers." In *Having Children: Philosophical and*

Legal Reflections on Parenthood, ed. Onora O'Neill and William Ruddick. New York: Oxford University Press, 1979.

———. "On Ronald Dworkin's Liberalism and Conservatism." In *Two Centuries of Philosophy in America,* ed. Peter Caws. London: Blackwell, 1980.

———. "The Political 'Testing' of Moral Theories." *Midwest Studies in Philosophy* 7 (Spring 1982): 343–63.

———. "The Division of Moral Labor and the Role of the Lawyer." In *The Good Lawyer,* ed. David Luban. Totowa, N.J.: Rowman and Allanheld, 1983.

———. "The Independence of Intellectuals." *Journal of Philosophy* 80 (October 1983): 572–82.

———. *Rights and Goods: Justifying Social Action.* New York: Free Press, 1984.

———. "Feminism and Epistemology: Recent Work on the Connection Between Gender and Knowledge." *Philosophy and Public Affairs* 14 (Summer 1985): 296–307.

———. "Access, Enablement, and the First Amendment." In *Philosophical Foundations of the Constitution,* ed. Diana T. Meyers and Kenneth Kipnis. Boulder, Colo.: Westview, 1988.

———. "Culture or Commerce: On the Liberation of Expression." *Philosophic Exchange* SUNY Brockport, nos. 19–20 (1988–89).

———. "Terrorism, Rights, and Political Goals." In *Violence, Terrorism, and Justice,* ed. R. G. Frey and Christopher W. Morris. Cambridge, Eng.: Cambridge University Press, 1991.

Heilbrun, Carolyn G. "Feminist Criticism in Departments of Literature." *Academe* 69 (September-October 1983): 11–14.

Hirsch, Marianne, and Evelyn Fox Keller, eds. *Conflicts in Feminism.* New York: Routledge, 1990.

Hoagland, Sarah Lucia. *Lesbian Ethics: Toward New Value.* Palo Alto, Calif.: Institute of Lesbian Studies, 1989.

Hobbes, Thomas. *The Citizen: Philosophical Rudiments Concerning Government and Society,* ed. B. Gert. Garden City, N.Y.: Doubleday, 1972. Originally published 1642.

———. *Leviathan,* ed. C. B. Macpherson Baltimore: Penguin Books, 1971. Originally published 1651.

Holstein, Constance Boucher. "Irreversible, Stepwise Sequence in the Development of Moral Judgment: A Longitudinal Study of Males and Females." *Child Development* 47 (March 1976): 51–61.

hooks, bell. *Feminist Theory: from Margin to Center.* Boston, South End Press, 1984.

Houston, Barbara. "Rescuing Womanly Virtues: Some Dangers of Moral Reclamation." In *Science, Morality and Feminist Theory,* ed. Marsha Hanen and Kai Nielsen. Calgary: University of Calgary Press, 1987.

Hull, Gloria T., Patricia Bell Scott, and Barbara Smith, eds. *All the Women Are White, All the Blacks Are Men, But Some of Us Are Brave.* New York: Feminist Press, 1982.

Hume, David. *Essays Moral, Political and Literary,* ed. T. H. Green and T. H. Grose. London: Longmans, 1898. Originally published 2 vols., 1741, 1742.

Huston, Nancy. "Tales of War and Tears of Women." In *Women and Men's Wars,* ed. Judith Stiehm. New York: Pergamon Press, 1983.

Huyssen, Andreas. *After the Great Divide: Modernism, Mass Culture, Postmodernism.* Bloomington: Indiana University Press, 1986.

Ishiguro, Hide. "Imagination." In *British Analytic Philosophy*, ed. B. Williams and A. Montefiore. New York: Humanities Press, 1966.

Jaggar, Alison M. *Feminist Politics and Human Nature.* Totowa, N.J.: Rowman and Allanheld, 1983.

———. "Human Biology in Feminist Theory: Sexual Equality Reconsidered." In *Beyond Domination*, ed. Carol Gould. Totowa, N.J.: Rowman and Allanheld, 1983.

———. "Feminist Ethics: Some Issues for the Nineties." *Journal of Social Philosophy* 20 (Spring-Fall 1989): 91–107.

———. "Love and Knowledge: Emotion in Feminist Epistemology." *Inquiry* 32 (June 1989): 151–76.

———. "Feminist Ethics: Projects, Problems, Prospects." In *Feminist Ethics,* ed. Claudia Card. Lawrence: University Press of Kansas, 1991.

———. "Taking Consent Seriously: Feminist Ethics and Actual Moral Dialogue." In *The Applied Ethics Reader,* ed. Earl Winkler and Jerrold Coombs. Oxford: Blackwell, 1993.

Jaggar, Alison M., and William L. McBride. "'Reproduction' as Male Ideology." *Women's Studies International Forum* (Hypatia) 8, no. 3 (1985): 185–96.

Jameson, Frederic. "Postmodernism, or the Cultural Logic of Late Capitalism." *New Left Review* 146 (July-August 1984): 53–93.

Johnson, Richard. "What Is Cultural Studies Anyway?" *Social Text: Theory/Culture/Ideology* 16 (Winter 1986–87): 38–80.

Jordan, Brigitte. *Birth in Four Cultures: A Cross-cultural Investigation of Childbirth in Yucatan, Holland, Sweden and the United States.* Montreal: Eden Press, 1980.

Jordan, Judith. "The Meaning of Mutuality." Wellesley, Mass.: Stone Center Working Paper No. 23, 1986.

Kaplan, E. Ann. *Rocking around the Clock: Music, Television, Postmodernism, and Consumer Culture.* New York: Methuen, 1987.

Kelly, Joan. "Did Women Have a Renaissance?" In *Becoming Visible: Women in European History.* ed. Renate Bridenthal and Claudia Koonz. New York: Houghton Mifflin, 1977.

Kenny, Anthony. *Action, Emotion and the Will.* London: Routledge, 1963.

Kessler-Harris, Alice. "The View from Women's Studies." *Signs* 17 (Summer 1992): 781–805.

King, Ynestra. Afterword. *Rocking the Ship of State,* ed. Adrienne Harris and Ynestra King. Boulder, Colo.: Westview, 1989.

Kittay, Eva Feder. "Womb Envy: An Explanatory Concept." In *Mothering,* ed. Joyce Trebilcot. Totowa, N.J.: Rowman and Allanheld, 1984.

———. "Woman as Metaphor." *Hypatia* 3 (Summer 1988): 63–86.

Kittay, Eva Feder, and Diana T. Meyers, eds. *Women and Moral Theory.* Totowa, N.J.: Rowman and Littlefield, 1987.

Kline, Stephen. "Limits to the Imagination: Marketing and Children's Culture." In *Cultural Politics in Contemporary America,* ed. Ian Angus and Sut Jhally. New York: Routledge, 1989.

Kohlberg, Lawrence. *The Philosophy of Moral Development.* San Francisco: Harper and Row, 1981.

Kohlberg, Lawrence, and Kramer, R. "Continuities and Discontinuities in Child and Adult Moral Development." *Human Development* 12, no. 2 (1969): 93–120.

Kolenda, Konstantin. "Facing Death: Four Literary Accounts." *Philosophic Exchange* SUNY Brockport, nos. 14–15 (1984–85).

Lange, Lynda. "On (Re)Claiming Feminism: Postmodern Doubts and Political Amnesia." Paper presented at the annual meeting of the American Philosophical Association, Central Division. Chicago. April 1991.

Larmore, Charles. *Patterns of Moral Complexity.* Cambridge, Eng.: Cambridge University Press, 1987.

Lapidus, Gail Warshofsky. *Women in Soviet Society: Equality, Development, and Social Change.* Berkeley: University of California Press, 1978.

Lazaro, Reyes. "Feminism and Motherhood: O'Brien vs. Beauvoir." *Hypatia* 1 (Fall 1986): 87–102.

Lazere, Donald, ed. *American Media and Mass Culture: Left Perspectives.* Berkeley: University of California Press, 1987.

Leavitt, Judith Walzer. *Brought to Bed: Childbearing in America 1750 to 1950.* New York: Oxford University Press, 1986.

Lerner, Gerda. *The Majority Finds Its Past: Placing Women in History.* New York: Oxford University Press, 1979.

Littleton, Christine A. "Reconstructing Sexual Equality." *California Law Review* 75 (1987): 201–59.

Lloyd, Genevieve. "Reason, Gender, and Morality in the History of Philosophy." *Social Research* 50 (Autumn 1983): 490–513.

———. *The Man of Reason: "Male" and "Female" in Western Philosophy.* Minneapolis: University of Minnesota Press, 1984.

Locke, John. *Two Treatises of Government,* ed. P. Laslett. New York: Mentor, 1965. Originally published 1690.

Lugones, Maria C., and Elizabeth V. Spelman, "Have We Got a Theory for You! Feminist Theory, Cultural Imperialism and the Demand for 'The Woman's Voice.'" *Women's Studies International Forum* (*Hypatia*) 6, no. 6 (1983): 573–81.

MacCallum, Gerald. "Negative and Positive Freedom." *Philosophical Review* 76 (July 1967): 312–34.

Machiavelli, Niccolo. *The Prince,* trans. G. Bull. New York: Penguin, 1961. (Originally published 1532.)

MacIntyre, Alasdair. *After Virtue: A Study in Moral Theory.* Notre Dame, Ind.: University of Notre Dame Press, 1981.

Mackie, J. L. *Inventing Right and Wrong.* New York: Penguin, 1977.

MacKinnon, Catharine A. *Feminism Unmodified: Discourses on Life and Law.* Cambridge: Harvard University Press, 1987.

———. *Toward a Feminist Theory of the State.* Cambridge: Harvard University Press, 1989.

Macoby, Eleanor Emmons, and Carol Nagy Jacklin. *The Psychology of Sex Differences.* Stanford, Calif.: Stanford University Press, 1974.

Macpherson, C. B. *The Political Theory of Possessive Individualism.* New York: Oxford University Press, 1972.

———. *Democratic Theory: Essays in Retrieval.* Oxford: Clarendon Press, 1973.

———. *The Life and Times of Liberal Democracy.* New York: Oxford University Press, 1977.

———. *The Rise and Fall of Economic Justice, and Other Papers.* New York: Oxford University Press, 1985.

Mahowald, Mary, ed. *Philosophy of Woman: Classical to Current Concepts.* Indianapolis, Ind.: Hackett, 1978.

Mansbridge, Jane. *Beyond Adversary Democracy*. Chicago: University of Chicago Press, 1983.

———. *Why We Lost the ERA*. Chicago: University of Chicago Press, 1986.

———, ed. *Beyond Self-Interest*. Chicago: University of Chicago Press, 1990.

Markowitz, Sally. "Abortion and Feminism." *Social Theory and Practice* 16 (Spring 1990): 1–17.

Martin, Emily. *The Woman in the Body: A Cultural Analysis of Reproduction*. Boston: Beacon Press, 1987.

Martin, Jane Roland. "Methodological Essentialism and Other Dangerous Traps." Paper presented to the Society for Women in Philosophy. New York, December 1991.

Matsuda, Mari J. "Liberal Jurisprudence and Abstracted Visions of Human Nature." *New Mexico Law Review* 16 (Fall 1986): 613–30.

———. "Affirmative Action and Legal Knowledge: Planting Seeds in Plowed-Up Ground." *Harvard Women's Law Journal* 11 (Spring 1988): 1–17.

May, Larry. *The Morality of Groups: Collective Responsibility, Group-Based Harm, and Corporate Rights*. Notre Dame, Ind.: University of Notre Dame Press, 1987.

Mayne, Judith. "L.A. Law and Prime-Time Feminism." *Discourse: Journal for Theoretical Studies in Media and Culture* 10 (Spring-Summer 1988): 30–47.

Mellema, Gregory. *Individuals, Groups, and Shared Moral Responsibility*. New York: Peter Lang, 1988.

Mellencamp, Patricia. "Situation Comedy, Feminism, and Freud: Discourses of Gracie and Lucy." In *Studies in Entertainment: Critical Approaches to Mass Culture,* ed. Tania Modleski. Bloomington, Ind.: Indiana University Press, 1986.

———. "Video Politics: Guerrilla TV, Ant Farm, Eternal Frame." *Discourse* 10 (Spring-Summer 1988): 78–100.

Menkiti, Ifeanyi. "Person and Community in African Traditional Thought." In *African Philosophy: An Introduction. 3d ed.,* ed. Richard A. Wright. New York: University Press of America, 1984.

Merchant, Carolyn. *The Death of Nature: Woman, Ecology, and the Scientific Revolution*. New York: Harper and Row, 1982.

Meyers, Diana T. *Self, Society, and Personal Choice*. New York: Columbia University Press, 1989.

Mill, John Stuart. *On Liberty,* ed. E. Rapaport. Indianapolis, Ind.: Hackett, 1978. Originally published 1859.

Miller, Jean Baker. *Toward a New Psychology of Women*. Boston: Beacon Press, 1976.

———. "The Development of Women's Sense of Self." Wellesley, Mass.: Stone Center Working Paper No. 12, 1984.

Miller, Mark Crispin. *Boxed In: The Culture of TV*. Evanston, Ill.: Northwestern University Press, 1988.

———. *Seeing through Movies*. New York: Pantheon, 1990.

Minow, Martha. *Making All the Difference: Inclusion, Exclusion, and American Law*. Ithaca, N.Y.: Cornell University Press, 1990.

Modleski, Tania, ed. *Studies in Entertainment: Critical Approaches to Mass Culture*. Bloomington: Indiana University Press, 1986.

———. "A Father Is Being Beaten: Male Feminism and the War Film." *Discourse* 10 (Spring-Summer 1988): 62–77.

Mohanty, Chandra Talpade. "On Race and Voice: Challenges for Liberal Education in the 1990's." *Cultural Critique* 14 (Winter 1989–90): 179–208.

Moraga, Cherrie, and Gloria Anzaldua, eds. *This Bridge Called My Back: Writings by Radical Women of Color*. New York: Kitchen Table Press, 1981.

Morgan, Kathryn Pauly. "Women and Moral Madness." In *Science, Morality and Feminist Theory*, ed. Marsha Hanen and Kai Nielsen. Calgary: University of Calgary Press, 1987.

———. "Strangers in a Strange Land: Feminists Visit Relativists." In *Perspectives on Relativism*, ed. D. Odegaard and C. Stewart. Toronto: Agathon Press, 1990.

Morgan, Michael. "Television and Democracy." In *Cultural Politics in Contemporary America*, ed. Ian Angus and Sut Jhally. New York: Routledge, 1989.

Morris, Meaghan. "Banality in Cultural Studies." *Discourse* 10 (Spring-Summer 1988): 3–29.

Nagel, Thomas. *Mortal Questions*. Cambridge, Eng.: Cambridge University Press, 1979.

———. *The View from Nowhere*. New York: Oxford University Press, 1986.

Nails, Debra. "Social-Scientific Sexism: Gilligan's Mismeasure of Man." *Social Research* 50 (Autumn 1983): 643–64.

Narayan, Uma. "Working across Difference: Some Considerations on Emotions and Political Practice." *Hypatia* 3 (Summer 1988): 31–47.

National Academy of Sciences. *Who Cares for America's Children?* Washington D.C.: National Academy Press, 1990.

National Commission on Children. *Beyond Rhetoric: A New American Agenda for Children and Families*. Washington, D.C.: U.S. Government Printing Office, 1991.

Nedelsky, Jennifer. "Reconceiving Autonomy: Sources, Thoughts and Possibilities." *Yale Journal of Law and Feminism* 1 (Spring 1989): 7–36.

———. "Law, Boundaries, and the Bounded Self." *Representations* 30 (Spring 1990): 162–89.

Nehamas, Alexander. "Plato and the Mass Media." *Monist* 71 (April 1988): 214–34.

Nicholson, Linda J. *Gender and History: The Limits of Social Theory in the Age of the Family*. New York: Columbia University Press, 1986.

———, ed. *Feminism/Postmodernism*. New York: Routledge, 1990.

Noddings, Nel. *Caring: A Feminine Approach to Ethics and Moral Education*. Berkeley: University of California Press, 1984.

Nova, Mica. "Consumerism and Its Contradictions." *Cultural Studies* 1 (May 1987): 204–10.

O'Brien, Mary. "Reproducing Marxist Man." In *The Sexism of Social and Political Theory*, ed. Lorenne Clark and Lynda Lange. Toronto: University of Toronto Press, 1979.

———. *The Politics of Reproduction*. London: Routledge, 1983.

Okin, Susan Moller. *Women in Western Political Thought*. Princeton: Princeton University Press, 1979.

———. *Justice, Gender, and the Family*. New York: Basic Books, 1989.

Olsen, Tillie. *Silences*. New York: Delacorte, 1979.

Omolade, Barbara. "We Speak for the Planet." In *Rocking the Ship of State*, ed. Adrienne Harris and Ynestra King. Boulder, Colo.: Westview, 1989.

Ortner, Sherry B. "Is Female to Male as Nature Is to Culture?" In *Woman, Culture and Society*, ed. Michelle Z. Rosaldo and Louise Lamphere. Stanford, Calif.: Stanford University Press, 1974.

Paige, K. E., and J. M. Paige. *The Politics of Reproductive Ritual.* Berkeley: University of California Press, 1981.

Parenti, Michael. *Power and the Powerless.* New York: St. Martin's Press, 1978.

―――. *Inventing Reality: The Politics of the Mass Media.* New York: St. Martin's Press, 1986.

Pateman, Carole. *The Problem of Political Obligation: A Critique of Liberal Theory.* Berkeley: University of California Press, 1985.

―――. *The Sexual Contract.* Stanford, Calif.: Stanford University Press, 1988.

―――. *The Disorder of Women: Democracy, Feminism, and Political Theory.* Stanford, Calif.: Stanford University Press, 1989.

Phillips, Anne. *Engendering Democracy.* University Park, Pa.: Pennsylvania State University Press, 1991.

Pierce, Christine. "Natural Law Language and Women." In *Woman in Sexist Society,* ed. Vivian Gornick and Barbara K. Moran. New York: Basic Books, 1971.

Piercy, Marge. *Woman on the Edge of Time.* New York: Fawcett, 1976.

Polan, Dana. "Brief Encounters: Mass Culture and the Evacuation of Sense." In *Studies in Entertainment,* ed. Tania Modleski. Bloomington: Indiana University Press, 1986.

Postman, Neil. *Amusing Ourselves to Death: Public Discourse in the Age of Show Business.* New York: Penguin, 1985.

Postow, B. C. "Economic Dependence and Self-Respect." *Philosophical Forum* 10 (1978–79): 181–205.

Purdy, Laura M. *In Their Best Interest? The Case against Equal Rights for Children.* Ithaca, N.Y.: Cornell University Press, 1992.

Railton, Peter. "Moral Theory as a Moral Practice." *Noûs* 25 (April 1991): 185–90.

Rapaport, Elizabeth. "Generalizing Gender: Reason and Essence in the Legal Thought of Catharine MacKinnon." In *A Mind of One's Own,* ed. Louise Antony and Charlotte Witt. Boulder, Colo.: Westview Press, 1992.

Rawls, John. *A Theory of Justice.* Cambridge: Harvard University Press, 1971.

―――. "Justice as Fairness: Political not Metaphysical," *Philosophy and Public Affairs* 14 (Summer 1985): 251–75.

Raymond, Janice. *A Passion for Friends: Toward a Philosophy of Female Affection.* Boston: Beacon Press, 1986.

Reardon, Betty. *Sexism and the War System.* New York: Teachers College Press, 1985.

Rich, Adrienne. *Of Woman Born: Motherhood as Experience and Institution.* New York: Bantam, 1977.

Roberts, Barbara. "The Death of Machothink: Feminist Research and the Transformation of Peace Studies." *Women's Studies International Forum* 7, no. 4 (1984): 195–200.

Rohrlick, Ruby. "Prehistoric Puzzles." *Women's Review of Books* 7 (June 1990): 14–16.

Rooney, Phillis. "Gendered Reason: Sex Metaphor and Conceptions of Reason." *Hypatia* 6 (Summer 1991): 77–103.

Rorty, Amélie Oksenberg, ed. *Explaining Emotions.* Berkeley: University of California Press, 1980.

―――. "Imagination and Power." In *Mind in Action: Essays in the Philosophy of Mind.* Boston: Beacon Press, 1988.

―――. *Mind in Action.* Boston: Beacon Press, 1988.

Rosaldo, Michelle Z., and Louise Lamphere, eds. *Woman, Culture, and Society.* Stanford, Calif.: Stanford University Press, 1974.

Rothman, Barbara Katz. *Recreating Motherhood: Ideology and Technology in Patriarchal Society.* New York: Norton, 1989.

Rousseau, Jean Jacques. *Emile,* trans. B. Foxley. New York: Dutton, 1911. Originally published 1762.

———. *The Social Contract,* ed. Charles Frankel. New York: Hafner, 1947. Originally published 1762.

Ruddick, Sara. "Maternal Thinking." *Feminist Studies* 6 (Summer 1980): 342–67.

———. "Remarks on the Sexual Politics of Reason." In *Women and Moral Theory,* ed. Eva Feder Kittay and Diana T. Meyers. Totowa, N.J.: Rowman and Littlefield, 1987.

———. *Maternal Thinking: Toward a Politics of Peace.* Boston: Beacon Press, 1989.

Russell, Diana. *The Secret Trauma: Incestuous Abuse of Women and Girls.* New York: Basic Books, 1986.

Russell, Diana, and Nancy Howell, "The Prevalence of Rape in the United States Revisited." *Signs* 8 (Summer 1983): 668–95.

Ryan, Alan. "Distrusting Economics." *New York Review of Books* 18 May 1989, 25–27.

Sandel, Michael J. *Liberalism and the Limits of Justice.* Cambridge, Eng.: Cambridge University Press, 1982.

Sargent, Lydia, ed. *Women and Revolution.* Boston: South End Press, 1981.

Sayre-McCord, Geoffrey, ed. *Essays on Moral Realism.* Ithaca, N.Y.: Cornell University Press, 1988.

Schauer, Frederick. *Free Speech: A Philosophical Inquiry.* Cambridge, Eng.: Cambridge University Press, 1982.

Scheman, Naomi. "Individualism and the Objects of Psychology." In *Discovering Reality,* ed. Sandra Harding and Merrill B. Hintikka. Dordrecht, Holland: Reidel, 1983.

Schwarzenbach, Sibyl. "A Political Reading of the Reproductive Soul in Aristotle." *History of Philosophy Quarterly* 9 (July 1992): 243–64.

Scott, Joan. "The New University: Beyond Political Correctness." *Boston Review,* March 1992, 9.

Shanley, Mary Lyndon. *Feminism, Marriage, and the Law in Victorian England: 1850–1895.* Princeton: Princeton University Press, 1989.

Shanley, Mary Lyndon, and Carole Pateman, eds. *Feminist Interpretations and Political Theory.* University Park, Pa.: Pennsylvania State University Press, 1991.

Sher, George. "Three Grades of Social Involvement." *Philosophy and Public Affairs* 18 (Spring 1989): 133–57.

Sherwin, Susan. "Feminist and Medical Ethics: Two Different Approaches to Contextual Ethics." *Hypatia* 4 (Summer 1989): 57–72.

Simons, Margaret A. "Motherhood, Feminism and Identity." *Women's Studies International Forum (Hypatia)* 7, no. 5 (1984): 349–59.

Slote, Michael. "Morality and Self-Other Asymmetry." *Journal of Philosophy* 1 (April 1984): 179–92.

Smith, Adam. *The Wealth of Nations,* ed. M. Lerner. New York: Random House, 1937. Originally published 1776.

Smyth, Ailbhe. "A (Political) Postcard from a Peripheral Pre-Postmodern State (of Mind) or How Alliteration and Parentheses Can Knock You Down Dead in Women's Studies." *Women's Studies International Forum* 15 (May-June 1992): 331–37.

Snitow, Ann. "A Gender Diary." In *Rocking the Ship of State,* ed. Adrienne Harris and Ynestra King. Boulder, Colo.: Westview, 1989.

Spelman, Elizabeth V. *Inessential Woman: Problems of Exclusion in Feminist Thought.* Boston: Beacon Press, 1988.

Spiro, Melford E. *Gender and Culture: Kibbutz Women Revisited.* New York: Schocken Books, 1980.

Stiehm, Judith, ed. *Women and Men's Wars.* New York: Pergamon Press, 1983.

———, ed. *Women's Views of the Political World of Men.* Dobbs Ferry, N.Y.: Transnational Publishers, 1984.

Stimpson, Catharine R. *Where the Meanings Are: Feminism and Cultural Spaces.* New York: Routledge, 1990.

———. "Multiculturalism: A Big Word at the Presses." *New York Times Book Review* 22 September 1991.

Surrey, Janet. "The 'Self-in-Relation': A Theory of Women's Development." Wellesley, Mass.: Stone Center Working Paper No. 13, 1985.

Swerdlow, Amy. "Pure Milk, Not Poison: Women Strike for Peace and the Test Ban Treaty of 1963." In *Rocking the Ship of State,* ed. Adrienne Harris and Ynestra King. Boulder, Colo.: Westview, 1989.

Tannen, Deborah. *You Just Don't Understand: Women and Men in Conversation.* New York: Ballantine Books, 1991.

Thalberg, Irving. *Perception, Emotion and Action.* Oxford: Blackwell, 1977.

Theweleit, Klaus. *Male Fantasies. Vol. 1, Women, Floods, Bodies, History,* trans. S. Conway. Minneapolis: University of Minnesota Press, 1987.

Thomas, Laurence. "Trust, Affirmation and Moral Character." In *Identity, Character, and Morality,* ed. Owen Flanagan and Amélie Oksenberg Rorty. Cambridge: MIT Press, 1990.

Thorne, Barrie, ed. *Rethinking the Family: Some Feminist Questions.* New York: Longman, 1982.

Trebilcot, Joyce, ed. *Mothering: Essays in Feminist Theory.* Totowa, N.J.: Rowman and Allanheld, 1984.

Tronto, Joan C. "Beyond Gender Difference to a Theory of Care." *Signs* 12 (Summer 1987): 644–63.

Tylee, Claire M. "'Maleness Run Riot'—The Great War and Women's Resistance to Militarism." *Women's Studies International Forum* 11, n. 3 (1988): 199–210.

Walker, Lawrence J. "Sex Differences in the Development of Moral Reasoning: A Critical Review." *Child Development* 55 (June 1984): 677–91.

Walker, Margaret Urban. "Moral Understandings: Alternative 'Epistemology' for a Feminist Ethics." *Hypatia* 4 (Summer 1989): 15–28.

Warren, Karen. "Feminism and Ecology: Making Connections." *Environmental Ethics* 9 (1987): 3–20.

Westkott, Marcia. "Female Relationality and the Idealized Self." *American Journal of Psychoanalysis* 49 (September 1989): 239–50.

Whitbeck, Caroline. "Feminist Ontology: A Different Reality." In *Beyond Domination,* ed. Carol Gould. Totowa, N.J.: Rowman and Allanheld, 1983.

Williams, Bernard. *Moral Luck: Philosophical Papers 1973–1980.* Cambridge, Eng.: Cambridge University Press, 1981.

———. *Ethics and the Limits of Philosophy.* Cambridge: Harvard University Press, 1985.

Williams, Patricia J. *The Alchemy of Race and Rights.* Cambridge: Harvard University Press, 1991.

Williams, Raymond. *Problems in Materialism and Culture.* London: Verso, 1980.

Williamson, Judith. "Woman Is an Island: Femininity and Colonization." In *Studies in Entertainment,* ed. Tania Modleski. Bloomington: Indiana University Press, 1986.

Wolff, Robert Paul. *In Defense of Anarchism.* New York: Harper, 1970.

Wollheim, Richard. *On Art and the Mind.* Cambridge: Harvard University Press, 1974.

———. *The Thread of Life.* Cambridge: Harvard University Press, 1984.

Wright, Richard A., ed. *African Philosophy: An Introduction.* 3d ed. New York: University Press of America, 1984.

Wylie, Alison. "The Philosophy of Ambivalence" In *Science, Morality and Feminist Theory,* ed. Marsha Hanen and Kai Nielsen. Calgary: University of Calgary Press, 1987.

Young, Iris Marion. "Humanism, Gynocentrism and Feminist Politics." *Women's Studies International Forum (Hypatia)* 8, no. 3 (1985): 173–83.

———. "The Ideal of Community and the Politics of Difference." *Social Theory and Practice* 12 (Spring 1986): 1–26.

———. "Impartiality and the Civic Public." In *Feminism as Critique,* ed. Seyla Benhabib and Drucilla Cornell. Minneapolis: University of Minnesota Press, 1987.

———. "Pregnant Embodiment: Subjectivity and Alienation." *Journal of Medicine and Philosophy* 9 (February 1984): 45–62.

Zalk, Sue Rosenberg, and Janice Gordon-Kelter, eds. *Revolutions in Knowledge: Feminism in the Social Sciences.* Boulder, Colo.: Westview Press, 1992.

Credits

Grateful acknowledgment is hereby given for permission to use in some chapters of this book earlier versions of parts of the following: "Feminism and Moral Theory," in *Women and Moral Theory*, ed. Eva Feder Kittay and Diana T. Meyers (Totowa, N.J.: Rowman and Littlefield, 1987), 111–28; "Non-Contractual Society," in *Science, Morality and Feminist Theory*, ed. Marsha Hanen and Kai Nielsen (Calgary: University of Calgary Press, 1987), 111–37; "Birth and Death," *Ethics* 99 (January 1989): 362–88; "Gender as an Influence on Cultural Norms Relating to War and the Environment," in *Cultural Norms, War and the Environment*, ed. Arthur H. Westing (Oxford: Oxford University Press, 1988), 44–52 (courtesy of Stockholm International Peace Research Institute); "Feminist Transformations of Moral Theory," *Philosophy and Phenomenological Research* 50 (Supplement, Fall 1990): 321–44; and "Freedom and Feminism," in *Democracy and Possessive Individualism*, ed. Joseph H. Carens (Albany: State University of New York Press, in press).

Index

Abortion, 27–28, 66, 81–82, 115

Abraham, 86

Abstract: alternatives, 73; principles and mothering, 210–11

Academic freedom, 106

Achilles, 149

Action: as opposed to reflection, 74–75, 77, 79; group, 93

Actual: context, 210; persons, 169, 198, 210; society, 194; vs. hypothetical, 66, 74–75, 77–78, 112, 201, 211

Adler, Jonathan, 74

Adoption, 84

Adorno, Theodor, 96

Advertising, 8, 98, 100, 103, 108, 141; economic censorship and, 240–41n.14

Affective bonds, 58

Affiliation: desire for, 59; desire for, and morality, 60

Affordable housing, 164

Africa, 74

African American women, 41–42, 105, 157, 253–54n.24

Agent: abstract rational, 35–40, 42, 46–47, 226; actual vs. hypothetical, 40; atomistic, 48; "cared for" as, 228; impartial, 40, in traditional moral theory, 48

Agreement: consensual vs. principled, 40–41

Aggression: male tendency towards, 138; violence and, 139

Alcoff, Linda, 13

Alienation, 165

All the Women are White, All the Blacks are Men, But Some of Us Are Brave: Black Women's Studies, 42

Ancient Greece and Greeks, 43, 45, 128–29, 143, 149

Arendt, Hannah, 126, 132, 134

Aristotle, 44–46, 87, 89, 135

Art, 16; the evolution of feminist consciousness and, 102

Attachments, 32

Aubrey, John, 192

Autonomous agent, 35; citizen as, 62

Autonomy, 32, 42, 188; feminist conception of, 61; interdependence and, 62; law and, 61–62; traditional liberal notion of, 62; valuing of, 60

Avarice, 201

Baier, Annette, 19, 37, 47, 51, 53, 86, 224

Baron, Marcia, 82

Barracks community, 143, 144, 216

Barry, Brian, 183

Bartky, Sandra Lee, 177–78

Beauvoir, Simone de, 125–26, 132, 134

Becker, Ernest, 149

Bentham, Jeremy, 183

Bible, 192

Biological determinism, 152

Biology: attitudes and, 150–51; birth and, 126–27, 130, 132; contrasted with society, 124

Biomedical ethics: feminism and, 52–53

Birth, 18, 81–84, 86, 112, 118, 120–22, 160, 171, 243n.9; as creative metaphor for women, 135; as natural and not fully human, 120, 124–26, 128, 131, 134–35; choice and, 114–18, 172; conscious awareness and, 118–20; cultural conception of, 121, 123, 130–31, 135; cultural vs. biological aspects of, 123–26; economic impact of, 124; feminist theory and, 132, 242n.1; from mother's point of view, 120–21; giving birth as fully human, 127–29, 133–34, 199; human vs. animal, 125–26; imaginative representation and, 121–22, 172; male and female conceptions of, 131–32; natural vs. divine conceptions of, 113, 121; rituals,

275